# Reviewing Culture Online

Maarit Jaakkola

# Reviewing Culture Online

## Post-Institutional Cultural Critique across Platforms

palgrave
macmillan

Maarit Jaakkola
Department of Journalism, Media and Communication
University of Gothenburg
Gothenburg, Sweden

ISBN 978-3-030-84847-7 ISBN 978-3-030-84848-4 (eBook)
https://doi.org/10.1007/978-3-030-84848-4



This Palgrave Macmillan imprint is published by the registered company Springer Nature Switzerland AG.
The registered company address is: Gewerbestrasse 11, 6330 Cham, Switzerland

# Acknowledgements

The findings and conclusions presented in this book draw heavily on the work I have carried out in the past few years in my two roles as researcher at Nordicom, a Centre for Nordic Media Research at the University of Gothenburg in Sweden, and as a lecturer in journalism at Tampere University in Finland. A research grant from the Finnish Cultural Foundation enabled me to turn my findings from that work into the present book. I am most grateful for the opportunity these institutions have given me to both conduct my research and present it to wider audiences.

Throughout this book, I keep referring back to my doctoral dissertation 'The Contested Autonomy of Arts and Journalism: Change and Continuity of the Dual Professionalism of Cultural Journalism', published by the University of Tampere in 2015. In addition, some of the results of the case studies in Chap. 6 have been published previously as follows:

Section 6.1 is partly based on the journal article 'From Re-viewers to Me-viewers: The #Bookstagram Review Sphere on Instagram and the Perceived Uses of the Platform and Genre Affordances', published in 2019 in *Interactions: Studies in Communication and Culture*, vol. 10, no. 1–2, pp. 91–110. A Finnish-language journal article on this topic, complemented with a dataset containing Finnish-language Instagram posts, was published in 2020 in *Kulttuurintutkimus*, vol. 36, no. 3–4, pp. 31–44.

Section 6.2 is partly based on the journal article 'Useful Creativity: Vernacular Reviewing on the Video-sharing Platform Vimeo', published in 2020 in *Culture Unbound: Journal of Current Cultural Research*, vol. 12, no. 2, pp. 373–392.

Section 6.3 is partly based on the journal article 'From Vernacularized Commercialism to Kidbait: Toy Review Videos on YouTube and the Problematics of the Mash-up Genre', published in 2019 in the *Journal of Children and Media*, vol. 14, no. 2, pp. 237–254.

Section 6.4 is partly based on the journal article 'Vernacular Reviews as a Form of Co-consumption: User-generated Review Videos on YouTube', published in *MedieKultur – Journal of Media and Communication Research*, vol. 34, no. 65, pp. 10–30.

I thank the publishers of these journals for permission to revise and republish parts of this material. The journals' editors and anonymous peer reviewers played an invaluable role in being the first scanners of my ideas, confirming to me their relevance and validity.

I would furthermore like to express my gratitude to my collaborator Pasi Luostarinen, a Finnish software engineer and programmer who made automated collection of big data possible, and my research assistants, Haitham Othman and Neha Sharma, who proved indispensable in helping me with the practicalities of data collection on Instagram.

My thanks also go to my networks of colleagues in cultural journalism and criticism for their inspiration, support and critical comments. Especially the collegial Nordic network on cultural journalism that has emerged and established itself over recent decade has often provided me with an excellent platform for sounding out my ideas. In particular, I would like to acknowledge Professor Nete Nørgaard Kristensen at the University of Copenhagen, with whom I have had the privilege of collaborating on a number of different occasions.

Finally, I want to extend my thanks to my friends and family: my personal language consultant Timo Lyyra, my husband Erik, my son Alvin, grandparents in Finland who patiently entertained the five-year-old on WhatsApp on remote work days during the COVID-19 pandemic, as well as the families of Fahlgren-Gastambide, Heimonen-Wathne and Karlsson-Lilliebjelke, who kindly offered me writing retreats when needed.

# Contents

# List of Figures

# List of Tables

CHAPTER 1

# Cultural Consumers Becoming Reviewers

In the twenty-first century, everyone can be a reviewer. People like you and me can review books, films, music, concerts, live performances, food, beverages, candy, restaurants, cosmetics, welfare products, clothes, shoes, toys, collectibles, furniture, vehicles, bicycles, motorcycles, sports gear, fishing gear, tech gadgets, computer software and mobile apps, games, craft tools, hotels, conference venues, travel destinations or rollercoasters, to name but a few. Reviewers can focus on a specific subgenre such as hip hop, pizza or a specific cosmetics brand. Reviews created by cultural consumers are flourishing from dedicated amateur reviewer platforms such as Rotten Tomatoes to product platforms such as Amazon and Google, and reviews are employed by companies such as Trustpilot and TripAdvisor.

Our consumer behaviour and the related evaluative actions have become mediatized, which means that private actions that were previously restricted to small groups of people, like friends and family, are now visible to others in the digital environment (Hjarvard, 2013). Within a couple of decades, we have been drawn into the circles of product mediation in a way that was not possible before the arrival of new technologies (Bolin, 2011). After a customer experience, we are asked to push a button when leaving the boutique or pharmacy, or after reading a journalistic article online we are asked to respond to a mentimeter that measures our feelings. Restaurants, hotels and spas are asking us to write a review afterward we leave, preferably to 'recommend' a good service to peers and potential customers (rather than describing a negative experience). Reviews, as


M. Jaakkola, *Reviewing Culture Online*,
https://doi.org/10.1007/978-3-030-84848-4_1

conscious accounts based on encounters with products and services, are part of the grand collective—critics would add, neoliberal—pursuit to find the best product on the market and identify quality. This common mission is a Janus-faced task: On one hand, it is an organized effort by organizations and service providers to collect data and receive feedback, which can be used to tailor and enhance a customer experience, but can also be sold to third parties who can use it to target relevant people. On the other hand, sharing personal experiences and ideas may help identify quality in huge amounts of supply available on the market and in this way facilitate purchasing and consumption decisions, and contribute to the refinement of discourses and taste cultures maintained in the digital democratic public sphere.

Reviews adhere to consumption, and thus also to the production of products aimed to be consumed, in a profound way. Reviews play a role in helping consumers and citizens construct a value for a product and related experience. Before you invest in a car, or a freezer, or pick up a restaurant order or a software plug-in, you may be interested in taking a look at what has been written on the specific brand by those who have been in contact with it. Previously, the public evaluation of works was a task conducted by a few professionals dedicated to monitoring a certain field. Nowadays, evaluation based on accumulated experience or spontaneous reactions is offered by a wider circle of people who want to be recognized as public evaluators, or reviewers.

If we take the statement of everyone being a reviewer seriously—which is an adaptation of Novalis' classic remark of everyone being an artist, taken up by the artist Joseph Beuys (Mesch & Michely, 2007)—we need to take a closer look at how ordinary people are involved in reviewing new cultural products in society. In today's technological landscape, anyone can technically become a reviewer; to become a legitimated, recognized, appreciated or productive reviewer, or to become heard, receive a voluminous audience and make an impact, or to gain any other similar qualities, is another question. Nevertheless, technically, the reception process can be extended to production of messages. The consumer has thus truly become what Alvin Toffler, in an anticipating manner a couple of decades ago in his book *The Third Wave* (1980), called a 'prosumer' (consumer and producer), a person not only consuming products but also sharing his or her instant experiences with others by producing messages that create meaning. The hybrid form of online engagement that characterizes the reception and creation of user-generated content has also been described as being a 'produser' (user and producer) (Bruns, 2008; Bruns, 2016). While the twenty-first-century prosumership and produsership can be celebrated as a democratic accomplishment, the new digital communication environment calls forth new implications that in turn call for multiple considerations.

Literature on institutional criticism seems to be unanimous in its message concerning the ramifications of the citizen-led evolvements: the monopoly of the traditional institutional criticism has been challenged. Technological and cultural changes have made it possible for children and young people, senior citizens, bookworms, tech nerds and ordinary people to become reviewers, and even reach out to millions of followers or receive billions of views. The reviewsphere has become more plural, more voices are shouting, which to some appears as an indication of the democratization of opinion (McWhirther, 2016). At the same time, the Habermasian cultural sphere, centred upon the private space of home, has now been exposed to mass audiences, and discussions by rational citizens that used to unfold and remained within coffee houses now unfold in public by a multitude of persons with different backgrounds (Eberly, 2000). The mediatization of reception processes, for example, of play and individual habitus (Hjarvard, 2013), has resulted in an almost limitless ways of talking about products, embedded in different lifestyles. Voices from the ivory tower have been mixed with voices from the street.

For an individual citizen this development means that evaluating products that he or she encounters has the potential to become an everyday activity supported by a community, and to provide an individual with identity as a cultural content producer. Negotiating between the position of being part of an extended marketing strategy and democratic achievement of cultural engagement, as well as between a sheer amateur and a professional with expertise, the reviewer needs to develop new competences. Contemporary and future cultural consumers need to develop more advanced skills for identifying situations where they act, and for recognizing the implications of their evaluative acts. They need to be able to incorporate competences related to reviewing, both as a receiver of others' messages and a producer of messages of one's own, into the agency that is needed for responsible cultural citizenship and consumership. While the calls for media education have traditionally been preoccupied with texts (see, e.g., Masterman, 1985; Kellner & Share, 2019), reviewing needs consideration of consumer behaviour, organizational production context and wider contexts of production. Reviewing is not just producing a message, it is being engaged and involved in a process of meaning making where the prosuming subject needs to actively position itself towards the industry, the infrastructures of production, and his or her audiences.

This book focuses on reviewers who are engaged in producing public assessments of cultural products and are thus embedded in the circulation of goods and services. Blank (2007, p. 14), outlining a 'sociology of the review', remarked more than a decade ago that the most work on reviews is 'narrowly focused on specific high-cultural genres' and 'it is particularly unclear how the results may generalize to non-high-culture genres or to other categories of cultural consumption'—according to him, there were 'no studies of commercial genres' and 'no one' had 'attempted to synthetize the field'. Since then, studies on different forms of reviewing have emerged, but the synthetizing attempts are still lacking. This book tries to answer that call and makes an attempt to expand the scope of reviewing. The book aims to indicate that reviewing is an increasingly prolific activity in social networking sites and their online communities, not only on dedicated amateur review platforms and in professional news outlets. Therefore, we need to ask what kind of activity reviewing is, seen as a broader phenomenon than confined to the professional-institutional framework. How can we understand and acknowledge vernacular reviewing in its own right, not just as a continuation of or a challenge to the traditional forms of reviewing carried out by cultural desks of legacy media? On which premises and in which ways is it being conducted in social networking settings? How does non-institutional reviewing, an activity carried out by a heterogeneous people ranging from ordinary citizens to professionals in different fields, alter our picture of what we have understood as 'criticism' or 'reviewing'? How do understandings of vernacular reviewing add to our knowledge about user-generated content and online communities?

My research interest focuses on increasing our understandings of the young forms of reviewing that have emerged online. I want to ask how they are connected to what we know already about reviewing and criticism and how they are potentially altering our conceptions of the very idea and concept of reviews and reviewing. I am trying to do something that may arouse controversial reactions; reviewing is not a strictly defined area, not the least in its vernacular forms. The platforms and their cultures of communication are changing rapidly, and it may feel almost impossible to deliver an adequate picture of what reviewing is and what is it not. However, my aim is less to deliver a detailed picture of possibilities on a certain platform than to make the effort to identify reviewing as a diversity of practices, possibly to be distinguished from influencing, promotion and other forms of online communication. Moreover, I am less interested in whether online reviews 'work', that is, whether they have an impact on sales (see, e.g., Duan et al., 2008). Instead of this instrumental perspective on reviews and reviewing, the most prevalent in studies of customer reviewing, I intend to clarify how the evaluative behaviour of online users works in the everyday and how it can be further developed and directed towards more democratic, inclusive and ethical ends. Reviews generate huge amounts of data that can be sold and utilized for different purposes of targeted communication and marketing, but my ambition is rather to counteract this development and reveal paths for looking at user reviewing as a cultural phenomenon instead of a product. This means that my book presents an attempt to negotiate between traditions that celebrate user reviewing as everyday creativity and traditions that are solely connecting reviewing to the purpose of facilitating customers' and consumers' word-of-mouth communication on their way towards making purchasing choices. By searching for mediating views, I want to remind the reader of the possibilities of discovering reviewing as a space of democratic discussion, individual growth and development, *while* struggling with obstacles that contradict these aims.

However, what do we talk about when we talk about reviews and reviewing—how is the area to be delimited? Reviewing is a special genre that implies a distinct mode of speaking and acting, with pertinent assumptions, values and practices. At the beginning of 2021, the Annenberg School of Journalism at the University of Southern California was searching for an instructor for a course on writing film reviews and described reviewing in the announcements as follows: 'Reviewing is a way of looking at art and encountering the world. It is also a way to learn the art and discipline of the written word. The norms of reviewing are the same across all the arts. Given appropriate knowledge, if you can effectively review one at, you can review others. Therefore, not every student needs to come with a background in film, but they must [show] an interest in the discipline of being a daily or weekly art, entertainment & culture critic'. This description refers to the idea of reviewing as a special epistemic form of mediation, applying the principles of journalism. While emphasizing the need for mastering the form of mediation, it also expresses the idea that mere knowledge about the substance is not enough for those who want to become reviewers. There is a certain 'way of looking at art and encountering the world' that needs to—and can—be learned.

As a professional product, review has been relatively easy to identify as it has been identical to the genre, and reviewers have been those who have been recruited to write texts in this genre. Reviews are typically marked by a certain type of layout that differs it from, for example, news articles and columns. In its online form, reviewing is not synonymous with every evaluation or judgement. We may make public assessments of cultural products, phenomena, persons and institutions as part of any communication. Reviewing, above all, in the way it is conceived of in this book, is understood as a specific form of communication in which an individual self-identifies as a reviewer and intends to create a reviewer profile.

Reviewing thus implies conscious and continuous human activity to address cultural products of choice. It needs to be differentiated from other forms of evaluative acts. *Rating* means assigning stars, numbers or similar attributes to an object, but it doesn't require any continuous basis, let alone motivation or contextualization of the choice. *Recommending* means passing on an advisement or suggestion, based on a judgement of a product as worth trying, to someone who is presupposed to be interested in that product. Recommending has been prolific for product reviews, in which word of mouth (WOM) has become an influential marketing strategy (Kozinets et al., 2010). Recommending can even occur in the form of curation or aggregation, either fully or half-automatically, as, for example, in the form of music playlists or literature reading lists. Thus, neither rating nor recommendation needs to be a subjective human action but rather a measure based on popularity or some other ranking of an item, based on an algorithm. For example, the review aggregator platform Metacritic, launched in 1999, uses advanced conversions of data, giving each review a score that is weighted according to the writer's popularity, stature and volume of review production. For consumer products there are a number of review sites such as the Swedish Testfreaks (launched in 2007), as well as the US Consumer Reports (launched in 1936), The Wirecutter (launched in 2011) and Honest Product Reviews (launched in 2018), collecting information on reviews available on the internet to produce an unbiased rating on products as different as vacuum cleaners, blood pressure monitors, drones, gaming mouses, bike helmets, airlines and home security systems. Moreover, all popular social media platforms from YouTube to Instagram and Facebook to Twitter and from Spotify to TikTok conduct algorithmic recommendations built into their systems.

Individual users may also make evaluations in their contributions to online discussions, such as in debates or updates in discussion groups and forums, blogs, on Twitter and Facebook, in mail lists and so on. These do not qualify as reviews, however critical and argumentative they may be. Even if written by reviewers they are more appropriately regarded as supplemental communication related to reviewing, as part of the professional communication or relational labour (Baym, 2015) reviewers, among other professionals, are doing. For example, if we look at literature, it has become an established distinction to draw a line between book reviews and other forms such as book discussion (Boot, 2011), book blogging (Steiner, 2010) and 'bookish' online engagement (Rodger, 2019).

In this book I am mainly interested in new and emerging forms of reviewing rather than the more established and medium-specific forms of 'amateur' reviewing, previously richly discussed as platform communication, like blogging (Steiner, 2010; Tryon, 2009), vlogging (Ashton & Patel, 2018; Khalil, 2015), podcasting (Bolden & Nahachewsky, 2015) and writing amateur reviews on dedicated amateur platforms such as Internet Movie Database (IMDb) or Amazon (see Sect. 4.2 User Reviewing in Chap. 4). Instead, and while, of course, not completely dismissing the previous digital forms of reviewing either, I will place more stress on newer 'amateur' or 'lay' reviewer communities in social media that develop practices that more dramatically detach from the classical understandings of the review (see Chap. 6. Vernacular Reviewers' Communities). In doing this, my focus lies in something that I have conceptualized as vernacular creatorship, a critical user production agency that can be developed and is typically employed across different platforms. Vernacular creatorship combines elements of reception and (user-generated) production in a way that is often easily dismissed by discussions on user-generated content that tend to be less genre-sensitive and more medium- or platform-centric. Likewise, previous discussions on reviewing have centred on professional and amateur identities, characteristics of online cultures and methods of communication. These discussions have not paid much attention to production knowledge and or elements that would be equivalent to the professional production knowledge of traditional industries. The reason for disregarding the production structures and their central role may be a result of conceptualizations of users as 'formerly audiences', which pays more attention to their receiver position rather than their role as an active producer and manager of their own medium. By looking at new and emerging vernacular creatorship as post-professional agency we can try to reconfigure the user positionings in a way that enables us to overcome the user reviewers' subordination to the professional reviewers. This helps us better see reviewers as part of not only the democratic communication that unfolds in society but also of the symbolic value production in which intermediary actors are engaged.

Online engagement similar to what reviewers are involved in has been characterized in academic literature as a participatory culture (Jenkins, 2006, 2007), vernacular creativity (Burgess et al., 2006; Edensor et al., 2009) and platform vernacular(s) (Gibbs et al., 2015). These ideas refer to the idea of ordinary people creating meaning in interaction with each other and collaborating with each other. The communication work carried out by users with different competences and profiles has also been characterized as digital, creative or unpaid or free labour (Terranova, 2004; Hesmondhalgh, 2015), and aspirational or relational labour (Baym, 2015; Duffy, 2017). All of these terms address different dimensions of cultural online engagement but they are too general to remain sensitive to the special characteristics of reviewing. While illuminating the creative, productive, collaborative and economic aspects of online engagement, none of these concepts fully manages to capture the work rooted in subjectivity and authority. This is, above all, because reviewing is a specific genre, mode and practice that differs from other forms of participation and engagement on different platforms. While reviewing may incorporate many features of creative, aspirational, relational and affective labour across online platforms, it cannot fully be returned to the general activities of vlogging, blogging, tweeting or platform-specific subgenres such as unboxing, mukbang, making play-throughs or tutorials. The signature trait of reviewing, which is not necessarily present in the abovementioned forms, is the evaluative aim of finding out whether something is good or bad in its category, or discovering the possible worth or value of a product (Blank, 2007). Furthermore, reviewing, as a more or less systematic and iterative activity, fulfils a specific function that reaches beyond the platform vernaculars; it is also connected to the more institutionalized forms of criticism and needs to be examined as its counterpart, even if it may significantly depart from the objectives and conditions of the institutional criticism.

However, the vernacular practices of reviewing are still very young and evidently subject to change. Social networking sites and digital tools develop quickly, and we do not know which of the most frequently used will exist within the next five, 10 or 15 years, if at all. Successful services are purchased, services are merged, the users' habits shift. For example, only just over a decade ago, a great extent of amateur criticism was conducted on discussion boards (e.g. by Yahoo!), and many review platforms were absorbed into a functionality on platforms with a broader scope; for example, the customer review service Epinions was merged into eBay. However, to keep the theoretical ground for examining these diverging landscapes we need documentation even of the very early forms and synthetizing that enables us to examine these developments from a more broad-brush perspective. This book presents findings from the 2010s, negotiating between insights from the early beginnings of social media and a slightly more mature stage of these platforms, and tries to bridge gaps from theories that were created in the pre-digital era to pave the way for further research on user-generated reviewing. Instead of focusing on technical aspects and details, I try to outline more long-evolving trends.

## 1.1 Studies of Reviews

Reviews, in their classical institutional form, emerged as early as the modern newspaper came into being, and there has been a decades-long scholarly interest in reviews within the humanities and social sciences. While Blank (2007) remarked in his seminal book Critics, ratings, and society: The sociology of reviews that the body of research concerning reviewing is rather scarce, there has been a significant increase in interest in the field since the emergence and establishment of amateur and customer reviewing. However, the scholarly interest in reviews and reviewing has not always been directed to reviewing in itself and in its own right but, instead, many times the interest of inquiry has departed from seeing review in a more instrumental way, as a carrier of something, such as cultural preferences or mediated canon, or consumer behaviour and attitudes. The highest interest in reviews has been found in studies of media and culture within social sciences, film and game studies, philosophy, literary criticism and literature studies, as well as consumer and marketing research and computer science. In this chapter I will identify some relevant academic literature on reviews; this being said, I will not focus on the wide body of literature concerning criticism but only on the more limited field of reviewing (for delimitations, see Chap. 4 Reviewing in Genre and Practice). The critical studies that define criticism as a disciplinary or philosophical practice have developed cogent postmodern ideas that have also affected ways of conceiving of reviewing in the journalistic environment, including post-colonial criticism (Moore-Gilbert et al., 2014), feminist criticism (Donovan, 2014) and ecocriticism (Garrard, 2014). They illuminate the interaction between criticism and reviewing, and are likely to guide practices of reviewing in terms of the notions of diversity, ethics and structures of power, affecting the ideas of symbolic boundaries, cultural canons, embodiment of practices and so on.

Studies on journalistic reviewing, to begin with, have formulated the basic understandings of review as a media genre and practice. The landmark studies based on empirical work on reviewing by journalistic outlets find the foundations for reviewing at three levels: reviewing as an institution (e.g. Hohendahl, 1982; Walmsley-Evans, 2018), a genre (e.g. Titchener, 1998) and a practice (e.g. Janssen, 1997). Art-related reviewers and the institution and practice of reviewing have been of interest, above all, in journalism studies, sociology of arts, studies of culture, as well as philosophy and aesthetics, which have contributed to the conceptualization of the genre and its dynamics. A central narrative that has both motivated and framed the study of reviews and been detected or negated by these studies has been the crisis of the journalistic review. Accompanied by pamphlet-oriented essay literature that has been focused on discussing the crisis of reviewing during both decades of the turn of the millennium (see, e.g., Elkins, 2003; McDonald, 2007; Elkins & Newman, 2008; for more contextualizing treatments of crisis discourse, see Jaakkola, 2015, Frey, 2014; McWhirther, 2016), the development of journalistic reviews in newspapers has been traced with the help of content analyses, to find out whether their share has dropped as anticipated in the crisis discourse. Analyses on the review format itself and its production conditions have reported a certain constancy (Heikkilä & Gronow, 2018; Jaakkola, 2015; Weibull & Nilsson, 2010). Studies with a wider scope where reviews have been examined as part of other cultural journalistic content have explored reviewing as part of the cultural change that professional cultural journalism has been undergoing (Jaakkola, 2015; Purhonen et al., 2019), often in comparative designs and in terms of global metaprocesses affecting journalism such as globalization and digitalization, with popularization and entertainization as ramifications (Janssen et al., 2008).

In addition, the empirical studies focused on journalistic reviewing have predominantly directed their attention to reviewers' professional identities (Boenisch, 2008; Chong, 2020), practices of reviewing (Janssen, 1997; Shrum Jr., 1996), and review content and its changes, as symptomatic of a wider cultural change (Purhonen et al., 2019; van Venrooij & Schmutz, 2010). Studies on review content have been focused on how certain cultural forms such as Hollywood films (Baumann, 2007) or forms of popular music (Fürsich & Avant-Mier, 2012; Lindberg et al., 2005; Schmutz, 2009) have become legitimized and part of the cultural canon.

Only recently has scholarly interest been directed to the 'amateur critics' of the internet. With the help of content analyses of published content and interviews with informants, studies have traced the identity of the 'everyday amateur expert', attempting to outline and understand them in conjunction with the more professional identities (de Jong & Burgers, 2013; Kammer, 2015). Studies have analysed the structural characteristics of reviews such as the degree of demonstrated expertise (McAuley & Leskovec, 2013; Verboord, 2010), the articulation of experience in review texts (Savolainen, 2019; Vásquez, 2014) or emotions or sentiments, tracing whether a review constructs a positive or a negative opinion (Brownfield & Zhou, 2020; Suhariyanto & Sarno, 2018; Tiwari et al., 2020). A prevalent framework has been participation in fan cultures (see, e.g., Galuszka, 2015; Baym & Burnett, 2009; Jenkins, 2006).

Studies on user reviews may deliver very different pictures of the user-generated review if the phenomenon is contextualized as part of citizen-journalistic efforts or individuals' consumer behaviour (for an insightful analysis underlining this viewpoint, see Lobato et al., 2011). One strain of research dedicated to amateur reviewers constitutes studies exploring consumer behaviour in marketing research. The basic assumption of cultural consumership is that consumption is a collective phenomenon that provides individuals, embedded in networks of social relations that are enacted through certain behaviour, with constructive agency to add value to products and services (Cova & Dalli, 2018, p. 235). The sociocultural, experiential, symbolic and ideological aspects of consumption have been studied in scholarship of cultural consumption that is often referred to as consumer culture theory (CCT) or interpretive consumer research (Arnould & Thompson, 2005; Kravets et al., 2018), as well as within cultural sociology or the sociology of cultural consumption (McQuarrie et al., 2012).

After a gradual increase of initial interest after the turn of the millennium (see, e.g., Chatterjee, 2001; Liu et al., 2008; Duan et al., 2008), research on customer or consumer reviews has become prolific only during the recent decade. The focus areas in customer reviews research have been the expertise and motivations of writing customer reviews (Mackiewicz, 2010; McAuley & Leskovec, 2013), the perceived usefulness or helpfulness of customer reviews (Filieri, 2015; Ketelaar et al., 2015; Kim et al., 2011; Mudambi & Schuff, 2010; Purnawirawan et al., 2015; Schindler & Bickart, 2012; Willemsen et al., 2011; Wu, 2013), and the impact of customer reviews on individual purchases and, accordingly, sales or product returns (Dewenter & Heimeshoff, 2015; Duan et al., 2008; Floyd et al., 2014; Minnema et al., 2016; Vermeulen & Seegers, 2009; Wu et al., 2020; Zhu & Zhang, 2010; Zou et al., 2011). Even in these studies, expertise, often in the form of 'customer expertise' (Alba & Hutchinson, 1987), connected to the persuasiveness and influence of the review, has been the key term. Compared to studies of arts reviews, the approach to reviews has been instrumental, attaching reviews and reviewing to the framework of sales, marketing and business, within a specific field such as retail marketing or tourism. Reviews have typically been perceived in connection to the tradition of word of mouth (WOM), referred to as e-WOM in online environments, and the central question has been how to develop marketing strategies that would eliminate the risk of failure and maximize the use of customer voices.

In addition, reviews have been intensively studied in computer sciences, typically by applying computer-assisted methods such as data mining and sentiment analysis, to examine their linguistic features, experiences, opinions or impact (see, e.g., Genc-Nayebi & Abran, 2017). The study of recommendation systems has also been relevant for understanding the accumulation of expertise in user reviewing (McAuley & Leskovec, 2013). The interest in reviews has been motivated by examining the reviews' impact on retail sales and marketing, to detect changes and trends in consumers' lifeworlds and, in this way, to be able to forecast future trends.

Typically, art reviews, focused on forms of high art, and customer reviews, centred upon consumer goods, have been discussed separately. Between these two categories, there has been a fluctuating category of reviews on popular products and lifestyle-related commodities and services, that have not really found an established place in journalistic reviewing and, accordingly, in academic research. An evident reason for distinguishing between aesthetic and consumer, or cultural and customer, reviews is the more profound historically rooted distinction between products of arts and consumer products and their consumption. The very essence of art, and, accordingly, the community producing and consuming it, has largely relied upon a conception of its extraordinary character and distinction from non-art. The very identity and essence of art has, in other words, been based on the condition of being separated from life (Carroll, 2009). Scholars like cultural researcher Felski (2020) and pragmatic philosopher Shusterman (1992) have challenged the critical disinterestedness as the governing principle of reviewing arts, turning to

Dewey's (2005/1934) organic understanding of aesthetic experience and somaesthetics as underlying the principles of reviewing. Within journalism, the genre of review has been tightly connected to the ontological boundaries of arts. Reviewing, perhaps partly to fulfil its journalistic function of showing immediacy and newsworthiness, has adopted a connection to the monitoring of the launch of new products in the field of arts. A corollary to this has been the limitation of the review text to covering an artistic object, as well as the time of its release and period of public access. Review production has adopted an organizational structure of specialized writers each following their own area of expertise. In the structure of the daily newspaper, consumer product reviews have to a large extent been left to other sections beyond arts and culture; reviews of cars and sports gear, restaurants, food and wine, and fashion and cosmetics have been published in consumer, leisure sections and produced by writers not connected to the organizational unit of arts and culture, with its related extra-organizational networks. The production of these reviews has not been supported by any professional communities as in the field of arts where art reviewers and critics have a long tradition of their own professional unions, maintaining and developing the professional standards and advancing their position in society.

When discussing professional and amateur reviews, discussions on nascent online cultural critique still tend to be collapsed into an oversimplified division between professionals and amateurs, or the category of amateurs has been either very general, encompassing an abundance of different genres, communication modes and media platforms, or very specific, focusing on amateurism in one type of cultural form only. In established discourses on professionalism the mutually exclusive categories of 'professionals' and 'amateurs' have typically been set against each other, the one seen as challenging or even threatening to the other. While professionals have been envisioned as an exclusive group of knowledgeable public connoisseurs (Said, 1994), amateurs may have been downplayed as actors of ignorance and low quality (Keen, 2007). Alternatively, amateurs have been celebrated as the renewing force (Jenkins, 2007; Leadbeater, 2007), pushing professionals into a crisis (e.g. McDonald, 2007). These narratives, which are not part of the past but still maintained in everyday discourse, need to be deconstructed and re-thought in order to overcome the dichotomy that does not do any justice to the more diverse reality in online communities. The increasing body of research concerning user-generated content and online content creators has, indeed, started recognizing expertise as a process of learning instead of being a stable category, addressing processes of formalization of amateur media (Burgess, 2012) and professionalization of amateurs (McAuley & Leskovec, 2013).

## 1.2 Contexts of User Reviewing

What has enabled the emergence of reviewing carried out by an increasing number of sociocultural groups and not just media professionals? A simple answer would be the technological development that enables access to production for basically everyone. However, there are more fundamental epistemological shifts that have affected the intellectual discourses and informed action in the twenty-first century. In the previous section I described how reviewing, as a social phenomenon and an object of study, has been strongly connected to legacy media, professional organizations, professional identities and expertise, while the evolution revolution at hand calls for expansion of scope. In its online and ordinary forms, reviewing is part of vernacular creativity (Burgess, 2006) and entertainment (Baym, 2021). Göran Bolin has outlined a model for understanding the value production of television production (Bolin, 2004) and journalistic production (2007), in which the cultural economy of production is negotiated in four spheres of power: the political, economic, cultural and academic (Bolin, 2011, p. 31). In the following, I will discuss the central contexts of reviewing according to these dimensions.

The central contexts for reviewing in its non-institutional and non-professional forms can be identified in four areas: policies, public pedagogies, practices and academic research. International and national policy work, along with aligned applications and implementations at lower regional and local levels, sets a framework for citizens' creation of content. Policies are centred around the freedom of expression and cultural rights, while simultaneously stressing the protection of individuals' rights to immaterial work and of vulnerable groups from risk and harm. Policies consist of a number of documents with different degrees of binding content, ranging from legislation to recommendations. Public pedagogies refer to critical practices advancing learning in its informal contexts, that is, beyond the formal school curricula (Sandlin et al., 2010). These include learning in unconventional sites such as those of everyday and popular culture, from streets to museums, and from online cultures to activism events, supported and advanced by a diverse number of groups such as public intellectuals and cultural organizations. Practices are established sets of values, norms and routines to get things done in communities of practice (Wenger, 1998). Finally, research to a central degree contributes to conceptualizations of the phenomena at stake, and with this conceptual work makes us see the world in certain ways in the other three areas, which applies, for example, to the idea of audiences, cultural agency and media production. The central contexts in which the conditions for reviewing are formed, with some central concepts, are shown in Fig. 1.1.

In the *policy domain*, especially in culture- and media-related issues, nation states attempt to collect and prepare intellectual resources to support the agency of the individual at different levels. Central notions to individuals who engage as public reviewers are cultural citizenship and consumership, which go hand in hand, even if often discussed in different strands. Cultural citizenship has been expanded from its initial emphases on citizen's legal rights and formal membership of a nation state to cover global struggles for societal inclusion of and justice for marginalized groups (Beaman, 2016). Cultural citizenship refers to individuals' fundamental rights to belong to the participatory processes of democratic society, while having their differences recognized (Rosaldo, 1994). According to Klaus and Lünenborg (2012, p. 204), cultural citizenship 'entails all those cultural practices that allow competent participation in society and includes the rights to be represented and to speak actively'. Individuals' cultural rights include 'the right to symbolic presence and visibility (vs. marginalisation); the right to unhindered and dignified representation (vs.

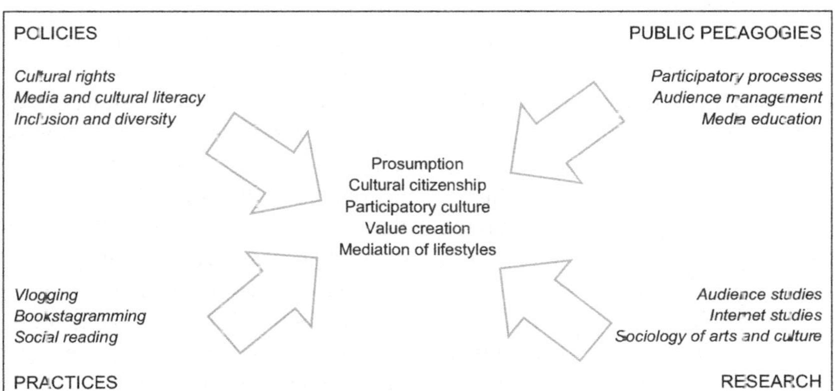


**Fig. 1.1** Central contexts and concepts of user reviewing

stigmatisation)', as well as 'the right to propagation and maintenance of distinct cultural identities and lifestyles (vs. assimilation)' (Pakulski, 2007, p. 77). In late modern or postmodern society, cultural citizenship is firmly connected to—ideally critical—cultural consumership and participation in entertainment and everyday culture (Burgess, 2006; Burgess, 2007; Burgess et al., 2006). In Murdock's (1999) words, central to the cultural citizenship are the rights of information, experiences, knowledge and participation, the latter referring to acting out one's cultural practices and ideas as part of meaning making in society. Delanty (2003) links learning as an essential ingredient to cultural citizenship, suggesting that cultural citizenship implies more a process than a static label.

Supporting cultural inclusion with regard to the possibilities for expressing one's 'lifestyle identity' and manifesting it publicly in the cultural sphere (McGuigan, 1996) has been the mission of many transnational policy efforts of the last century. These efforts have centred upon individuals' rights to freedom of speech and expression and national policy aspirations for citizen-consumers' ability to make an informed judgement. The promotion of human rights, based on the United Nations' Universal Declaration of Human Rights (1948), developed further in specific groups' rights such as minorities' (Thornberry & Martín Estébanez, 2004) and children's rights (OHCHR, 1989), and even minors' digital rights for expression (UN, 2021). According to article 13 of the Convention on the Rights of the Child (OHCHR, 1989), every child 'shall have the right to freedom of expression' and this right 'shall include freedom to seek, receive and impart information and ideas of all kinds, regardless of frontiers, either orally, in writing or in print, in the form of art, or through any other media of the child's choice'.

Based on these ideas, in 2011, UNESCO initiated a framework for media and information literacy (Grizzle et al., 2013) in which civic media competences are seen as a tool for sustainable democracy and intercultural dialogue. In the tradition of literacy and related research, cultural competence has been seen as a pivotal ingredient of being able to become a literate citizen and consumer. National media and educational policies alienated to the aim of developing media literacy pursue advancing a democratic environment in which the key feature is freedom of speech, transparency and trust in scientific knowledge, while at the same time protecting citizens from harmful influences and risky behaviour (UNESCO, 2013). Ethical regulation of content production on social media platforms and networks has, however, turned out to be less under the control of national states, imposing more responsibility on users themselves.

In supporting media literacy, the emphasis has throughout the history of the very concept of 'being media literate' been on receiving, interpreting, deconstructing and analysing messages, that is, on dimensions of critical reception as part of media (and information) literacy. Based on the US Aspen Media Literacy Leadership Institute's early definition from the 1992 media literacy conference (Aufderheide & Firestone, 1993), media literacy is defined as the ability to access, evaluate, analyse and create media in a variety of forms (UNESCO, 2013; Livingstone, 2004; Aufderheide & Firestone, 1993). The interpretation of media literacy has in practice put greater emphasis on reception qualities, which are the most fundamental and apply to the majority of citizens, while only a number of citizens are producing media themselves. The National Association for Media Literacy Education (NAMLE, 2020) declares that media literacy 'is about helping students become competent, critical and literate in all media forms so that they control the interpretation of what they see or hear rather than letting the interpretation control them'. They believe that the construction of critical autonomy, to use Masterman's (1985) vocabulary, is the ultimate aim of media literacy. According to the association's formulation, 'without this fundamental ability [of media literacy], an individual cannot have full dignity as a human person or exercise citizenship in a democratic society where to be a citizen is to both ***understand*** and ***contribute*** to the debates of the time' (NAMLE, 2020).

However, the focus being on the reception, evaluation and use of facts and information, the production knowledge, such as the knowledge needed in reviewing culture online, is more loosely articulated in policy frameworks, and the knowledge produced concerning the aspect of lay production and production cultures is often relatively case-specific. This may be because production is a matter for minorities of users—user studies in general tend to point to the fact that only about 10 per cent produce content—and often connected to professional identities rather than ordinary citizenship. Still, we have to ask how the specific communication environments in which messages are created affect and direct the citizens, who are attracted by others' attention, entertainment and emotions and not only rational fact-seeking. What kind of producer identities, comparable to professional identities, as well as norms, values, practices and routines, exist, or should exist, for the citizen producers, similar to the professional equivalents, and what competences are needed to construct and maintain these? One could even question the aim of creation and ask to which extent the creation of public messages is an aspiration for every citizen. When is the creation of published messages relevant, and on which conditions? Aren't there grades of contribution that all require different self-awareness related to the creatorship of messages, ranging from simple reacting and commenting to producing stand-alone pieces of work? The construction of theories concerning the production knowledge should not be left to case studies; rather, more general theoretical frameworks, followed by practical recommendations and successive policies, should be pursued.

In the *public pedagogies* domain, the emergence of the idea of participation and pertinent participatory practices marks an important development. The diverse practices that occur outside formal schooling can be brought together under the umbrella construct of public pedagogies (Burdick et al., 2014). Cultural organizations, especially media organizations and high-cultural organizations such as theatres and the LAM sector (libraries, archives, museums), have adopted approaches that to an increasing degree aim at including ordinary citizens and cultural consumers in their work. The curatorial turn of cultural organizations (O'Neill, 2007) entails the idea of an increase and development of curatorial practices, interactivity, as well as community and audience management and development. Audience development refers to the strategic work carried out by the management of cultural organizations aimed at increasing the outreach of their output (Kawashima, 2000). Kawashima (2000) distinguishes between four types of audience development: audience education, taste cultivation, extended marketing and work for cultural inclusion. Audience education and taste cultivation target existing audiences, while extended marketing addresses potential and culturally inclusive unlikely audiences. The same development towards inclusivity and participation can be seen on the market where private and commercial actors have become interested in co-creation with customers and consumers, or customer management. In an era where information retrieval can ideally be based on big data, the extensive numbers of customer reviews play a key role in providing information on trends in customer preferences and behaviour.

As for the *practices*, what is particularly relevant for new forms of reviewing are the forms of social and cultural engagement as well as platform-specific communication that have started emerging because of the socio-technological changes of the twenty-first century. Even before the development of the internet and social media, there were forms of socializing that were based on mutual interaction, collaboration and exchange between enthusiasts in a specific cultural domain. For example, zines of different kinds may have involved elements of hobbyist reviewing (Knobel & Lankshear, 2002). In literature, literature cafes, book clubs and practices of social reading (Eberly, 2000; Fuller & DeNel Rehberg, 2013; Long, 2003) prepared the rise of reviewing online, which is still very much based on social contacts and interaction. The recent development of platformization (see Sect. 3.4 Platformized Cultural Production in Chap. 3), the centralization of communication to social networking sites controlled by GAFAM, or the Big Five—the global media giants Google, Apple, Facebook, Amazon and Microsoft—has involved the emergence of communication led by platform users that is constantly adapted to the affordances of the specific platforms. Reviewing is being developed in conjunction with and within the more general forms of blogging, vlogging, Instagramming and image sharing, and podcasting. Critical discussions similar to the content of reviewing are also seen in status updates, posts and discussion threads of social networking sites and communication tools with varying degrees of publicness. The new platforms enable not only user-led content production and horizontal ties between users, but also multimodal communication that results in practices that have been more or less foreign to the genre of reviewing, the entire tradition of which has essentially been argumentation-based and logocentric.

The most popular social media platforms worldwide in October 2020, with public community features (in contrast to limited-group and semi-private functions such as on WhatsApp, Facebook Messenger and so on), were the multi-purpose social networking site Facebook (2.7 billion active users), the video platform YouTube (2.0 billion), the visual app Instagram (1.2 billion) and the video app TikTok (689 million) (Statista, 2020d). The user-generated content is thus centrally characterized by the publishing and sharing of visual and audiovisual materials. Average time spent daily on the internet worldwide has been on a continuous increase since the last decade, having increased from 75 to 192 minutes (Statista, 2020a). Video and entertainment have gained more ground in global social media consumption patterns, increasing from 13 per cent in 2016 to 21 per cent in 2019 of the total time spent using social media, at the cost of general social interaction and communication as well as game playing, which have slightly decreased (Statista, 2020b). For the development of reviewing practices, the platforms with highest relevance at the time of writing are

YouTube, Instagram and TikTok, as well as the internally diverse spheres of blogs and podcasts, because these include the possibility to publish stand-alone public works that can be identified as reviews and contribute to the societal functions of reviewing and criticism.

When it comes to *academic research*, research that has identified the 'people formerly known as the audience' (as noted by Jeff Jarvis) as its object of inquiry have paved the way for examining user reviewing as a phenomenon in its own right. What has played a specific role is the fact that academic research has significantly contributed to recognizing the societal worth of, and the worth of studying, active audiences, popular culture, entertainment and 'lower' and more mundane forms of culture, all of which are important dimensions of user reviewing. The emergence of new interdisciplinary areas of inquiry such as cultural studies, feminisms and media literacy has entailed an explicit *mission* to change the prevailing disciplinary structures by producing knowledge that enables new knowledge to be generated, which has benefited the study of non-legitimized and non-professional epistemology, and 'smaller' and ordinary agency and consumption. The shifts in academic research, such as the cultural (e.g. Ray & Sayer, 1999), participatory (e.g. Bherer et al., 2016) and affective (e.g. Clough & Halley, 2007) turn, have influenced the development of methodologies, and with the help of nethnography it has become possible to explore citizen and consumer communities. Understanding the role of large metaprocesses transforming societies, such as mediatization (Hjarvard, 2013), has helped in dedicating scholarly attention to the small agency and expertise of citizens and consumers. Both converging and diverging metaprocesses have been identified. Converging metaprocesses have brought nation states, cultures and perspectives together, as in globalization, digitalization and media convergence, accelerating people's access to cultural resources. Diverging metaprocesses such as individualization, democratization and neoliberalization have an effect of increasing differentiation and diversity, undermining the monopoly of institutional reviewing.

Academic research has shed light on the conditions in which phenomena such as user reviewing occur. In postmodern cultural economies, relationships formerly untainted by commerce have increasingly become commercialized and aesthethized (Featherstone, 2007/1991). In 'hybrid economies' (Scaraboto, 2015), 'sharing economies' (Botsman & Rogers, 2010), 'attention' or 'like economies' (Gerlitz & Helmond, 2013), or 'experience economies' (Pine II & Gilmore, 2011), market and non-market practices interact; lifestyle communities, as consumer communities, are acting in market exchange systems while simultaneously being able to act as agents of change. Lash and Urry (1994) use the term 'reflexive accumulation' to denote the condition in which economic and cultural processes are more closely interwoven than in earlier phases of modern capitalism. Sociology of consumption has produced insightful theories on reviews (Blank, 2007) and tastes (Wright, 2015) that can be applied to user reviewers' engagement. In culturally oriented media studies, Bolin (2011) has made a valuable effort in theoretically outlining the conditions of consumption, or productive consumption as he calls value creation, in different media environments. The recent cultural and communication research on platformized cultural production in online environments (Sect. 3.4 Platformized Cultural Production in Chap. 3) has high relevance in understanding how the cultural economy of user reviewing works.

One of the most discernible insights of recent decades has been the conviction articulated in media and cultural studies that the audience, or actually the 'public', is active and critical, consisting of passive receivers, and also able to produce messages. The shift from passive to active, or consuming to creative, audience was initially developed in television studies and more recently in internet studies, accompanied by neologisms that hybridize the new and old positionings. The user reviewers are what Bruns (2008) has labelled 'produsers' and Toffler (1980) almost three decades earlier characterized as 'prosumers' (see also Bird, 2011; Bruns, 2016; Ritzer et al., 2012; Ritzer & Jurgenson, 2010). Prosumer, as a consumer of the post-industrial age, refers to an individual who produces many of their own goods and services. Since then, the active and creative consumers have been called protagonists, value co-creators and consum'actors, all of whom have in common that their involvement in branding and production empowers them to 'create their own lives and contribute positively to companies' (Cova & Dalli, 2018, p. 248).

Because the hybrid neologisms of produsage and prosumption couple reception with production roles, they enable seeing users as both citizens and consumers, and both receivers and producers at the same time. Those citizen-consumers who choose not only to remain private receivers but start producing messages become public agents making processes of reception and consumption visible. They are participating in processes that are normative, hermeneutic and transformative. Normative connects to the creation of value to a product or a lifestyle; by addressing cultural products user reviewers are figuring out the uses of literature, music, food, toys, comics or whatever the object of their reviewing is. By articulating positions of consumption and sharing them in a community that essentially has an affirmative relationship with the reviewer, the user reviews are doing normative work, working as value, quality or taste detectors. They are also developing discourses that add to the meaning making around cultural products, constructing meaningful identities as fans, admirers and enthusiasts, and citizens and consumers. Sharing and mutual exchange also essentially imply a learning process, where meaning about cultural products, forms and lifestyles is collaboratively discovered and elaborated.

The user reviewers may constitute marginal, biased or diverse groups, and their output cannot be taken as representative, which is a normal presumption in institutional reviewers' work (see 4. Reviewing in Genre and Practice). What cultural citizenship and consumership have in common is the fact that they set up symbolic boundaries with inclusion and exclusion, and users with certain features become more popular and influential in their communities than others. Belonging to an online community is not synonymous with having media literacy agency, refined taste or advanced understanding of the field of monitoring, and neither does media literacy agency automatically imply 'good agency', that is, having liberal, egalitarian, peace-promoting, non-racist, inclusive or non-biased aims (McDougall, 2017).

Still, user reviewers' communities provide us with windows into how lifestyles are practised and how cultural products are connected to everyday life and individuals' identities. To address the user reviewers' embeddedness in networked communities, I am using the term *lifestyle community* (see Sect. 2.2 Online Lifestyle Communities in Chap. 2). It intends to bridge the gap between the disinterested, democracy-oriented discourses of citizen communities and the commercially oriented consumer discourses. Users in online lifestyle communities have a common interest in a specific cultural area and are maintaining a same kind of engagement in this cultural domain, whether it is reading books, using cosmetic products or playing same type of video game. Central to users in online lifestyle communities are the performative practices of preferred or fantasized cultural citizenship and/or consumership, based on inclusion in material and symbolic conditions of consumption. Ways of being a citizen-consumer are lived out in roles that require knowledge and competence, and this competence needs to be recognized by others in the community, whether the community deals with book culture, beauty or video games. Practices related to lifestyle communities are partly documentary, recording an experience or encounter with a particular product; partly evaluative, testing and assessing a product or service; and partly performative, following ideals and norms of being a certain kind of cultural citizen-consumer. In practising their cultural citizenship, or a specific area of it like literary citizenship of a certain kind, reviewers are users who transform their insights from receiving products into self-created coverage, which entails a profound act of self-expression. This lifestyle work, rooted in the ordinary consumption of everyday life, has been called 'leisure-work' (Bell & Hollows, 2005), which invites consumers to play with their identities through lifestyle choices and choices to share these choices with others. The lifestylization of everyday life is a product of social, economic and cultural processes and can be seen as complementary to the mediation of lifestyle that was previously conducted by 'lifestyle media' to the consumers. The mediated leisure work done by cultural prosumption implies turning the existing properties of lifestyles into the situated context of one's own lifeworld. The lifestyle communities are places for such 'aesthetic practices' (Vinogradovs, 2021), spaces for identity formation, reflection and re-formation.

The online lifestyle communities practising reviewing of new cultural products are media-literate communities: the people who are involved in processes that are set as the aim of the current media literacy framework. When contrasted to professionals' content production, however, they are easily dismissed as low-quality, contingent and heterogeneous content production communities. However, their potential lies in being open to everyone, allowing different levels and standards of participation, and providing entry points into public engagement that can turn freedom of expression into something real. Processes may be important for individuals involved in them, and their public activity may be inspiring to others, initiating constructive and transformative learning processes. Instead of assessing lifestyle communities solely in terms of the quality of conduct and outcome, they could be, above all, conceived of as processes of learning. The postmodern communication culture invites even traditional intermediaries, who were previously positioned in expert roles, into such a dialogical learner's role, or 'gardeners', as Bauman (1987) puts it.

To see both traditional professional intermediaries and the vernacular intermediaries as cultivators of contemporary cultures is the pursuit of this book. The context of this book is formed by what I at a general level call post-institutional cultural production (see Chap. 3. Reviewing as

Post-Institutional Cultural), and the functions of cultural intermediaries are connected to it through the post-professional framework. It is the focal interest of this book to examine the altered and entirely new professionalisms that emerge through the newer professionalization processes. In essence, this book discusses two phenomena, a very old (classical reviewing of arts) and a very young (user-generated reviewing), trying to create a synthesis and a broad-brush perspective that would help us recognize the traits of both phenomena. The book aims to examine reviewing from an emic perspective, that is, a perspective that arises from within the reviewer communities, rather than constructing an etic, an outside observer's, perspective (Whitaker, 2017). This means that we cannot impose the standards of institutional reviewing, let alone criticism, on the emerging and new forms of user-generated reviewing; rather, the latter needs to be identified, understood and conceptualized in its own right. By identifying the differences and similarities among the various forms of reviewing we can try to put them onto the same map, but without losing their distinctive features. In this way we can also learn to see the worth of different groups of reviewers in the political economy of reviewing, who may exert different functions, fulfilling different yet parallel needs at different levels of education and socioeconomic hierarchy, and setting up different standards of quality. I will frame the new and emerging forms of reviewing as post-institutional and post-professional cultural production; the two fundamental dimensions thus include the changes in the institutional environment in which reviewing is being conducted, and the professionalizing identity politics that form different groups of actors, sustained in self-identified reviewing communities.

## 1.3 Methodological Background

The object of study is cultural audiences that consist of consumers of cultural products who want to take an active role as public communicators by sharing their experiences by producing messages online in the specific genre of review. This book is thus anchored in media studies with a connection to online cultures, drawing on audience studies, and studies of cultural engagement and lifestyles, as examined across interdisciplinary areas of subdisciplines in social sciences. With regard to the multifaceted character of the object of study, I will borrow concepts and theories from kinship disciplines such as cultural studies and study of culture, sociology (in particular, sociology of arts) and consumer research (in particular, studies on consumer cultures). My focus will be on the communicative and aesthetic aspects of cultural communication during the second decade of the twenty-first century, crystallized in the user-defined concept of genre, instead of the actual content of mediated culture, cultural content or cultural change.

This book is based on my studies on reviewers in 2010–2020. My point of departure is essentially the fact that I started my journey by studying the media professionals—reviewers in legacy media—having worked as a professional cultural journalist myself (Jaakkola, 2015). After this, the increased online activity in reviewing drew my attention and I wanted to outline the communities of reviewing as seen beyond the institutional settings. My intention is not to make direct comparisons between these two forms; rather, my argument is that continuities and similarities, as well as contradictions and differences, may help us understand the two profoundly different phenomena in a better way. I also want to underline the conviction that one phenomenon is not a threat to the other, even if vernacular reviewing is often seen as subordinated or even as a threat to the institutional activities.

The individual studies that this book is based upon, published as separate analyses in international peer-reviewed journals, deal with reviewers on Instagram, YouTube and Vimeo. These platforms present the most popular networking sites at the time of writing, and are also the most relevant with regard to platformized cultural production and vernacular reviewing as a case of this. More specifically, I have studied book reviewers on Instagram (Jaakkola, 2019), video reviewers on YouTube (Jaakkola, 2018), children's toy reviewers on YouTube (Jaakkola, 2020a), child reviewers across platforms (Jaakkola, 2020c, 2020d) and film gadget reviewers on Vimeo (Jaakkola, 2020b, 2020c). These reviewing communities not only represent the most extensive and influential reviewer communities, but also communities that have been less studied in terms of cultural (inter)mediation. They can to an essential degree be complemented with knowledge retrieved from studies on gamers and gaming (e.g. Lin et al., 2019) and film cultures (e.g. McAuley & Leskovec, 2013; McWhirther, 2016) and consumer product reviews that have been more richly studied as platformized production than those selected by me, and bear relevance to the phenomenon of reviewing culture online.

In previous articles, I have presented qualitative analyses of reviews of different types. The empirical work is based on automatic retrieval of an extensive amount of data, which has made it possible to outline these communities better than with purposive sampling. Identifying the most popular users—or, as in this case, reviewers—is relevant because online communities are strongly influenced by those who act at the top of the genre hierarchies (Himma-Kadakas et al., 2019). Genres applied by the most popular channels appear to be continuously reproduced and imitated by YouTubers placed lower in the hierarchy, that is, with fewer subscribers. This suggests that re-invention of genres most probably occurs on the most subscribed channels rather than on recently created channels that are more likely to follow and mimic the conventionalized practices and genre norms established by already successful channels.

With automated scripts it is possible—despite the increased restrictions imposed by platform providers—to collect data that are unbiased and not directed by the limitations of a user's everyday observations (Caliandro & Gandini, 2019). Automatic data retrieval makes it possible to sort and structure a community according to the metadata on users and content features. For example, a dataset can be sorted according to number of followers, subscribers, views, likes or other metadata, to identify the most attention-grabbing and thus influential users in the community. This is not possible with manual work, as the volumes are extensive and personalization of online content, based on algorithms that try to filter out content according to the receiver's preferences, makes content feeds look different to different users. However, with regard to the massive amounts of data, its analysis needs to be complemented with qualitative approaches, as in the case studies presented in Chap. 6 Vernacular Reviewers' Communities: Case Studies.

My analyses of Instagram book reviewers are based on a dataset consisting of public Instagram entries that used the hashtag #bookreview in 2019. The analysis covers public entries that are more permanent, that is, they are not 'stories'—a feature launched in August 2016, where entries are available on the user's profile for only 24 hours. The open software Instagram Scraper was used to collect the posts that were published on Instagram and provided with the given hashtag at a given point of time. Instagram Scraper is an application written in Python that scrapes and downloads Instagram users' photos and videos (http://github.com/rarcega/instagramscraper; see also Caliandro & Gandini, 2019).

To enable the retrieval of individual users and relevant information regarding the book-review posts, the script was enhanced by additional features. The script was written by Pasi Luostarinen (BeTeK) and the new script was released online as Instagram User Scraper (https://github.com/BeTeK/InstagramUserScraper). The script transferred the internal user-id to a user name and retrieved these users' metadata, which included user name, URL address of the post, caption, number of likes and comments per post, number of followers and users followed by a user, user handle ('bio') and rank of the hashtag #bookreview. The data retrieval occurred from 25 to 29 January 2019 (Instagram Scraper) and from 30 January to 3 February 2019 (the enhanced script).

The script retrieved 631,771 posts in which the hashtag #bookreview was used, from 199,568 unique users. Among these posts, we do not know for what purpose the hashtag was used, whether it was a reference to a book review published in traditional media, written by a professional reviewer, or whether the user was writing about book reviews in general, or perhaps happened to use #bookreview for promotion or spam. With such large amounts of data, it is impossible to sort out the original review posts, which should be conducted by manual coding, as the review cannot be reduced to some formalized characteristics. Therefore, the macro analysis could only address some formal characteristics of the use of the hashtag, and the purpose of the data retrieval was to track the general outline of the review community on Instagram. Among the 199,568 unique users identified as having used the hashtag #bookreview, 1381 (0.2 per cent) had set their profile as private, which disabled access to some parts of their data (the content of the post and the number of followers/following). With the majority ($N$ = 198,187) being public, though, the genre of review appears to be very community- and network-oriented. To minimize the number of fake or irrelevant entries, the dataset was further limited by excluding posts based on the following interaction criteria: likes≤5, followed≤20, following = 0. Thus, the data was limited to 594,804 posts in total, all public entries, by 65,534 individual users. When users with ≤10 posts in their account were eliminated—many of them still featuring spam or irrelevant topics and indicating no continuity which would be elementary to the reviewing—the number of posts was reduced to 163,269 entries and the number of users to 8474 individual users. In total, 1907 posts (1 per cent) were video posts and 161,362 (99 per cent) still images. The dataset was organized according to the posting volume (the highest number of review posts) and popularity (the highest number of followers), and analysed further with the help of mixed methods analysis. Content was analysed by applying the basic methods of thematic analysis (Guest et al., 2012) and visual analysis (Bell, 2000).

For an accompanying micro analysis, a sample of a local community was created by focusing on a geographically and culturally limited area of one country and a relatively small community of Finnish-speaking Finland (for a more detailed analysis of results, see Jaakkola, 2020b). There are 4.9 million native speakers of the Finnish language, and it was possible to get a comprehensive understanding of the local Kirjagram community that reflects and circulates the ideas of the global Bookstagram community. The data consists of entries from a Finnish book-reviewing community, in which the entries were hashtagged with #kirjaarvostelu ('book review') at the point of data collection. The hashtag corresponds, for example, to #bokrecension (7530 entries), #boganmeldelse (4699 entries), #buchrezension (8268 entries), #critiquedelivre (336 entries) and #recensionelibri (9645 entries) in other language communities. The data collection for this local sample occurred on 27–29 December 2018. There were 645 posts tagged with #kirjaarvostelu. Entries were manually collected and analysed by opening each image and using the entire post as a unit of analysis. Because the community was included in its entirety, personalization of the feed did not significantly influence the results. To gain an overview, 25 per cent—160 entries in total, from 65 users—of the Finnish book-review space with #kirjaarvostelu were allotted to a category that was developed from within the content. The coding occurred on 31 December 2018 and 3–4 January 2019. A quarter of the whole population was assessed as a saturated sample, as the rest of the material of the entire community was browsed through and did not show any further deviations from the coded material.

To contextualize findings from content analyses, an online questionnaire was released in 2020 and sent to the relevant Instagram book reviewers included in the global dataset. The questionnaire was compiled in the software Qualtrics and included 17 questions, which occupied 4 screen views on a mobile device. The invitation was directed to users with a minimum of 100 review posts published on their accounts ($N = 727$ individual users), and the highest and average number of posts were 11,046 and 245, respectively. While going through the list of users, I identified a total of 93 accounts that had been changed (deleted, made private or changed), and they were thus excluded. Accordingly, invitations were sent to 627 account holders, with a reminder after one week. The invitations were sent either through the internal messaging system of Instagram, so-called direct messages (DMs), or via e-mail. If the user had mentioned his or her e-mail in his or her profile, he or she was approached via e-mail. Otherwise, a DM was sent, with identical text to that in the e-mail. This hybrid strategy was adopted because Facebook restricted the sending of DMs; typically, you could only send four messages before getting blocked for a while. The invitations were sent between 2 April and 16 April 2020. This timeframe coincided with the coronavirus pandemic, during which many people were sitting at home in quarantine.

In total, I received 76 responses. Compared to the dataset used as the basis for invitations, the response rate was low at 12 per cent. However, as I used the invitations as a self-excluding method, many less serious users or users with no relevance for book reviewing denied the request, and the original dataset was highly diverse and heterogeneous, we can argue that the body of responses can be seen as valid for identifying some user behaviour behind the published content. All the responses were serious and provided detailed descriptions as responses to the open questions. All those who responded regarded book reviewing as relevant to their communication strategy. The majority of the questionnaire respondents, 45 per cent, were aged 20–30, 33 per cent were aged between 30 and 40, with 21 per cent aged over 40 and 1 per cent aged under 20. The great majority of those who responded (88 per cent) said that they were female. Of the respondents, 71 per cent were freelancers, 14 per cent were unemployed and 8 per cent were students. All respondents remained anonymous, as had been promised, and in the analysis I will thus refrain from mentioning individual account names.

To further extend the analysis of Instagram book reviewers, I analysed text material, retrieved as part of the dataset, from 727 users' handles. Even if the list of users analysed was not fully identical to the survey respondents' profiles, the extensive volume of these most active Bookstagram book reviewers' self-presentations could give an overview of the most frequently occurring themes, terms and expressions. The handle texts were deconstructed with a simple automated text analysis, identifying key terms in the word frequency analysis and visualization tool WordArt.

Besides Instagram, I was interested in reviewing on the popular video-sharing platform YouTube. The collection of data on YouTube was executed, with channels as a unit of analysis, by means of an automated script, that is, a program written by a computer programmer to perform data retrieval according to a set of ordered operations. The script retrieved an initial sample from the 5000 most subscribed to channels that automatically noted video counts, views, likes and dislikes. The script was released as open software on GitHub. Data retrieval occurred from 26–29 April

2017 and collected 4999 channels representing 6,697,639 videos, with an average of 1340 videos per channel.

The toy review sample (the case study in Sect. 6.3 At the Playstage: Toy Reviewers on YouTube in Chap. 6) was pulled from this larger dataset (for an analysis of the dataset, see Jaakkola, 2018) by manual coding (see below), to arrive at a limited sample consisting of 35 toy review channels including 29,037 individual videos. The manual coding was applied in a two-stage process. First, review channels were separated from non-review channels with the help of 'About' descriptions and examinations of the channel's front page. This procedure limited the sample to 200 review channels. Second, the remaining channels were coded according to the group of cultural objects the channel was mainly covering, such as toys, cosmetics or games. A sample of 35 toy review channels was extracted. (For a more detailed methodological description of the sampling and data management process, see Jaakkola, 2018.)

Thereafter, the sample of 35 toy review channels was subjected to a two-stage qualitative analysis. First, each channel was analysed in terms of its profile and channel characteristics, such as subscribers, views, likes and dislikes, to get an overview of these types of channels in general. Channels provided only a very rough overview and many of the individual videos on the review channels fell beyond the category of reviews. This is why the unit of analysis was switched from channels to videos. Second, using videos as the unit of analysis, five videos from each channel were selected that best fit the definition of a review and that were listed as a 'review' by the content producers themselves. This second stage of analysis was conducted, preferably, using in-built playlists that were specifically created for toy reviews by the content creators to contribute their accessibility. A subset of 180 toy review videos from the 35 content-producing channels were subjected to close reading and analysed with regard to the actors appearing in the videos (narrator) and the activities completed while conducting the review (method). In addition, the rhetorical strategies used by narrators when making an evaluation or an assessment were identified.

As for Vimeo (the case study in Sect. 6.2 Judging Gadgets: Filmmaker Reviewers on Vimeo in Chap. 6), the data were collected on the website Vimeo.com among published and thus publicly available video material. Based on the possibilities and restrictions provided by Vimeo's API, a script for Vimeo was created. The script, released as an open software on GitHub, automatically retrieved videos provided with the hashtag #review, limited to videos with a minimum of 10 likes. The retrieved information included the username, the user URL, the number of likes and the number of followers of the username, which are all public information. The data retrieval occurred in July 2017 and the output data is dated July 13 2017. The data collection retrieved a total of 1661 videos. Besides content that could be regarded as review videos, the sample included videos that did not show reviewing character even if tagged as #review: original films, film trailers to be reviewed later or elsewhere, PR material and other miscellaneous content that did not relate to the review genre. The sample was manually coded by separating review videos (1) from non-review videos (0). A review video was thus expected to show original content that comments on or otherwise builds a relationship with a cultural object or objects. The coding resulted in 1273 videos categorized as 'review videos', which formed the sample for further analysis. The qualitative analysis of videos was based on identification of the main types of review videos (What kind of cultural products were reviewed in the videos?) and their common characteristics, which are condensed around the concept of 'usefulness'.

As the sample is limited to videos with some or a high degree of interaction between the producers and viewers, seen in the number of likes (10–3879), the sample may overlook some reviews that would be relevant for theorizing about reviewing but have not built up any dialogical audience relationship (i.e. have nine or fewer likes). This might be the case with videos that have only been published on Vimeo but in fact consumed somewhere else by embedding the videos in external websites. However, due to the API restrictions causing it not to be possible to automatically retrieve the number of views per video, the sampling method could not be based on actual views. The number of likes and followers of individual producers may, nevertheless, function as some sort of quality control; videos with no interaction often turned out to be material of varied quality and with no clear connection to reviewing. Furthermore, it has been found that the more popularity the user reviewers gain, the more 'objective' their reviews tend to become (Goes et al., 2014). Besides, since reviewing is typically a continuous activity by someone who wants to profile as a reviewer, it can be assumed that a serious and continuous activity eventually brings forward at least some online interaction.

As noted, the material analysed in this sample is public: it has been published online and shared to an unlimited audience on Vimeo. While bearing in mind that the mere availability of data does not directly mean that it can be used for research purposes (see, e.g., Zimmer, 2010), in this case the producers under study explicitly position themselves as publishers of public content, making explicit claims for authorship, which means that they can be conceived of as publishers and their channels can be juxtaposed to public media. This condition differs from social networking sites where people appear in different and more private roles such as commentators in a virtual debate, possibly not even being aware of the public and performative character of their appearance. Nevertheless, to protect the privacy of individual reviewers, the producers' activities are described at a general level as much as possible instead of focusing on individuals who can be identified.

This book draws on observations based on empirical work, but creating a theoretical framework of reviewing, to show the social imaginary of this type of communication across different production spaces, is my main ambition. However, when talking about reviewing as an entity we have to be aware of the heterogeneousness and internal incoherence of this non-formalized 'field'. While all reviewing per se requires some sort of interest, knowledge and experience from the reviewer, the act of reviewing different products incorporates different emphases, methods and styles, and may sometimes be very fragmented and contingent. In addition, reviewing cultural products such as books and films, and consumer products like lipsticks and camera equipment, requires different kinds of approaches from the reviewer. Above all, the outcome of reviewing, the review text, needs to look different, as the content of books cannot be visualized and put into practice in the same way as, for example, lipsticks and mascara can be shown and tested. Different online reviewing communities develop different practices and standards for reviewing, and as an embedded practice (see 7. Characteristics of Vernacular Reviewing), reviewing is likely to adopt traits from online subcultures in which the reviewing unfolds.

When studying reviewing and cultural journalism more generally, the researcher has two fundamental choices at hand. The first way is to approach the object of study in a holistic or cross-genre and cross-medium way, or, as I have called it, as an integrative approach, combining different professional paradigms and coverage of different cultural forms, as well as examining content across different genres. The other option is to delimit the object of study by focusing on one cultural form (film) or subform (animation), or one genre (e.g. review) only. Both ways are essential in advancing the study of a certain field like cultural journalism or criticism. Study approaches should be alternated and insights retrieved from them should be compared and combined. For this book I have chosen the holistic way in order to gain a bigger picture.

Discussing both aesthetic user reviews and customer product reviews under the same umbrella term of reviewing is not fully unproblematic. I have chosen to do so because these types of user reviews have similarities to each other, and in online reviewing, especially in the open-participation platforms of social media, the boundary between an aesthetic and consumer product or service becomes porous. Previous research has often focused either on aesthetic or customer-related reviewing, which may result in unnecessary dualisms and construct obstacles for seeing what is important for the theories of reviewing. Many social media reviewers also adopt a hybrid of ambiguous positions with regard to the distinctions between aesthetic products vs. consumer products, or disinterestedness vs. consumerism, creating hybrid forms that we would easily miss if we only focused on one form of product. However, there is a discrepancy between aesthetic and consumer reviews traditions and, accordingly, practices. In customer reviewing it is not relevant to maintain a distinction between amateurs and professionals in the same way that it has been of importance in the aesthetic domain. Customers always remain non-professionals, comparable to amateurs, because customership does not imply a full-time occupation.

Last but not least, it has to be underscored that reviewing is truly global as a social phenomenon. Even if online cultures are globalized and trends travel across linguistic, cultural and geographical boundaries, there are many local online cultures and niche cultures as well. Studying cultures is always more or less ethnocentric, as one's own cultural anchoring, with all its boundaries in terms of mastering languages and cultural codes, affects the way culture is accessed. I have been and am working in the Nordic countries, which inevitably affects my way of viewing the topic under discussion by, for example, ethnocentrically prioritizing the 'Western' perspectives. However, when we are talking about internet use, the focus essentially lies on the 'Western' perspectives, and reviewing can at a general level be characterized as leisure work of the privileged, at least in its more advanced forms and in aesthetic fields that require cultural capital to be accessed. The global internet usage rate was about 54 per cent in 2020, developed countries such as those in Europe and the Americas showing the highest rate (87 per cent on average) (Statista, 2020e). The people enjoying the privilege of expressing their lifestyle online is limited. This group of users is not only relatively young and presumably middle-class but also globally oriented in their mindset. As in institutional professionalism, reviewers are no longer confined to their national languages and cultures; by choosing English or an alternative world language such as Spanish, Arabic, Russian or Mandarin Chinese, an individual content creator may reach wider audiences. English is, however, the global lingua franca, used by 26 per cent of internet users, leaving behind Chinese (19 per cent), Spanish (8 per cent) and Arabic (5 per cent) (Statista, 2020c). Simultaneously, there are national userspheres with smaller languages that may play an important role in lifestyle communities. Nevertheless, more and more users are following content across linguistic and thus even cultural boundaries, as the increased use of visuals and rapidly developing automatic translation functions enable intercultural dialogue that has not been possible in the same volume and with the same user-friendliness before.

## 1.4 The Structure of the Book

This book consists of seven chapters and is structured as follows. After the introduction setting the theoretical and methodological context for examining reviewing, Chap. 2 enquires into digital online communities, localizing the review communities as prosumptive communities of lifestyle and taste. Chapter 3 introduces the idea of platformized cultural production, and inserts the frequently addressed model of cultural mediation in this relatively young and still evolving landscape. A central concept is cultural intermediation, a term originally coined by Pierre Bourdieu, to describe reviewers' role as bridging and translating functions spanning different communities and organizations. I agree that the critique put forward towards the all-purpose use of the term does not do any justice to the multifaceted landscape of cultural mediators, and we have to keep different functions apart, developing a more nuanced vocabulary for addressing the boundary-spanning actors. This is why the chapter further introduces and discusses the concept of cultural intramediation, and develops more sensitivity towards different flows of mediation that are important for a deepened understanding of different reviewers operating in different institutional and non-institutional contexts.

Cultural intermediation and intramediation are to a central extent dependent on understandings on the genre of review, and its traditions, modes and styles of expression. Chapter 4 describes the basic character of the genre of review, based on a sociocultural theory of genre, and distinguishes genre communities at different levels, identifying the sociocultural forms of criticism, journalistic reviewing and user reviewing as the main traditions. User reviewing is further divided into two basic forms according to their production environment: user reviewing on user-review sites and user reviewing on the social web. These two categories are based on different forms of knowledge production. The first one is hierarchically, top-down organized and controlled by a centralized structure showing the spaces and imposing the rules of communication on users, which links it to institutional structures. This form of user reviewing, indeed, forms the basis of what I later call institutional amateurism. The second one, based on the basic idea of social media or Web 2.0, is less guided by a central review organization structure and rather organized through loose structuration in online communities, based on users' content production, mutual interaction and exchange. This form of user reviewing is defined as the vernacular web, which is the most recent and, in the scope of this book, interesting form of post-professional reviewing.

Chapter 5 continues from here and outlines a general framework for examining reviewers in different communication environments, institutional and non-institutional (vernacular). The chapter describes a typology of reviewers, distinguishing between institutionalized professional and amateur reviewers, as well as vernacular amateurs and professionals, and discussing the central traits of each. The overarching theoretical framework of cultural intermediation is thus specified by identifying the main groups of reviewers according to the vantage points of institutional attachment and professionalization, with a focus on the reviewers' expertise. The framework is further specified and concretized in Chap. 6, which consists of case studies examining the major vernacular reviewing communities on popular social media platforms. The communities addressed in this context include four different but potentially innovative signature practices of reviewing that illustrate different dimensions of the practice and purpose of vernacular reviewing.

As for the case studies, as the first case, I will take a look at book reviewers who are active as part of the Bookstagram community on the mobile visual app Instagram, in which it has become commonplace to address 'bookish' things and cherish book-related lifestyle culture. Instagram book reviewers, although they are a specific group of reviewers using visual means of communication, essentially connect to other central book platforms such as blogs as well as review and advance reading copy services. Second, I have chosen the filmmaker and film gadget reviewers on the video-sharing platform Vimeo as a showcase community, as they show a professional dimension of reviewing while being different from the classical connoisseur tradition manifest in institutional criticism and also seen in the vernacular domain. The third group of reviewers are children, who are typically creating content in a family context, which is popular on YouTube. Toy reviewers are important not only because they constitute a large group of content creators but also because they expose the ethical problems related to reviewing in a tangible and illuminating way. Last but not least, I will examine the heterogeneous category of reviewtainment that is scattered around all popular social media platforms and is more an overall category or mode than a delineable community. However, reviewtainers constitute an increasingly influential form of presenting and evaluating everyday products of wide interest and relevance to us all living in an experience economy.

After the observations drawing on empirical analyses of reviewers' communities, I will bring different threads together by subsuming some of the most relevant characteristics of the evaluative user-generated content and content production that is seen in non-professional—vernacular and amateur—reviewing. Chapter 7 characterizes non-professional reviewing with the key concepts of 'co-consumption', 'me-viewing' and 're-creational work'. My summarizing argument here is that vernacular reviewing is self-centred, shared, affective work carried out in the contexts of shared consumption and leisure time in a close dialogue with like-minded groups of people, with an intention to work on one's own relationship with a specific form of culture. This contrasts non-professional reviewing to professional reviewing, the main mission of which, roughly put, is to define the socio-aesthetic and historical value of new art and culture. This division clearly shows how post-institutional and post-professional reviewing is located in both production and reception paradigms. In addition, I briefly discuss the phenomenon of fake and pseudo reviews, which has emerged along with the increased volumes of non-professional reviewing.

Finally, Chap. 8 concludes by envisioning user reviewing as consisting of pedagogical potential and outlining a pedagogical agenda for the development of this diverse field. The book does not aim at defining the ultimate value of user-generated reviewing, which would not even be possible, as the forms, types and structures are undergoing constant and increasingly rapid change. However, it aspires to document reviewing at a certain point in time, in which the concept of social media is still of a relatively recent vintage, hardly two decades old. By doing this, it takes a step further in studying criticism and reviewing in profoundly new circumstances where the classical institutions no longer dictate the rules but where you and I can be involved in figuring out new creative directions for the value creation of culture.

## References

Alba, J. W., & Hutchinson, W. (1987). Dimensions of consumer expertise. *Journal of Consumer Research, 13*(4), 411–454.

Arnould, E. J., & Thompson, C. J. (2005). Consumer culture theory (CCT): Twenty years of research. *Journal of Consumer Research, 31*(4), 868–882.

Ashton, D., & Patel, K. (2018). Vlogging careers: Everyday expertise, collaboration and authenticity. In S. Taylor & S. Luckman (Eds.), *The new normal of working lives: Dynamics of virtual work* (pp. 147–169). Palgrave Macmillan.

Aufderheide, P., & Firestone, C. M. (1993). *Media literacy: A report of the National Leadership Conference on media literacy*. Aspen Institute.

Bauman, Z. (1987). *Legislators and interpreters: On modernity, post-modernity and intellectuals*. Polity Press.

Baumann, S. (2007). *Hollywood highbrow: From entertainment to art*. Princeton University Press.

Baym, N. K. (2015). Connect with your audience! The relational labor of connection. *The Communication Review, 18*(1), 14–22. https://doi.org/10.1080/10714421.2015.996401

Baym, N. K. (Ed.). (2021). *Creator culture: An introduction to global social media entertainment*. New York University Press.

Baym, N. K., & Burnett, R. (2009). Amateur experts: International fan labour in Swedish independent music. *International Journal of Cultural Studies, 25*(5), 433–449.

Beaman, J. (2016). Citizenship as cultural: Towards a theory of cultural citizenship. *Sociology Compass, 10*(10), 849–857.

Bell, D., & Hollows, J. (Eds.). (2005). *Ordinary lifestyles: Popular media, consumption and taste*. Open University Press.

Bell, P. (2000). Content analysis of visual images. In T. Van Leeuwen & C. Jewitt (Eds.), *The handbook of visual analysis* (pp. 10–34). Sage.

Bherer, L., Dufour, P., & Montambeault, F. (Eds.). (2016). *The participatory democracy turn*. Routledge.

Bird, S. E. (2011). Are we all produsers now? *Cultural Studies, 25*(4–5), 502–516.

Blank, G. (2007). *Critics, ratings, and society: The sociology of reviews*. Rowman & Littlefield Publishers.

Boenisch, V. (2008). *Krise der Kritik? Was Theaterkritiker denken – und ihre Leser erwarten.* [Crisis of criticism? What theatre critics think – and their readers expect.] Recherchen 63. Theater der Zeit.

Bolden, B., & Nahachewsky, J. (2015). Podcast creation as transformative music engagement. *Music Education Research, 17*(1), 17–33. https://doi.org/10.1080/14613808.2014.969219

Bolin, G. (2004). *The value of being public service: The shifting of power relations in Swedish television production.Media Culture and Society, 26*(2), 277–287.

Bolin, G. (2007). The politics of cultural production: The journalistic field, television and politics. In K. Riegert, (Ed.), *Politicotainment: Television's take on the real* (pp. 59–82). New York: Peter Lang.

Bolin, G. (2011). *Value and the media: Cultural production and consumption in digital markets.* Routledge.

Boot, P. (2011). *Towards a genre analysis of online book discussion: Socializing, participation and publication in the Dutch booksphere.* Selected papers of internet research. Association of Internet Researchers (AoIR).

Botsman, R., & Rogers, R. (2010). *What's mine is yours: The rise of collaborative consumption.* Harper Collins.

Brownfield, S., & Zhou, J. (2020). Sentiment analysis of Amazon product reviews. In R. Silhavy, P. Silhavy, & Z. Prokopova (Eds.), *Software engineering perspectives in intelligent systems.* CoMeSySo 2020: Advances in intelligent systems and computing, vol. 1295. Published online before print 15 December 2020. Springer. https://doi.org/10.1007/978-3-030-63319-6_68

Bruns, A. (2008). *Blogs, Wikipedia, Second Life and beyond.* Peter Lang.

Bruns, A. (2016). User-generated content. In K. B. Jensen, R. T. Craig, J. D. Pooley, & E. W. Rothenbuhler (Eds.), *The international encyclopedia of communication theory and philosophy* (pp. 1–5). Wiley-Blackwell.

Burdick, J., Sandlin, J. A., & O'Malley, M. P. (Eds.). (2014). *Problematizing public pedagogy.* Routledge.

Burgess, J. (2006). Hearing ordinary voices: Cultural studies, vernacular creativity and digital storytelling. *Continuum: Journal of Media & Cultural Studies, 20*(2), 201–214. https://doi.org/10.1080/10304310600641737

Burgess, J. (2007). *Vernacular creativity and new media.* Doctoral dissertation, Queensland University of Technology, Brisbane.

Burgess, J. (2012). YouTube and the formalisation of amateur media. In D. Hunter, R. Lobato, M. Richardson, &Thomas, J. (Eds.), *Amateur media: Social, cultural and legal perspectives* (pp. 53–58). London: Routledge.

Burgess, J., Foth, M., & Klaebe, H. (2006). Everyday creativity as civic engagement: A cultural citizenship view of new media. In F. Papandrea (Ed.), *Proceedings 2006 communications policy & research forum* (pp. 1–16). Network Insight Institute.

Caliandro, A., & Gandini, A. (2019). *Qualitative research in digital environments: A research toolkit*. New York:Routledge.
Carroll, N. (2009). *On criticism: Thinking in action*. New York: Routledge.
Chatterjee, P. (2001). Online reviews: Do consumers use them? In M. C. Gilly & J. Myers-Levy (Eds.), *ACR 2001 proceedings* (pp. 129–134). Association for Consumer Research.
Chong, P. K. (2020). *Inside the critics' circle: Book reviewing on uncertain times*. Princeton University Press.
Clough, P. T., & Halley, J. (Eds.). (2007). *The affective turn: Theoretizing the social*. Duke University Press.
Cova, B., & Dalli, D. (2018). Prosumption tribes: How consumers collectively rework brands, products, services and markets. In O. Kravets, P. Maclaran, S. Miles, & A. Venkatesh (Eds.), *The SAGE handbook of consumer culture* (pp. 235–255). Sage.
de Jong, I. K. E., & Burgers, C. (2013). Do consumer critics write differently from professional critics? A genre analysis of online film reviews. *Discourse, Context & Media*, *2*(2), 75–83.
Delanty, G. (2003). Citizenship as a learning process: Disciplinary citizenship versus cultural citizenship. *International Journal of Lifelong Education*, *22*(6), 597–605.
Dewenter, R., & Heimeshoff, U. (2015). Do expert reviews really drive demand? Evidence from a German car magazine. *Applied Economics Letters*, *22*(14), 1150–1153. https://doi.org/10.1080/13504851.2015.1011304
Dewey, J. (2005/1934). *Art as experience*. Penguin Books.
Donovan, J. (Ed.). (2014). *Feminist literary criticism: Explorations in theory* (2n ed.). The University Press of Kentucky.
Duan, W., Gu, B., & Whinston, A. B. (2008). Do online reviews matter? An empirical investigation of panel data. *Decision Support Systems*, *48*(1), 1007–1016.
Duffy, B. E. (2017). *(Not) getting paid to do what you love: Gender, social media, and aspirational work*. Yale University Press.
Eberly, R. A. (Ed.). (2000). *Citizen critics: Literary public spheres*. University of Illinois Press.
Edensor, T., Leslie, D., Millington, S., & Rantisi, N. (Eds.). (2009). *Spaces of vernacular creativity: Rethinking the cultural economy*. Routledge.
Elkins, J. (2003). *What happened to arts criticism?* Prickly Paradigm Bristol University Presses.
Elkins, J., & Newman, M. (Eds.). (2008). *The state of art criticism*. Routledge.
Featherstone, M. (2007/1991). *Consumer culture and postmodernism* (2nd ed.). Sage.

Felski, R. (2020). *Hooked: Art and attachment.* The University of Chicago Press.

Filieri, R. (2015). What makes online reviews helpful? A diagnosticity-adoption framework to explain informational and normative influences in e-WOM. *Journal of Business Research, 68*(6), 1261–1270.

Floyd, K., Freling, R., Alhogail, S., Cho, H. Y., & Freling, T. (2014). How online product reviews affect retail sales: A meta-analysis. *Journal of Retailing, 90*(2), 217–232. https://doi.org/10.1016/j.jretai.2014.04.004

Frey, M. (2014). *The permanent crisis of film criticism: The anxiety of authority.* Amsterdam University Press.

Fuller, D., & DeNel Rehberg, S. (2013). *Reading beyond the book: The social practices of contemporary literary culture.* Routledge.

Fürsich, E., & Avant-Mier, R. (2012). Popular journalism and cultural change: The discourse of globalization in world music reviews. *International Journal of Cultural Studies, 16*(2), 101–118.

Galuszka, P. (2015). New economy of fandom. *Popular Music and Society, 38*(1), 25–43. https://doi.org/10.1080/03007766.2014.974325

Garrard, G. (Ed.). (2014). *The Oxford handbook of ecocriticism.* Oxford University Press.

Genc-Nayebi, N., & Abran, A. (2017). A systematic literature review: Opinion mining studies from mobile app store user reviews. *Journal of Systems and Software, 125*, 207–219.

Gerlitz, C., & Helmond, A. (2013). The like economy: Social buttons and the data intensive web. *New Media & Society, 15*(8), 1348–1365.

Gibbs, M., Meese, J., Arnold, M., Nansen, B., & Carter, M. (2015). #Funeral and Instagram: Death, social media, and platform vernacular. *Information, Communication & Society, 18*(3), 255–268.

Goes, P. B., Lin, M., & Yeung, C. A. (2014). Popularity effect in user-generated content: Evidence from online product reviews. *Information Systems Research, 25*(2), 222–238.

Grizzle, A., Moore, P., Dezuanni, M., Asthana, S., Wilson, C., Banda, F., & Onumah, C. (2013). *Media and information literacy: Policy and strategy guidelines.* UNESCO.

Guest, G., MacQueen, K. M., & Namey, E. E. (2012). *Applied thematic analysis.* Sage Publications.

Harries, G., & Wahl-Jorgensen, K. (2007). The culture of arts journalists: Elitists, saviors or manic depressives? *Journalism: Theory. Practice and Criticism, 8*(6), 619–639.

Heikkilä, R., & Gronow, J. (2018). Stability and change in the style and standards of European newspapers' arts reviews, 1960–2010. *Journalism Practice, 12*(5), 624–639. https://doi.org/10.1080/17512786.2017.1330664

Hesmondhalgh, D. (2015). Exploitation and media labor. In R. Maxwell (Ed.), The Routledge companion to laborand media (pp. 30–39). New York: Routledge.

Himma-Kadakas, M., Rajavee, A., Orgmets, M., Eensaar, L., & Kõuts-Klemm, R. (2019). The food chain of YouTubers: Engaging audiences with formats and genres. *Observatorio, 41*(12), 54–75. https://doi.org/10.15847/obsOBS0001385

Hjarvard, S. (2013). *The mediatization of culture and society*. Routledge.

Hohendahl, P. U. (1982). *Institution of criticism*. Cornell University Press.

Jaakkola, M. (2015). *The contested autonomy of arts and journalism: Change and continuity of the dual professionalism of cultural journalism*. Doctoral dissertation, Tampere University Press, Tampere.

Jaakkola, M. (2018). Vernacular reviews as a form of co-consumption: User-generated review videos on YouTube. *MedieKultur – Journal of Media and Communication Research, 34*(65), 10–30.

Jaakkola, M. (2019). From re-viewers to me-viewers: The #Bookstagram review sphere on Instagram and the perceived uses of the platform and genre affordances. *Interactions: Studies in Communication and Culture, 10*(1–2), 91–110.

Jaakkola, M. (2020a). From vernacularized commercialism to kidbait: Toy review videos on YouTube and the problematics of the mash-up genre. *Journal of Children and Media, 14*(2), 237–254.

Jaakkola, M. (2020b). Oman lukukokemuksensa visualisoijat: käyttäjälähtöiset kirjallisuusarvostelut Instagramissa. [Visualizers of their own reading experience: The user-generated literature reviews on Instagram.] *Kulttuurintutkimus*, 36(3–4), 31–44.

Jaakkola, M. (2020c). Useful creativity: Vernacular reviewing on the video-sharing platform Vimeo. *Culture Unbound: Journal of Current Cultural Research, 12*(2), 373–392.

Jaakkola, M. (2020d). Young voices, new insights? Child reviewers and vernacular reviewing of cultural products. In N. N. Kristensen, U. From, & H. K. Haastrup (Eds.), *Rethinking cultural critique: New voices in the digital age* (pp. 185–208). Palgrave Macmillan.

Janssen, S. (1997). Reviewing as social practice: Institutional constraints on critics' attention for contemporary fiction. *Poetics, 24*(5), 275–297.

Janssen, S., Kuipers, G., & Verboord, M. (2008). Cultural globalization and arts journalism: The international orientation of arts and culture coverage in Dutch, French, German, and U.S. newspapers, 1995 to 2005. *American Sociological Review, 73*(5), 719–740.

Jenkins, H. (2006). *Fans, bloggers, and gamers: Exploring participatory culture*. New York University Press.

Jenkins, H. (2007). Confronting the challenges of participatory culture: Media education for the 21st century (part one). *Nordic Journal of Digital Literacy, 2*, 23–33.

Kammer, A. (2015). Post-industrial cultural criticism: The everyday amateur expert and the online cultural public sphere. *Journalism Practice, 9*(6), 872–889. https://doi.org/10.1080/17512786.2015.1051371

Kawashima, N. (2000). *Beyond the division of attenders vs. non-attenders: A study into audience development in policy and practice*. Research Papers No 6. Centre for Cultural Policy Studies, the University of Warwick.

Keen, A. (2007). *The cult of the amateur: How blogs, MySpace, YouTube and the rest of today's user generatedmedia are killing our culture and economy*. New York: Doubleday.

Kellner, D., & Share, J. (2019). *The critical media literacy guide: Engaging media and transforming education*. Leiden: Brill Sense.

Ketelaar, P. E., Willemsen, L. M., Sleven, L., & Kerkhof, P. (2015). The good, the bad, and the expert: How consumer expertise affects review valence effects on purchase intentions in online product reviews. *Journal of Computer-Mediated Communication, 20*(6), 649–666.

Khalil, B. (2015). Vlogging: YouTube book reviewers. *School Librarian, 63*(4), 212–218.

Kim, E. E. K., Mattila, A. S., & Baloglu, S. (2011). Effects of gender and expertise on consumers' motivation to read online hotel reviews. *Cornell Hospitality Quarterly, 52*(4), 399–406.

Klaus, E., & Lünenborg, M. (2012). Cultural citizenship: Participation by and through media. In E. Zobl & R. Drake (Eds.), *Feminist media: Participatory spaces, networks and cultural citizenship* (pp. 197–212). Transcript Verlag.

Knobel, M., & Lankshear, C. (2002). Cut, paste, publish: The production and consumption of zines. In D. E. Alvermann (Ed.), *Adolescents and literacies in a digital world* (pp. 164–185). Peter Lang.

Kozinets, R. V., de Valck, K., Wojnicki, A. C., et al. (2010). Networked narratives: Understanding word-of-mouth marketing in online communities. *Journal of Marketing, 74*(2), 71–89.

Kravets, O., Maclaran, P., Miles, S., & Venkatesh, A. (Eds.). (2018). *The SAGE handbook of consumer culture*. Sage.

Lash. S., & Urry, J. (1994). *Economies of signs and space*. London: Sage.

Leadbeater, C. (2007). *We think: Why mass creativity is the next big thing*. http://charlesleadbeater.net/wp-content/uploads/2010/01/We-Think-charles-full-draft.pdf

Lin, D., Bezemer, C. P., Zou, Y., & Hassan, A. E. (2019). An empirical study of game reviews on the Steam platform. *Empirical Software Engineering, 24*, 170–207. https://doi.org/10.1007/s10664-018-9627-4

Lindberg, U., Gudmundsson, G., Michelsen, M., & Weisethaunet, H. (2005). *Rock criticism from the beginning: Amusers, bruisers and cool-headed cruisers*. Peter Lang.

Liu, Y., Huang, X., An, A., & Yu, X. (2008). Modeling and predicting the helpfulness of online reviews. *Eighth IEEE international conference on data mining*, Pisa, 2008, pp. 443–452.

Livingstone, S. (2004). What is media literacy? *Intermedia, 32*(3), 18–20.

Lobato, R., Thomas, J., & Hunter, D. (2011). Histories of user-generated content: Between formal and informal media economies. https://ssrn.com/abstract=1749803

Long, E. (2003). *Women and the uses of reading in everyday life*. The University of Chicago Press.

Mackiewicz, J. (2010). Assertions of expertise in online product reviews. *Journal of Business and Technical Communication, 24*(1), 3–28.

Masterman, L. (1985). *Teaching the media*. Comedia Books.

McAuley, J. J., & Leskovec, J. (2013). From amateurs to connoisseurs Modeling the evolution of user expertise through online reviews. *WWW'13: Proceedings of the 22nd international conference on World Wide Web*, May 2013, pp 897–908.

McDonald, R. (2007). *The death of the critic*. London: Continuum.

McDougall, J. (2017). Media literacy for good agency: If Jez we could. *Journal of Media Literacy, 64*(1–2), 20–26.

McGuigan, J. (1996). *Culture and the public sphere*. Routledge.

McQuarrie, E. F., Miller, J., & Phillips, B. (2012). The megaphone effect: Taste and audience in fashion blogging. *Journal of Consumer Research, 40*(1), 136–157.

McWhirther, A. (2016). *Film criticism and digital cultures: Journalism, social media and the democratisation of opinion*. I.B. Tauris.

Mesch, C., & Michely, V. (Eds.). (2007). *Joseph Beuys: The reader*. London: I.B. Tauris.

Minnema, A., Bijmolt, T. H. A., Gensler, S., & Wiesel, T. (2016). To keep or not to keep: Effects of online customer reviews on product returns. *Journal of Retailing, 92*(3), 253–267. https://doi.org/10.1016/j.jretai.2016.03.001

Moore-Gilbert, B., Stanton, G., & Maley, W. (Eds.). (2014). *Postcolonial criticism*. Routledge.

Mudambi, S. M., & Schuff, D. (2010). Research note: What makes a helpful online review? A study of customer reviews on Amazon.com. *MIS Quarterly, 34*(1), 185–200.

Murdock, G. (1999). Rights and representations: Public discourse and cultural citizenship. In J. Gripsrud (Ed.), *Television and common knowledge* (pp. 7–17). Routledge.

NAMLE, National Association for Media Literacy Education. (2020). *Media literacy defined*. https://namle.net/publications/media-literacy-definitions/

O'Neill. (2007). The curatorial turn: From practice to discourse. In J. Rugg & M. Sedgwick (Eds.), *Issues in curating contemporary art and performance* (pp. 13–28). Intellect Books.

OHCHR, the Office of the High Commissioner for Human Rights. (1989). *Convention on the rights of the child*. United Nations.

Pakulski, J. (2007). Cultural citizenship. *Citizenship Studies, 1*(1), 73–86. https://doi.org/10.1080/13621029708420648

Pine, J. P., II, & Gilmore, J. H. (2011). *The experience economy: Work is theatre and every business a stage*. Harvard Business Review Press.

Purhonen, S., Heikkilä, R., Karademir Hazir, I., Lauronen, T., Rodríguez, C. J. F., & Gronow, J. (2019). *Enter culture, exit arts? The transformation of cultural hierarchies in European newspaper culture sections, 1960–2010*. Routledge.

Purnawirawan, N., Eisend, M., De Pelsmacker, P., & Dens, N. (2015). A meta-analytic investigation of the role of valence in online reviews. *Journal of Interactive Marketing, 31*(1), 17–27.

Ray, L., & Sayer, A. (Eds.). (1999). *Culture and economy after the cultural turn*. Sage.

Ritzer, G., Dean, P., & Jurgenson, N. (2012). The coming of age of the prosumer. *American Behavioral Scientist, 56*(4), 379–398.

Ritzer, G., & Jurgenson, N. (2010). Production, consumption, prosumption: The nature of capitalism in the age of the digital 'prosumer'. *Journal of Consumer Culture, 10*(1), 13–36.

Rodger, N. (2019). From bookshelf porn and shelfies to #bookfacefriday: How readers use Pinterest to promote their bookishness. *Participations, 16*(1), 473–495.

Rosaldo, R. (1994). Cultural citizenship and educational democracy. *Cultural Anthropology, 9*(3), 402–411.

Said, E. W. (1994). *Representations of the intellectual: The 1993 Reith lectures*. Vintage Books.

Sandlin, J. A., Schultz, B. D., & Burdick, J. (Eds.). (2010). *Handbook of public pedagogy: Education and learning beyond schooling*. Routledge.

Savolainen, R. (2019). Sharing information through book reviews in blogs: The viewpoint of Rosenblatt's reader-response theory. *Journal of Documentation, 76*(2), 440–461. https://doi.org/10.1108/JD-08-2019-0161

Scaraboto, D. (2015). Selling, sharing, and everything in between: The hybrid economies of collaborative networks. *Journal of Consumer Research, 42*(1), 152–176.

Schindler, R. M., & Bickart, B. (2012). Perceived helpfulness of online consumer reviews: The role of message content and style. *Journal of Consumer Behaviour, 11*(3), 234–243.

Schmutz, V. C. (2009). *The classification and consecration of popular music: Critical discourse and cultural hierarchies*. Doctoral dissertation, Erasmus University of Rotterdam, Rotterdam.

Shrum, W. M., Jr. (1996). *Fringe and fortune: The role of critics in high and popular art*. Princeton University Press.

Shusterman, R. (1992). *Pragmatist aesthetics: Living beauty, rethinking art*. Oxford: Blackwell

Statista. (2020a). Average daily time spent per capita with the internet worldwide from 2011 to 2021. https://www.statista.com/statistics/1009455/daily-time-per-capita-internet-worldwide/

Statista. (2020b). Distribution of global hours spent on mobile from 2016 to 2019, by category. https://www.statista.com/statistics/435324/share-app-time-category/

Statista. (2020c). Most common languages used on the internet as of January 2020, by share of internet users. https://www.statista.com/statistics/262946/share-of-the-most-common-languages-on-the-internet/

Statista. (2020d). Most popular social networks worldwide as of October 2020, ranked by number of active users. https://www.statista.com/statistics/272014/global-social-networks-ranked-by-number-of-users/

Statista. (2020e). Percentage of individuals using the internet worldwide in 2019, by region. https://www.statista.com/statistics/333879/individuals-using-the-internet-worldwide-region/

Steiner, A. (2010). Personal readings and public texts: Book blogs and online writing about literature. *Culture Unbound: Journal of Current Cultural Research, 2*(2), 471–494.

Suhariyanto, F. A., & Sarno, R. (2018). Prediction of movie sentiment based on reviews and score on Rotten Tomatoes using SentiWordnet. *International Seminar on Application for Technology of Information and Communication, Semarang, 2018*, 202–206. https://doi.org/10.1109/ISEMANTIC.2018.8549704

Terranova, T. (2004). *Network culture: Politics for the information age*. Pluto Press.

Thornberry, P., & Martín Estébanez, M. A. (2004). *Minority rights in Europe: A review of the work and rights of the Council of Europe*. Council of Europe Publishing.

Titchener, C. B. (1998). *Reviewing the arts* (3rd ed.). Lawrence Erlbaum.

Tiwari, P., Mishra, B. K., Kumar, S., & Kumar, V. (2020). Implementation of n-gram methodology for Rotten Tomatoes review dataset sentiment analysis. In M. Khosrow-Pour (Ed.), *Cognitive analytics: Concepts, methodologies, tools, and applications* (pp. 689–701). IGI Global. https://doi.org/10.4018/978-1-7998-2460-2

Toffler, A. (1980). *The third wave*. Collins.

Tryon, C. (2009). *Reinventing cinema: Movies in the age of media convergence*. Rutgers University Press.
UN, the Committee on the Rights of the Child. (2021). *General comment on children's rights in relation to the digital environment*. https://www.ohchr.org/EN/HRBodies/CRC/Pages/GCChildrensRightsRelationDigitalEnvironment.aspx
UNESCO. (2013). *Global media and information literacy assessment framework: country readiness and competencies*. UNESCO.
van Venrooij, A., & Schmutz, V. (2010). The evaluation of popular music in the United States, Germany and the Netherlands: A comparison of the use of high art and popular aesthetic criteria. *Cultural Sociology, 4*(3), 395–421.
Vásquez, C. (2014). *The discourse of online consumer reviews*. Bloomsbury.
Verboord, M. N. M. (2010). The legitimacy of book critics in the age of the Internet and omnivorousness: Expert critics, Internet critics and peer critics in Flanders and the Netherlands. *European Sociological Review, 26*(6), 623–637. https://doi.org/10.1093/esr/jcp039
Vermeulen, I. E., & Seegers, D. (2009). Tried and tested: The impact of online hotel reviews on consumer consideration. *Tourism Management, 30*(1), 123–127.
Vinogradovs, V. (Ed.). (2021). *Aesthetic literacy: A book for everyone*. Mont Publishing.
Walmsley-Evans, H. (2018). *Film criticism as a cultural institution*. Routledge.
Weibull, L., & Nilsson, Å. (2010). Four decades of European newspapers: Structure and content. In J. Gripsrud & L. Weibull (Eds.), *Media, markets & public spheres* (pp. 39–70). Intellect.
Wenger, E. (1998). *Communities of practice: Learning, meaning, and identity*. Cambridge: Cambridge UniversityPress.
Whitaker, E. M. (2017). Emic and etic analysis. In B. S. Turner (Ed.), *The Wiley-Blackwell Encyclopedia of Social Theory* (pp. 1–2) https://doi.org/10.1002/9781118430873.est0640
Willemsen, L. M., Neijens, P. C., Bronner, F., & de Ridder, J. A. (2011). 'Highly recommended!' The content characteristics and perceived usefulness of online consumer reviews. *Journal of Computer-Mediated Communication, 17*(1), 19–38.
Wright, D. (2015). *Understanding cultural taste: Sensation, skill and sensibility*. Palgrave Macmillan.
Wu, P. F. (2013). In search of negativity bias: An empirical study of perceived helpfulness of online reviews. *Psychology & Marketing, 30*(11), 971–984.
Wu, X., Jin, L., & Xu, Q. (2020). Expertise makes perfect: How the variance of a reviewer's historical ratings influences the persuasiveness of online reviews. *Journal of Retailing*. Published online before print 24 June 2020.

Zhu, F., & Zhang, X. (2010). Impact of online consumer reviews on sales: The moderating role of product and consumer characteristics. *Journal of Marketing, 74*(2), 133–148.

Zimmer, M. (2010). But the data is already public: On the ethics of research in Facebook. *Ethics and Information Technology, 12*(4), 313–325.

Zou, O., Yu, B., & Hao, Y. (2011). Does the valence of online consumer reviews matter for consumer decision making? The moderating role of consumer expertise. *Journal of Computers, 6*(3), 484–488.

CHAPTER 2

# Cultural Online Engagement

Living in online cultures has become possible since online technologies have enabled self-expression and interaction as we know it in today's connective world. Cultural online engagement refers to online communication that mediates culture. Online engagement consists of communicative activities to create content, or content that is typically specified as 'user-generated content' (Bruns, 2016). User reviewing is thus one specific form of cultural online engagement. Central concepts for forms of digital-native reviewing are the terms 'culture' and 'lifestyle' as carriers of a certain form of culture. In this chapter I will thus briefly discuss the concept of culture and how it is manifest in reviewing communities, and the character of reviewing communities, which I summarize as 'lifestyle communities'.

## 2.1 Mediatized Culture

Reviewing is a channel for mediating a certain type of culture. Before going any further in examining reviewing we need to dedicate some attention to the word 'culture'. Reviewing is a form of (inter)mediation of a certain form of culture, whether it is film (or, more specifically, romantic comedies) or literature (more specifically, so-called chick lit). Reviewers may focus on a broad or wide definition of the form of culture, but a typical reviewer hardly reviews anything; there is always a delimitation of the area of coverage at play. My primary interest lies in the (inter)mediation


M. Jaakkola, *Reviewing Culture Online*,
https://doi.org/10.1007/978-3-030-84848-4_2

(and what I later will call intramediation) of *culture* that is comparable to the area for which cultural desks of daily newspapers and cultural magazines, as part of journalism, have had the institutional responsibility to mediate. I am thus excluding reviews of user products, because they typically need another kind of an approach and are more often infiltrated in everyday discourses and practices of, for example, vlogging that require no distinct reviewer identity. My scope thus covers cultural engagement and cultural consumership, or cultural prosumption or cultural usership—crystallized in the self-labelled activity of 'reviewing' cultural products—that would be more or less equivalent to the work that cultural journalists and critics are doing within the institutional domain.

Defining culture is far from a simple task, as it is a multidiscursive term that is frequently used and mobilized in very different contexts, with different extensions in semantic meaning and often not even explicitly clarified by the communicator. Indeed, Raymond Williams (1976, p. 76) characterized the term as one of the most complicated words in modern English. Eagleton (2000, p. 32) saw the word as 'both too broad and too narrow to be greatly useful'. The anthropologists Alfred Kroeber and Clyde Kluckhohn (1952, p. 119) identified 156 different meanings for the term in popular and academic discourse, categorizing meanings into descriptive, historical, normative, psychological, structural and genetic definitions. The Latin roots of culture (*cultura* from the verb *colere*, 'to inhabit, cultivate, protect, honour with worship') were initially connected with concrete things such as agriculture (*cultura agri*) and idolatry or cult (*cultus*) before undergoing a metaphor transformation where culture was regarded as a field of inner life and spirituality (*cultura animi*). This understanding of culture as a process, cultivation, holds relevance even today, as it brings a semantic dimension to the concept of 'tending of something' (Williams, 1976, p. 77). As such, the term serves to articulate inner coherence and unity in various social practices through which a society reproduces itself as a stable and self-identical whole. Along with the processual dimension of culture, Williams (1993/1958) also distinguishes two other meanings of the concept which refer to an objectified sense: first, a general state of mind or consciousness, and second, the artefacts or products of the processes of consciousness, which refers to the socially transmitted results of cultivation such as artworks and art institutions (ibid., p. 11).

Further, Fornäs (2017) identifies three different concepts of culture: the anthropological, aesthetic and hermeneutic. The anthropological concept refers to cultures as lived entities that are learned and transferred from generation to generation, implying certain norms, values and traditions. The aesthetic concept of culture entails culture as intellectual or artistic activity, supported by institutions and industries. The hermeneutic concept, which in a way attempts to reconcile the two previous concepts, refers to culture as meaning making that is manifest in human interaction through material artefacts in different societal contexts. Reviewing communities can be approached from all these directions. In the anthropological sense, the anatomies of the online cultures can be dissected into a set of norms, values and practices adopted by users, supporting the reviewing function. In the aesthetic sense, reviewing cultures are mediating and reproducing arts and culture(s), as do institutional actors such as mass media. In addition, they also generate their own aesthetics to support the act of mediation. As for the hermeneutic understanding of culture, reviewers in online communities are to a great extent part of meaning-making communities, attached to the material artefacts of the culture they are making sense of, and even exerting a societal or democratic function of refining opinion, preferences and taste.

There is an understanding of 'culture' underlying every act of cultural intermediation, even if it may not always be explicit and clearly defined by the communicators. Professional cultural journalists are involved in the work of newsrooms that adopt a certain concept of culture according to the framework provided by their media, which, for its part, is affected by the strategic decisions concerning the target audience, ways of expression, model of financing and so on. Cultural desks' concept of culture is constituted by work differentiation, according to which journalists and reviewers are specialized in monitoring certain fields of arts and culture. The conglomerate of cultural fields regularly covered is thus the sum of specialized professionals' work. In the same fashion, user reviewers delimit their field of inquiry by specializing in certain cultural forms, like comics, or even in a subgenre such as comics by female artists, which becomes their field of monitoring. Monitoring means reacting to new releases and more or less systematically covering them to find out how they are related to previous production.

In the concept of culture, we can identify a horizontal and vertical dimension. The horizontal dimension relies on the extension aspect of culture, seeing it in a narrow way by just focusing on high arts or in a broader way by including popular culture, lifestyle, celebrity culture and everyday culture. The vertical dimension implies a construction of hierarchies: preferences and a cultural canon of works where some are supposed to display higher quality according to someone, or personal preferences of the spectator. In constructing mediated concepts of culture individuals act as gatekeepers, by selecting certain forms or fields of culture and picking up distinct cultural products within them, and tastemakers, by defining which works are better than others. The mediators of culture are thus exerting definitional power. Media organizations like daily newspapers and cultural magazines have institutional power that is based on their influential position in a geocultural area, while user reviewers are constituted of their own micromedia and may, as individuals, not automatically have such power at hand. However, user reviewers affect the communities around them and can gradually acquire an influential position in defining certain cultural forms and individual works, including effects on institutional actors.

In online cultural engagement, the dynamics of the delimitation of 'culture' are thus different from the institutional cultural reporting. The cultural public sphere of cultural consumers (McGuigan, 1996) is based on the interests, ambitions and predispositions of an individual. The concept of culture that is being mediated and intermediated (or, as I will argue later, intramediated) does not have to be coherent, broad or representative by any means. Cultural consumers are following the cultural areas that happen to interest and appeal to them, without any promises about exhaustive or systematic monitoring. As boundaries between high and low cultures have been blurring and cultural consumers have increasingly become cultural omnivores (Peterson & Kern, 1996), crossing these boundaries, the cultures mediated online have become mixed and hybridized.

Nevertheless, published reviews are products that count as reified mediated culture, the delimitative (horizontal-extensional) and evaluative (vertical-hierarchical) aspects as two central culture-defining dimensions. Reviews of arts or cultural products such as literature, music, theatre, films and comics typically imply a definition of culture as an aesthetic area. Culture is understood as a form of culture that can be categorized with regard to its aesthetic features, traditions and production and consumption structures. Customer reviews, in contrast, rather rely on an anthropological definition of culture. Customer reviews are part of ordinary consumption that is not disconnected from everyday life in the same way as the field of (high) arts. In user reviews, the reviewers' relationship with cultural goods, whether of artistic-aesthetic or everyday-ordinary character, is typically connected to the consumption cultures, the lifestyle communities' work on their identity and field of consumption, or everyday life. This unfolds through the positioning of the user reviewer as a cultural intramediator, discussed later, for whom the proximity with the reception dimension in the chain of mediation is an important factor.

## 2.2 Online Lifestyle Communities

Reviewing, as a discernment of the persons' individual choices and preferences, aligns itself to agency and identity construction work (Holland et al., 2001) that finds its special character in displaying individuality and sense of style, as part of the individualization processes of late modernity (Giddens, 1991). Consumer cultures have typically been discussed in sociology in the frame of post-Fordist production (Bell & Hollows, 2005), consumption and lifestyle (Bell & Hollows, 2006; Storey, 1999). Expressions of lifestyle are related to processes of the increased role of sign value that Featherstone (2007/1991) calls aesthetization of everyday life. Production of messages in reviewing communities is also essentially connected to taste, the attribution of cultural, artistic or aesthetic worth to a cultural object (Wright, 2015).

The theorists of contemporary consumer culture have conceived the issue of lifestyle as a matter of consumption and its manifestation, through 'assembling goods, clothes, practices, experiences, appearance and bodily dispositions' to be 'designed together into a lifestyle' (Featherstone, 2007/1991, p. 86), typically by following mass media. Lifestyle has thus been discussed in conjunction with consumer behaviour where consumers' active choices and the structuration of such actions have been the focus. Online reviewing implies a step further, the consumer entering the position of a producer of mediated manifestations of lifestyle and related meanings. The productive consumption (Bolin, 2011) or *prosumption* of lifestyles is to a great extent based on online communities that, for their part, are accommodated on different social networking sites and online fora.

Reviewing is a community-based activity where communication rests upon an expectation of others doing the same or being interested in the same. Book communities such as Bookstagram on Instagram, Goodreads, BookTube on YouTube and the #bookish communities across a variety of platforms flourish from the idea of an imagined community (Anderson, 1991/1983; see also Litt, 2012; Pressman, 2020). Community may in some way replace the idea of a work contract issued by a media organization to a professional legacy-media reviewer; it functions as a motivation to keep up with an activity that is supported by hundreds of thousands or even millions of other producers, by assigning a meaningful role to a user in the cultural ecology. In supporting discussions on material, symbolic and sociocultural aspects of a certain area of culture, online communities arrive at promoting certain lifestyles. The communities affect the ways in which citizen and consumer identities, or childhood, expertise or readership in different local and global contexts is articulated. Interaction and content production in these communities convey ways of incorporating cultural goods into the maintenance of lifestyles in people's everyday lives. Reviewers are involved in developing individuals' relationships with certain groups or types of cultural products, genres, persons, institutions and brands. These relationships are often affective, as in fan communities and brand communities. Fandom can be expressed in relation to artists and other original creators, their output, or it can take on the form of production of fan output and its assessment such as fan fiction, including peer reviewing of fan-generated texts (Evans et al., 2017).

Consumer research and marketing theory have recognized that in societal micro-groups individuals entertain strong emotional bonds and common passions and social relationships are in fact more important than the goods, services and brands. They can be called co-consuming groups, of which Cova and Dalli (2018, p. 237) identify three types according to the strength of ties between consumers, the stability of the interaction (from ephemeral to long-established rituals) and the object of the shared interest: 'consumer tribes' that are a fluid group of people who share ephemeral experiences based on a particular product; 'subcultures of consumption' that refers to a group of people sharing ritualized experiences and commitment to a particular product, and 'brand communities' that are more stable groups of people sharing a way of thinking and tradition, as well as a religious zeal towards a focal brand.

Brand communities connect to distinct symbolic identities of products and product families that companies make (Coelho et al., 2019). Through these communities, 'consumers can discuss ideas and products or simply talk about their favorite brand with individuals who have the same feelings of ownership, admiration, and love toward that particular brand' (ibid.). Brand communities present an important marketing and customer relationship management tool for companies, as they maintain and intensify the emotional attachment of customers to brands and in this way create value for primary production by letting dedicated consumers control the meaning making that occurs around the consumership. Online communities with consumer orientation develop meaningful relationships with a brand and hone 'brand love', the degree of emotional and passionate affection that a satisfied consumer has towards a particular brand (Ahuvia, 2005). Based on these relationships, companies expect to more easily identify the desires and real needs of their customers.

What actually makes a community is an ambiguous question. A reviewing community can be formed in different ways, as seen in the chapter on platformized cultural production (Chap. 3). Whether an institution-led or a user-led community, users are involved in communities in different ways and to varying degrees. 'Communities' are far from homogeneous solid formations; they range from communities of like-minded people where a majority of users are actively involved in the production and development of content, like in fanfiction or user book-review sites, to communities where one person is the only active content-producing figure of his or her micromedia and others following him or her for multiple reasons. The reviewer, who acts as an opinion- and tastemaker, may attract groups of dedicated users such as followers and subscribers, but also more random members of audience who visit a channel and watch videos as they happen to appear in feeds through recommendation systems, and are thus less permanent and visible. On social media platforms, the genre of reviewing is practised by joining symbolic communities by using certain hashtags, and the outline of a community becomes more a symbolic one. Nevertheless, online lifestyle communities are an expression of a symbolic value community that has both a manifest form, consisting of a perceivable audience, and a latent form, consisting of an audience reached though metrics.

In other words, lifestyle communities endorse and transfer distinct values, regardless of whether the reviewers are aware of this dimension or not. However, as value-supporting communities, this dimension has societal ramifications and implications that need to be captured by institutions of formal and informal education. In the forms of reviewing that are more product- and purchase-centred, such as toy and beauty product reviews, users typically conform to supporting lifestyles that are very consumerist in their character. For example, in many consumer product reviews, the reviewers' activities are to a large extent based on exposing and recommending brands and in this way urging their followers to make another new purchase, often without discussing the consequences of such a lifestyle. As in toy reviews (see Sect. 6.3 At the Playstage: Toy Reviewers on YouTube in Chap. 6), children are exposed to such consumerist ideas from very early on, offering them identities that do not follow international and national policy directions set for the future, such as the goals of sustainable development, among which responsible consumption is explicitly mentioned (United Nations, 2015). In communities with a focus on cultural products that are more abstracted from the acts of purchasing things, for example in literature communities where books can also be borrowed from libraries or lent through book swapping or crossing practices, reviewers may position themselves as promoters of more sustainable values. They typically argue for cultural engagement as a feature of a healthy and balanced life, underscoring the importance of mental development, self-care and relaxation. There are also consciously critical communities, such as communities that aim at supporting feminist, green or minority values. These communities may create alternative ways of interpreting cultural content, such as among LGBTQ+ comic or film reviewers, child-centric children's literature reviewers or reviewers with a diasporic identity. Furthermore, online lifestyle communities can also be knowledge- or expertise-based, as in communities that to a high degree lean upon the exchange of experience, manifested as part of aspirational or relational labour. For example, film gadget reviewers (see Sect. 6.2 Judging Gadgets: Filmmaker Reviewers on Vimeo in Chap. 6) present such a community.

Online cultures of reviewing entail potential for users to take control of their consumer behaviour and practise more reflexive consumption. Their potentially transformative power lies in 'domesticating' a lifestyle concerning a form of a culture, or a cultural world. By adopting qualities of certain lifestyles and putting them into a situated context of an individual's own life, users concretely turn lifestyles into their own, and in this way shared, resource. By addressing cultural products through reviewing, users can cultivate reflexivity, express alternative ways of consuming and reacting to the products of cultural industries, and enhance self-identities that are different from those that are pre-imposed by the industries.

Online lifestyle communities with a connection to reviewing exist, or can exist, in all age groups, even if it is mostly adolescents who are the most active reviewers. Nevertheless, the concept of an online lifestyle community is not something that the practitioners themselves identify with; at the practical level, lifestyles are addressed through practices of vlogging, blogging, mediated play, gameplay, filmmaking and so on. In all these different forms of communication, lifestyles are at play, and reviewing is one channel for talking about community members' way of life. A relatively new dimension that is being introduced into the practice of reviewing through the activities of online communities is visual and audiovisual communication, coupled with aesthetics of bodily presence and performance, or somaesthetics (Wright, 2015; Shusterman, 2012). Material artefacts are portrayed and put into contexts of private spaces of reception in another way than what has been common in the cultures of reviewing before the internet, and visual and audiovisual practices such as vlogging and Instagramming foreground the reviewer as a human body, placed in the context of home or family, in a new way.

Online lifestyle communities, like their physical predecessors, entail gendered practices, some more powerfully structured than others, and some gender rifts can be seen (see, e.g., Ellis, 2019; Friman, 2015). In particular, the domains of film, tech gadget, comic book and video game reviews seem to be typically male-dominated, while the spheres of beauty and fashion are typically dominated by females. In cultural products, even differentiation into male and female product spheres can be seen, for example games like *The Sims* being more attractive to female gamers (Gee, 2010). Several studies on gender and emotion in online discussions have indicated that female users are likely to deliver and receive more positive attention than male users, while there is no difference for negative comments (Thelwall et al., 2009; see also Verboord, 2011, 2012). Gender differences in review cultures to a great extent boil down to gendered products and brands, and pertinent activities such as film watching and video game playing habits, which are subject to change (see, e.g., Jain et al., 2016), even consciously constructed ones such as waves of feminism and girl movements in gaming (Cassell & Jenkins, 1999). Practices such as video gameplay are for their part influenced by the character, plot and content design of games that have been observed to be dominated by male characters, while female characters have more often been sexually objectified, which undermines female self-perception or self-identification (Ivory, 2006). Nevertheless, reviewing can be a way of consuming, producing and re-producing gendered identity through distinct action, the genre-related communication practice of presenting, testing and evaluating a cultural product. Users can in their reviews explicitly focus on gender aspects, such as YouTube users reviewing LGBTQ+ products, female or male clothes and accessories, or female sex toys.

## References

Ahuvia, A. C. (2005). Beyond the extended self: Loved objects and consumers' identity narratives. *Journal of Consumer Research, 32*(1), 171–184.

Anderson, B. (1991/1983). *Imagined communities: Reflections on the origin and spread of nationalism* (Rev. ed.). Verso.

Bell, D., & Hollows, J. (2005). *Ordinary lifestyles: Popular media, consumption and taste*. Open University Press.

Bell, D., & Hollows, J. (Eds.) (2006). *Historicizing lifestyle: Mediating taste, consumption and identity from the 1900s to 1970s*. Ashgate Publishing Company.

Bolin, G. (2011). *Value and the media: Cultural production and consumption in digital markets*. Routledge.

Bruns, A. (2016). User-generated content. In K. B. Jensen, R. T. Craig, J. D. Pooley, & E. W. Rothenbuhler (Eds.), *The international encyclopedia of communication theory and philosophy* (pp. 1–5). Wiley-Blackwell.

Cassell, J., & Jenkins, H. (Eds.). (1999). *From Barbie to Mortal Kombat: Gender and computer games* (2nd ed.). MIT Press.

Coelho, A., Bairrada, C., & Peres, F. (2019). Brand communities' relational outcomes, through brand love. *Journal of Product & Brand Management, 28*(2), 154–165. https://doi.org/10.1108/JPBM-09-2017-1593

Cova, B., & Dalli, D. (2018). Prosumption tribes: How consumers collectively rework brands, products, services and markets. In O. Kravets, P. Maclaran, S. Miles, & A. Venkatesh (Eds.), *The SAGE handbook of consumer culture* (pp. 235–255). Sage.

Eagleton, T. (2000). *The idea of culture*. Blackwell Publishing.

Ellis, E. G. (2019). Why women are called 'influencers' and men 'creators'. *Wired*, May 29. https://www.wired.com/story/influencers-creators-gender-divide/

Evans, S., Davis, K., Evans, A., Campbell, J. A., Randall, D. P., Yin, K., & Aragon, C. (2017). More than peer production: Fanfiction communities as sites of distributed mentoring. In *Proceedings of the 2017 ACM Conference on Computer Supported Cooperative Work and Social Computing (CSCW '17)* (pp. 259–272). Association for Computing Machinery. https://doi.org/10.1145/2998181.2998342

Featherstone, M. (2007/1991). *Consumer culture and postmodernism* (2nd ed.). Sage.

Fornäs, J. (2017). *Defining culture: Conceptual foundations and contemporary debate*. Palgrave Macmillan.

Friman, U. (2015). The concept and research of gendered game culture. In: *DiGRA '15 – Proceedings of the 2015 DiGRA International Conference*. http://www.digra.org/digital-library/publications/the-concept-and-research-of-gendered-game-culture

Gee, J. P. (2010). *Women as gamers: The Sims and 21st century learning*. Palgrave Macmillan.

Giddens, A. (1991). *Modernity and self-identity: Self and society in the late modern age*. Stanford University Press.
Holland, D., Lachicotte, W. S., Jr., Skinner, D., & Cain, C. (2001). *Identity and agency in cultural worlds*. Harvard University Press.
Ivory, J. D. (2006). Still a man's game: Gender representation in online reviews of video games. *Mass Communication and Society, 9*(1), 103–114. https://doi.org/10.1207/s15327825mcs0901_6
Jain, V., Bharadwaj, K., Bansal, A., & Natarajan, V. S. (2016). Discovering the changes in gendering of products: Case of woman in 'Bikerni Community' in India. *Border Crossing, 6*(2), 169–194. https://doi.org/10.33182/bc.v6i2.490
Kroeber, A. L., & Kluckhohn, C. (1952). *Culture: A critical review of concepts and definitions*. Meridian Books.
Litt, E. (2012). Knock, knock, who's there? The imagined audience. *Journal of Broadcasting and Electronic Media, 56*(3), 330–345.
McGuigan, J. (1996). *Culture and the public sphere*. Routledge.
Peterson, R. A., & Kern, R. (1996). Changing highbrow taste: From snob to omnivore. *American Sociological Review, 61*(5), 900–907. https://doi.org/10.2307/2096460
Pressman, J. (2020). *Bookishness: Loving books in a digital age*. Columbia University Press.
Shusterman, R. (2012). *Thinking through the body: Essays in somaesthetics*. Cambridge University Press.
Storey, J. (1999). *Cultural consumption and everyday life*. Arnold.
Thelwall, M., Wilkinson, D., & Uppal, S. (2009). Data mining emotion in social network communication: Gender differences in Myspace. *Journal of the American Society for Information Science and Technology, 15*(1), 190–199.
Verboord, M. N. M. (2011). Cultural products go online: Comparing the internet and print media on distributions of gender, genre and commercial success. *Communications: The European Journal of Communication Research, 36*(4), 441–462. https://doi.org/10.1515/COMM.2011.022
Verboord, M. N. M. (2012). Exploring authority in the film blogosphere: Differences between male and female bloggers regarding blog content and structure. *Interactions: Studies in Communication & Culture, 2*(3), 243–259. https://doi.org/10.1386/iscc.2.3.243_1
Williams, R. (1976). *Keywords: A vocabulary of culture and society*. Oxford University Press.
Williams, R. (1993/1958). *Culture and society*. Hogarth Press.
Wright, D. (2015). *Understanding cultural taste: Sensation, skill and sensibility*. Palgrave Macmillan.
United Nations (2015). *UN Sustainable Development Goals*. Available at: https://sustainabledevelopment.un.org/sdgs

CHAPTER 3

# Reviewing as Post-Institutional Cultural Production

Cultural communication—the mediation of arts and culture from producers to audiences—has been frequently touched upon in the frameworks of mediation of culture, developed in the sociology of arts into a model of cultural mediation (Alexander, 2003) and discussed in studies of media and culture in the context of cultural industries (Hirsch, 2000) and creative industries (Hartley, 2005), or the political economy of culture (see, e.g., Hesmondhalgh, 2008). In this chapter, I intend to locate user reviewing within this infrastructural architecture where online platforms play a strategic role in how user reviewing is constituted. Discussing reviewing as cultural production implies taking a look at the specific structures that are typically referred to as the 'production context', and the bridging function in communication assigned for reviewers. In this chapter I will examine user reviewing as part of two influential and relevant frameworks, platformized cultural production and cultural intermediation, under the umbrella term post-institutional production of culture.

Cultural production includes the elementary components of production, texts and reception (Alexander, 2010). Production, cultural products, review texts and audiences are tightly bound together in the 'circuit of culture' (Johnson, 1986; Du Gay, 1997), the cultural meaning-making process that Du Gay (1997) has specified by singling out the elements of production, reception, representation, regulation and identity. Reviewing and similar activities of translation or bridging have come to be discussed as an intermediary function in the value chain that is constituted between


M. Jaakkola, *Reviewing Culture Online*,
https://doi.org/10.1007/978-3-030-84848-4_3

producers and receivers—artists as producers and audiences as receivers, and reviewers as actors in between (Alexander, 2003; Hirsch, 1977; Duncan, 1953). There has been a conviction that a value is built into a commodity in an exchange. This exchange or value transfer has been of interest in economic studies of valuation (Appadurai, 1986) and marketing theory, where the role of prosumers is seen in value co-creation (Cova & Dalli, 2018) or consumer-led creation of branded content (Muñiz & O'Guinn, 2001). In this context, cultural intramediation also resonates with the domain that Arsel (2015) refers to as recirculation markets. She identifies a domain where communities and networks create and transfer value for already used goods, as in book crossing or product swapping, finding a re-value in those products.

The institutional structures apply for media institutions but not for user reviewing where the intermediary organization is excluded or constituted in another form, as a 'platform'. The centrality of media organizations has been addressed from the post-industrial perspective of media industry. Post-industrial journalism refers to a condition where 'journalism is no longer organized around the norms of proximity to the machinery of production' (Anderson et al., 2017, p. 12). While post-industrial journalism is distinguished by media production beyond the traditional media organizations (Deuze & Witschge, 2020), post-industrial criticism is characterized in particular by amateurs' content production (Kammer, 2015). Beyond the structural order of media institutions, amateurs' production is characterized by a high heterogeneity in professional positionings, attachment to the objects of reporting and inclusion in the monetary mechanics of the platformized entertainment industry (see, e.g., Baym, 2021). In the humanities, the post-institutional communication landscape has been addressed as a question of developing new aesthetics and aesthetic agency, above all in post-digital literary studies and pragmatical aesthetics (Cramer, 2015, 2016; Thoburn, 2020; Felski, 2008).

I call the review production that has emerged in social media networks *post-institutional* to highlight the condition where reviewers are working in environments with different degrees of institutionalization and where institutionalization unfolds according to different principles. The institutional order of professional reviewing and criticism has traditionally been based on activities regulated by cultural institutions, including legacy or mass media, which essentially function as gatekeepers for reviewing and reviewers. In the post-institutional landscape of reviewing, in which almost anyone can enter the cultural public sphere and start reviewing culture in public, individuals can become reviewers without the authorization and legitimation of these gatekeeping institutions. The post-institutional frame thus accommodates two different logics, of which the institutional is based on a top-down regulation and the non-institutional on a bottom-up structure. I will argue that the institutional ways of reviewing typically underlie the model of cultural intermediation, while the non-institutional ways of reviewing are more typically centred upon a model that I will call cultural intramediation. In this section, we will start by looking at the model of cultural mediation, before proceeding to the intermediary functions on platforms.

## 3.1 Cultural Mediation

The mediation of cultural products, as a form of production of culture, is embedded in a framework that is typically referred to as cultural mediation (Alexander, 2003). According to this idea, individuals' and organizations' relationship with the culture is never direct but rather mediated, in multiple ways (Wilke, 2014). Production of culture shapes the symbolic elements of culture by the systems within which they are created, distributed, evaluated, taught and preserved (Crane, 1992). In the chain of mediation, there are certain critical stages that potentially affect and in their own way add to the symbolic value creation in which cultural products are mediated to audiences. It is of fundamental importance to recognize the number of different (inter)mediators in the horizontal chain.

Figure 3.1 shows the major flows as described in a model of cultural mediation. In general, *cultural mediation* (1) unfolds between the producer and

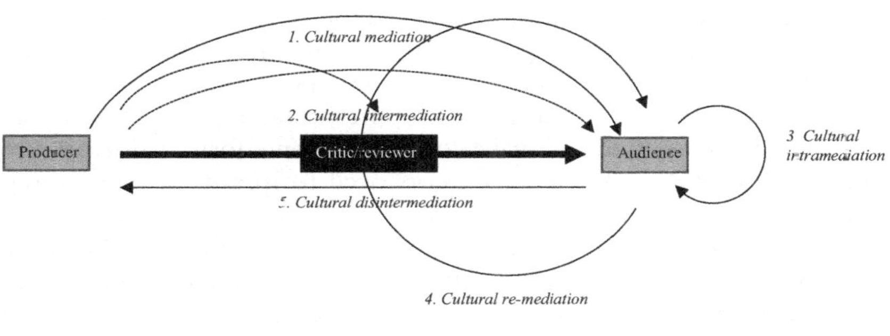


**Fig. 3.1** Cultural intermediation and interrelated processes of the mediation of culture

the receiver, and it describes the generation of shared culture at a general level. *Cultural intermediation* (2) is based on the fundamental components of the producer, cultural intermediary and receiver, where the cultural intermediary acts as a bridge between 'production' and 'reception' (Alexander, 2003; Duncan, 1953). In other words, the cultural intermediary positions himself or herself between the primary production (producer), such as the author and his or her publisher, and the audience (e.g. the reader, viewer, listener, user), attempting to decode a new work in the historical context of production (Orlik, 2016), yet preserving a critical distance from the producers and in this way delivering an independent evaluation of the work for the audience's benefit. *Cultural intermediation* (3) is an audience-based variant of cultural intermediation (see section "cultural Intramediation").

Besides the categories of production, intermediation and reception, the mediation chain can be described in more detail when it comes to the various mediation flows. However, the vocabulary here is less established, differing from author to author, the lines between production and consumption being less fixed. Some authors regard the work of content-producing audiences as secondary production (see, e.g., de Certeau, 1984), while—following Bourdieu's original line of thought that left the very definition of cultural intermediaries rather open—the term cultural intermediaries covers mediators from PR officers and marketers to professional critics, and even peer critics (see Sect. 3.2 Cultural Intermediation). For the purposes of recognizing the activities of reviewers of different types (see Chap. 4. Reviewing in Genre and Practice Hierarchies), it is appropriate to distinguish between mediators attached to primary production, mediators with an aim to sustain independence vis-à-vis primary production, and mediators with close ties to reception. Within primary production, the original creators of cultural products—the artists, writers and authors, filmmakers, performers—communicate by themselves, related to the objects of culture that have been produced. The smaller the size and scale of production, the more often creators need to adopt an entrepreneurial attitude and make communication efforts: artists need to engage in self-PR, and content creators need to spread the word about their own activities. Larger-scale primary production, however, typically involves organizational differentiation of functions, making use of separate units of strategic communication that create a communication and marketing plan, utilizing organizations' PR officers and communicators to enforce preferred messages. This group of communicators is typically conflated with the primary production, or sometimes included in the category of cultural intermediators, but to recognize their specific role in influencing cultural intermediaries and audiences they can more appropriately count as forces of secondary production. Secondary producers are thus second-stage mediators (artists and other primary producers being mediators of the first stage) that are closely connected to the primary production and fulfilling their needs to reach out to the market(s).

Agents of production have traditionally provided cultural intermediators such as journalists and reviewers with relevant information and, by acting both as sources and promoters, tried to get their preferred messages through but without any guarantee of it, as the guiding principle of cultural intermediators has been independence. The role of promotion and sales support applies for the activities of the increasing number of what in the prolific academic literature on cultural intermediation have often been called cultural intermediaries but what I here classify as secondary producers: literary and music agents, booksellers and marketers, art gallerists, culture promoters, lobbyists and producers, influencer marketing hubs. The second-stage mediators are not solely commercial and may also be cultural influencers in the name of non- and informal education, such as schools, libraries, authorities, associations and non-governmental organizations promoting different forms of cultural literacy to different audiences.

Finally, between cultural intermediators and receivers there can further be multiple mediators, forming a second stage of mediation, for example when an art reviewer's or journalist's message is re-mediated and filtered by users of social media (cultural intramediators) before reaching the final individual receiver. There are, of course, even other interdependencies between the actors. As a 'reverse' or audience-initiated type of mediation, processes and outcomes of cultural intramediation may be returned to mass media and become *re-mediated* (4), for example when events in the digital reviewsphere succeed in catching the traditional journalistic agents' attention and are addressed in traditional news outlets. Furthermore, primary producers are utilizing reviewers' and bloggers' views as part of their marketing material, as blurbs. Primary producers approach audience mediators with offerings for compensation of coverage: user reviewers are offered products for free if they promise to show them in their content. Primary producers also receive valuable feedback for their products from both inter- and intramediaries, even if the cultural intermediaries' discourses typically emphasize the fact that reviews are not for giving producers feedback but to teach audiences. On platforms, the 'feedback' is quantifiable in consumers' online behaviour data, and it is systematically collected.

If the scene of mediators is diverse, so are the audiences of culture. With regard to primary production, cultural audiences can be live audiences in immediate timely and physical contact with the arts or cultural product, or separated from the production in time and physical space. Even live audiences who share the time with primary production can be physical, such as people following a concert in a concert hall or a jazz club, or mediated, as in a streamed opera performance. Audiences may come into contact with the content of arts or culture by receiving artefacts such as recorded music albums or visiting an exhibition. Different forms of arts and culture pose their own specific conditions for reception. Even if audiences are very specialized and consist of experts similar to cultural intermediary, as is often the case in highly specialized topics, the intermediary intends to construct a position that addresses its audiences but does not inhabit them. Cultural intermediation thus implies a bridging position determined to seek neutrality, integrity and somehow democratic efforts to construct value for the common good. In cultural intermediation, audiences mark a separate group of receivers distinguished from cultural intermediaries.

The precondition for audiences' active participation and engagement is the process of ***cultural disintermediation*** (5). Disintermediation is a term borrowed from economics and refers to the removal of intermediaries in the supply chain, or to a condition where the customer is directly in contact with the supplier, without distributors, wholesalers or other agents of primary production (see, e.g., Langley & Leyshon, 2017). Cultural disintermediation thus means the elimination of cultural intermediaries due to the audiences' direct access to cultural events, products and services. Cultural disintermediation has become common because of the mediatization and digitalization of culture, as the agents of primary production can reach out to cultural consumers online and provide them with direct access to their products, without being dependent on any cultural intermediaries.

## 3.2 Cultural Intermediation

In academic literature on cultural production, professional reviewers of cultural products have frequently been conceptualized as cultural intermediaries, a term originally coined by the French sociologist Pierre Bourdieu. Bourdieu introduced the term in his book *Distinction* (1984) to refer to the growing class of new petite bourgeoisie workers engaged in occupations involving presentation and representation (Bourdieu, 1984, p. 359). In a two-way response with the readership—both leading them by introducing ideas and values and conforming to entrenched values—professional reviewers act in 'boundary spanning roles', as Hirsch (1972) puts it, to build the cultural frame for goods. Research on the intermediary aspect is intellectually indebted to the early mass media research that examined the industry based on transmission models and developed gatekeeper studies (Ettema & Whitney, 1982; DiMaggio & Hirsch, 1976). However, rather than just making choices of filtering flows of content as gatekeepers, the intermediaries' role in linking production and consumption is found in the active intervention they make in the process of producing meaning in the role of tastemakers. McQuail (1992, p. 278) amalgamates the institutions connected with education, the arts and sciences with cultural institutions the function of which is to provide legitimacy for their 'preference claims', under which 'the idea of hierarchy of aesthetic value' is the most prominent. He calls the cultural institutions along with cultural industries, political interests and pressure groups 'agents of preference' (ibid., pp. 278–279). Later studies on the general category of cultural intermediaries, leaning on the ideas of gatekeeping and tastemaking, have asserted that cultural intermediaries are differentiated by their locations within commodity chains, devices for gaining influence and claims to professional expertise in taste and value within specific cultural fields (Smith Maguire & Matthews, 2012).

In other words, cultural intermediation (Jones et al., 2019; Hutchinson, 2017; Smith Maguire & Matthews, 2014) refers to the construction of added symbolic value in the cultural value chain by actors placed between production (industry) and reception (audiences), whose role is to assign value to new art and aesthetics by framing the cultural goods produced by the industry for the consumers. Cultural intermediaries are involved in a translation of value from the production context to the reception context, and they conduct this transformation through their expertise in terms of taste and knowledge related to the cultural products that are being mediated by them. Cultural intermediaries are 'third parties who mediate between producers (writers and publishers) and audiences (readers), and whose interventions shape how the objects under scrutiny (books) subsequently become to be valued' (Chong, 2020, p. 1; Hirsch, 1972).

Scholarly debates have arisen about the usefulness of this general term, which has even been used interchangeably with the terms mediators (Alexander, 2003), brokers (DiMaggio, 1977) and boundary spanners

(Hirsch, 1972; Wenger, 1998), as it has been applied to groups as different as advertisers and consultants, booksellers, musicians and music managers, and personal trainers (Moor, 2008; Cronin, 2004; Hracs, 2015; Smith Maguire, 2008, 2010), emptying the term of its explanatory potential (Nixon & du Gay, 2002; Negus, 2002; McFall, 2010; Smith Maguire & Matthews, 2012). As the term, despite its weaknesses, continues to be employed in the study of journalistic professions, especially of cultural journalists and critics (Kristensen et al., 2019; Crosbie & Roberge, 2014; Mellor, 2008), it is essential to make it more nuanced. This is particularly important as no major critical voices have been raised against the idea that even cultural consumers, the 'people formerly known as the audience', as noted by Jay Rosen (2006; see McGuinness, 2016), count as 'cultural intermediaries' (Lee, 2012; Woo, 2012). However, our starting point is that it is counterproductive to place primary creators, distributors and produser/prosumer audiences, who should be considered as part of separate stages in the (cultural) value chain, in the same category.

The institutional forms of criticism and reviewing (see Sect. 4.1 From Criticism to Reviewing) are the most likely to clearly conform to the model of cultural intermediation (Blank, 2007). Cultural intermediaries, reviewers selected and employed by professional newsrooms, that is, (legacy) media organizations, position themselves neither as part of the production of art—referred to as primary production—nor as part of its reception, that is, the audiences of art. Instead, their position is distinguished by an in-betweenness, which manifests in a tendency for symbolic distance from the primary producers, such as artists and creators, the industry and their mediating mechanisms (such as museums and traders), supported by the journalistic norms of minimizing bias as well as fostering independence and accountability. At the same time, their discourse is based on the primary producers' understandings, and reviewing means placing new work in its historical and material context of production (Orlik, 2016). In constructing an independent assessment that anchors the value of the new work in the production context, integrity is the primary prerequisite (Carroll, 2009; Hohendahl, 1982). As for the audiences, reviewers are not ordinary receivers of either arts or culture, but because of their accumulated experience and public activity, they stand out from the cultural audience. Therefore, with their in-between positioning, cultural intermediaries intend to place a new cultural product in the production context (Orlik, 2016).

The intermediary processes operate on two principles that previous literature has considered as key dimensions in reviewing: the creation of critical autonomy (Blank, 2007; Orlik, 2016; Carroll, 2009), which occurs towards primary production, and the creation of critical authority (see, e.g., Klein, 2005; Verboord, 2012) targeted towards reception. Critical autonomy, sometimes described as 'critical proximity' (Simon, 2010), is a prerequisite for being critical or for the intermediary positioning that distinguishes cultural intermediaries from their promotional counterparts. Criticality means the construction of cultural distance from the ideas put forward by the primary producer by putting oneself in a position of relative distance—an outsider or an 'insider outsider'—regarding the producers. Critical authority in online environments is coupled and intertwined with endeavours towards authenticity (Glynn & Lounsbury, 2005) and negotiations of legitimacy (Verboord et al., 2015), including the construction of a voice that is taken seriously and legitimized by the audience.

## 3.3 Cultural Intramediation

Cultural intermediaries have an organization that guarantees freedom by separating content production from marketing and economic management via organizational differentiation of units and roles of the workers. Not all mediators of culture have this kind of freedom from financial constraints. In post-institutional reviewing, where platformized production makes the recruitment of reviewers different, user reviewers are not necessarily in the same position as cultural intermediators. They may construct critical distancefrom primary production, and they are influenced by the industry directly, and are free to choose how to position themselves towards primary production. Some reviewers choose to keep the distance, while others become agents of marketing, taking a more promotional role through partnerships and entrepreneurial efforts.

When the 'people formerly known as the audience' adopt intermediary functions, there is a greater diversity of positionings, and user reviewers are not always acting as cultural intermediaries as described above. While some user reviewers may seek the cultural intermediary position in the same fashion as professional journalists, the large majority of users practise mediation similar to peer-to-peer communication, in which the mediator and audience are part of the same group. 'Audience reviewers' do not typically regard showing the historical value as their primary mission, representative of a wider readership or a taste community, but intend to place the work in their own individual reception history and in this way hope to inspire and engage like-minded cultural consumers. The 'audience intermediary' and his or her audience are much closer to each other, and due to the absence of the creation of critical distance, the intermediation may even become extended marketing for the primary producers. This peer-to-peer mediation can be termed ***cultural intramediation*** (see 3 in Fig. 3.1) to make a contrast to the traditional cultural intermediation.

The central differences between cultural intermediation and cultural intramediation are summarized in Table 3.1. Cultural intramediation is based on a reviewer's positioning as part of the audience, or the community he or she is communicating with. Cultural intermediators are often described as being part of the art world, which Becker (1982, p. 34) defines as 'networks of people whose activities are necessary to the production of the characteristic works which that the world, possibly along with others, define as art'. Cultural intermediaries are thus seen as an integral part of the production machinery of arts and certain cultures, creating the essential discourses we use when addressing the cultural products, and generating the contemporaneity for also mediating their histories. Cultural intramediaries, who in the cultural intermediary discourse are demarcated as audiences or the receptive pole of the art world, do not necessarily see themselves as part of the chain; they are constructing their own lifeworlds and using cultural products available as war material. By putting one's own reactions, observations and experiences into words and by sharing these personal encounters, they aim at maintaining their connection to the

**Table 3.1** Cultural inter- and intramediation in comparison

| | *Cultural intermediation* | *Cultural intramediation* |
|---|---|---|
| *Position* | Between primary producers and receivers (cultural audience) | Receiver as part of cultural audience |
| *Function* | Putting new artistic/aesthetic/cultural content in its historically situated production context by public reception | The verbalization/externalization and sharing of one's own reception experience for the community construction |
| *Objective* | Assignment of a historical-aesthetic value to a new cultural product, informing and educating audiences about it | Peer encouragement, maintenance of a lifestyle though sharing related experiences |
| *Form* | Evaluation based on evidence and argumentation | Shared public reception, co-consumption |

reception community, or what I call the lifestyle community. At the same time, they create this community, which comes into existence by mediated encounters with culture.

Cultural intramediators are fan, peer or fellow communities, where the normative and ideal role of communicators is one of equals. In the common imaginary, communities are supportive, characterized by members' mutual engagement and continued motivation to participate. The communities also have an affective character, emphasizing shared passion, emotional investment or love of reading, watching or making films, and reviewing the cultural supply. One dominant mode in community communication is that of learning. The conception of learning processes underlying the community structures is thus horizontal peer-to-peer learning instead of, as in the case of cultural intermediaries, educating and informing, which occur from a teacher to the learners. The role of cultural products is also somewhat different. The focus not being on the artefact itself, artefacts become more like markers or points of reference of the continued and shared lifestyle work.

User reviewers may also position themselves as allies of primary production, becoming ***promotional intermediaries*** or intramediaries. Promotional intermediaries (Davis, 2006, 2013), often referred to as social influencers or micro-celebrities (e.g. Khamis et al., 2017), are positioned between the producer and audience, that is, belonging to neither of these entities, but seeking personal, predominantly economic or material profit through the investment of creating an added value for a cultural product. Besides the active practices of individuals—the promotional intermediaries—promotional cultures, which reach beyond mere advertising and marketing and play a role in 'historical transformations and in evolving social relations' (Davis, 2013, p. 1), are supported by promotional organizations, the 'promotional industries' such as lobbying, advertising, marketing and branding, and certain professional fields like publicists, agents and speech writers. Many theorists have pointed out that organizations of all kinds have become in general more promotionally oriented, and citizens, consumers, employees and media audiences have largely internalized the practices of self-promotion (Schwarzkopf, 2015; Davis, 2013; Einstein, 2016). This, together with platformization (see Sect. 3.4 Platformized Cultural Production), puts cultural intermediaries with democratic and disinterested intentions under increased pressure to keep the marketing forces at bay. User reviewers often need to create economically viable conditions for their continuing activity, and thus a sustainable agency implies becoming more promotional (Postigo, 2016; Kennedy, 2009). Cultural intramediators do not seek distance from primary production so they can utilize their role as a promoter for personal influence and reputation. Promotional intermediaries follow the principles of word of mouth and partisan marketing, inserting practices of product placement, commercial partnerships and memberships in affiliate programmes into their activities. Promotion is centrally connected to commercial biases; in a more democratic form, cultural inter- and intramediaries can become promoters of arts or, for example, healthy lifestyle, but this has not traditionally been perceived as being 'promotional' but as inherent in the role of the reviewer as an opinion- and tastemaker (Harries & Wahl-Jorgensen, 2007).

## 3.4 Platformized Cultural Production

Platformization refers to a development where the platform has become the dominant infrastructural and economic model of the social web (Helmond, 2015). The platform has been understood as a specific computational, economic and discursive model to organize social interaction, data and sell (Helmond, 2015). Beyond the institutions of reviewing and criticism, reviewing occurs on digital sites offered for users for their content production, and can be characterized as platformized cultural production (Poell et al., 2021; Nieborg & Poell, 2018; van Dijck & Poell, 2018).

Platforms are not a neutral element that the service providers only set up for the disposal of citizens and consumers. Platforms significantly direct the organization and structure of communication by offering certain possibilities and simultaneously limiting possibilities for communication. Users on platforms are subordinated to collection of data based on the information they leave and their actions. Platforms capitalize on users, but how the users can themselves make use of the platform-specific monetization principles to secure financial compensation for their activities and in this way also ensure continued existence as a communicator on the platform (Couldry & Mejias, 2019; Gillespie, 2019; Srnicek, 2016). Continued presence implies an increase in invested time and possibilities to develop the communication, which often means a step further towards deepened skills, established formats and enhanced interaction, which can be recognized as increased professionalism in communication. Communication is to a central degree governed by user attention where users in the 'like economy' (Gerlitz & Helmond, 2013) contribute to each other's attention value, and by datafication where almost everything can be built into measurable data sold to those who want to pay for it. As for published content, platformization has resulted in a messy output where 'democratic', 'disinterested' or 'unbiased' content can no longer easily be differentiated from interest-invested content, or content with commercial, political or personal bias. Einstein (2016) calls this condition 'content confusion', where the walls 'between church and state' have been broken down. At the same time even the boundaries between private and public action and message, as well as the categories of personal and professional, are becoming harder to maintain. For reviewing this means that the roles of a disinterested and promotional, and a private and public, mediator increasingly intermingle and are becoming inseparable. Platformized production applies primarily to vernacular reviewing (see Chap. 5. Post-Professional Reviewers), which occupies a central position when talking about non-professional reviewing, but even institutional amateurism is organized on sites that fit into the definition of a platform.

Platform-specific communication is to a great degree formed by platform policies, which are strategic choices put forward by the platform provider to select certain users while discouraging others and to divert these users' content production in a certain way. Furthermore, platform-specific communication is formed by affordances, which are platforms' socio-technical and aesthetic functionalities that on one hand support some features in communication and interaction ('affording' them), and on the other hand limit and hinder others. Platforms entail certain established ways of making use of perceived affordances of the platform, as well as the genre. In the conjunction of the platform use and genre formation, it is the perceived affordances (Norman, 1999) of the platform and of the genre that play a central role. According to Norman (1999, see also Gibson, 1979; McVeigh-Schultz & Baym, 2015), an affordance is the design aspect of an object, for example of the visual app Instagram, or the social convention of the review genre, which suggests how this more or less material 'object' should be used. To be effectively used, an affordance has to be perceived, that is, identified, and transformed into a functional feature.

The essential role of affordances can be seen if we compare how reviews look at different platforms. On the video-sharing platform YouTube, reviews can take on diverse forms, and the diversity of ways of expression boils down to the flexibility that the platform allows for the video format, practically, aesthetically and policy wise. A YouTube video in the vlogging style typically includes a creator addressing the viewer by speaking directly to the camera. Stylistically, what appears to separate the publications of YouTubers from other digital media is how a 'standardised YouTuber/vlog aesthetic, incorporating now familiar rapid-fire speech, jumpy and stylised editing, "insider" jokes, community shout-outs and collaborations' (Cunningham & Craig, 2017, p. 78), has become commonplace. Many reviewers apply the vlog style, talking in front of the camera at a high pace and embedding clips or images of the cultural product under review. Dominant modes of communication are entertainment and comedy, or everyday connectivity that is based on genres such as 'my day', 'haul' or 'tutorial', which involve not only informative but also confessional, intimate and educational elements (Torjesen, 2021). The length of the video is not regulated and does not affect reviews in any way, as verified users are allowed to upload videos of 12 hours' duration.

TikTok, or the Chinese variant Dǒuyīn duǎn shìpín ('Doyin Short Video'), in contrast, forces users to stick to a micro-format; initially, videos were limited to only 6 seconds in length, but the company ByteDance extended the limit to 15 and later to 60 seconds. Dance, comedy and education are the major themes, and the conventions of expression are influenced by another app that TikTok was merged with in 2018, Musical.ly, where bodily appearances, mainly dancing, occupied a central place. Written text is almost non-existent, and the culture of expression lies in oral and embodied communication.

A third video platform, Vimeo, is characterized by a non-commercial and alternative (to YouTube) as well as professionally oriented peer-support culture, underlined by high technical quality—'we were the first ones to support HD video'—and marketing towards the business sector—'the perfect video platform to keep your company organized, connected, and engaged from anywhere'. The video platform was created for 'creative professionals' and the company has explicitly sought distance from an entertainment orientation by, for example, excluding the gaming communities. In 2008–2014, gameplay videos, which are videos simply depicting individuals playing a video game, were not allowed on Vimeo because they did not comply with the quality requirements of 'creative expression'. Even though this ban was later lifted, gamers have adopted YouTube and the video live streaming service Twitch, a subsidiary of Amazon, on their platforms. Reviews that fit better into Vimeo's strategy are those made by filming professionals and serious hobbyists to test technical equipment and showcase their work, described in more detail as a case study in Sect. 6.2 Judging Gadgets: Filmmaker Reviewers on Vimeo.

Instagram is primarily based on uploading mobile photos that are accompanied with short texts under the pictures, but in 2018 Facebook, its owner since 2012, also introduced videos. The written text is clearly subordinated to visual material, as the texts are called captions and limited to 2000 characters. The use of hashtags is limited up to 30, links are not allowed and typographic formation of the text, such as the use of paragraphs, is not supported, which encourages the use of short texts and a central focus on the images. Full-length reviews are, indeed, often placed elsewhere, for example in a blog, and Instagram reviews adopt another character, becoming, above all, visual illustrations of reading processes, practices and preferences, with a strong connection to creating impressions and atmosphere. The short format in text also encourages users to make mini or quick reviews. The introduction of long-form video in the form of the IGTV application in 2018 also enables the elaboration of moving images on Instagram.

Finally, the use of perceived platform affordances is regulated and elaborated in communities, and platform strategies are constantly adapted to prevailing conditions in the cultural economy of the social web. The examples above, concerning the use of audiovisual material, show that on platforms, the different dimensions of multimodal communication are emphasized differently; in contrast to the pre-platformization era when a review was always a linear, argumentation-based, typically even monological text, reviews on the platformized social web can take on a diversity of forms using different media and user interaction, which is something profoundly new within the tradition of reviewing and criticism. Platforms are exist in a social media ecosystem where users travel across the community spaces established on them, and practices are interinfluenced by originally platform-specific conventions. For example, Goodreads have largely affected practices of social reading that are applied on Bookstagram and BookTube, as well as in the conjunct blogosphere and podcasts. And the idea of one-minute book reviews, which are at the time of writing occurring on all platforms, originated because of the limit of length, but now it has started living a life of its own, as a legitimate subgenre of reviewing in which the ultimate moment of suspension is formed by the challenge that a hard limit poses to the reviewer.

Platformized content production goes hand in hand with a shift in media uses, especially with the rapid growth of mobile technology. Ownership and use of handheld devices—smartphones and tablet computers—has increased during recent years, with 76 per cent of people in advanced economies and 45 per cent in developing economies owning a smartphone in 2018 (Taylor & Silver, 2019). This implies a radical difference from the reception culture prior to the era of user reviewing, as professional and amateur forms used to be read either on printed paper, as in the case of newspapers and culture magazines, or on a desktop, as in online magazines and even blogs. The mobile apps that are downloaded to devices encourage the use of smartphone or tablet, as some features may be limited or even entirely blocked in the desktop versions of the popular apps. Mobile technology benefits the use of visual and audiovisual modality, which is, indeed, a predominant feature of communication on the popular platforms of the social web. In 2021, mobile video has been anticipated to make up 78 per cent of total mobile traffic, an eightfold increase over 2015 (Cisco, 2017). At the same time, from a production perspective, mobile technology may contribute to the contexts of expression becoming more mundane, as it makes it simpler and easier to connect visual storytelling to everyday settings and the lives of the users (see, e.g., Sandvik et al., 2016); without any greater effort or preparation, mobile images and videos can be shot right where the cultural consumer happens to be.

In sum, platformized cultural production is the signature feature of post-institutional reviewing where the production of reviews is not guided by the centrality of an organization, or a newsroom. Platforms do not choose reviewers, but work more by pulling them in by providing a possibility to perform as a reviewer in public. Users who choose to do so are subjected to the platform mechanisms, and to be successful they need to find out ways to comply with the rules of the game. User reviewing is thus affected by platforms in varying ways. First, a central role is occupied by the platform policies, deriving from the company strategies, that define what kind of content production is allowed and encouraged and, accordingly, how the platform has been programmed to match these goals. Second, at a concrete level the platform affordances provide the user with certain avenues for their communication, and the social practices are formed in the user communities where influential users configure the reviewspace, setting the social, aesthetic and ethical rules that are feasible on the platform in question. Third, the social practices are largely driven by a certain community imaginary where users envision an imagined community to be a member of, for example, the book-related Bookstagram community on Instagram and BookTube on YouTube. Fourth, interplatform influence plays a strong role in forming policies, affordance systems and social practices, even encouraging reviewers to develop a critical cross-platform agency that leans less on one platform's offerings than the expertise and creativity attached to a reviewer's profile.

## References


Alexander, V. C. (2003). *Sociology of the arts: Exploring fine and popular forms*. Blackwell Publishing.

Alexander, V. D. (2010). Public institutions of "high" culture. In J. R. Hall & L. Lo. M.-G. Grindstaff (Eds.), *Handbook of cultural sociology* (368–377). Routledge.

Anderson, C. W., Bell, E. J., & Shirky, C. (2017). *Post-industrial journalism: Adapting to the present*. Tow Center for Digital Journalism.

Appadurai, A. (1986). *The social life of things: Commodities in cultural perspective*. Cambridge University Press.

Arsel, Z. (2015). Assembling markets and value. In R. Canniford & D. Bajde (Eds.), *Assembling consumption: Researching actors, networks and markets* (pp. 32–41). Routledge.

Baym, N. K. (Ed.). (2021). *Creator culture: An introduction to global social media entertainment*. New York University Press.

Becker, H. S. (1982). *Art worlds*. University of California Press.

Blank, G. (2007). *Critics, ratings, and society: The sociology of reviews*. Rowman & Littlefield Publishers.

Bourdieu, P. (1984). *Distinction: A social critique of the judgement of taste*. Harvard University Press.

Carroll, N. (2009). *On criticism: Thinking in action*. Routledge.

Chong, P. K. (2020). *Inside the critics' circle: Book reviewing on uncertain times*. Princeton University Press.

Cisco. (2017, March 28). *Cisco visual networking index: Global mobile data traffic forecast update, 2016–2021*. White paper. https://s3.amazonaws.com/media.mediapost.com/uploads/CiscoForecast.pdf

Couldry, N., & Mejias, U. A. (2019). *The cost of connectivity. How data is colonizing human life and appropriating it for capitalism*. Stanford University Press.

Cova, B., & Dalli, D. (2018). Prosumption tribes: How consumers collectively rework brands, products, services and markets. In O. Kravets, P. Maclaran, S. Miles, & A. Venkatesh (Eds.), *The SAGE handbook of consumer culture* (pp. 235–255). Sage.

Cramer, F. (2015). What is 'post-digital'? In D. M. Berry & M. Dieter (Eds.), *Postdigital aesthetics: Art, computation and design* (pp. 12–26). Palgrave Macmillan.

Cramer, F. (2016). Post-digital literary studies. *MATLIT: Materialidades da literatura, 4*(1), 11–27. https://doi.org/10.14195/2182-8830_4-1_1

Crane, D. (1992). *The production of culture: Media and the urban arts.* Sage.

Cronin, A. M. (2004). Regimes of mediation: Advertising practitioners as cultural intermediaries? *Consumption Markets & Culture, 7*(4), 349–369. https://doi.org/10.1080/1025386042000316315

Crosbie, T., & Roberge, J. (2014). Critics as cultural intermediaries. In C. Fleck & A. Hess (Eds.), *Knowledge for whom: Public sociology in the making* (pp. 275–298). Routledge.

Cunningham, S., & Craig, D. (2017). Being 'really real' on YouTube: Authenticity, community and brand culture in social media entertainment. *Media International Australia, 164*(1), 71–81. https://doi.org/10.1177/1329878X17709098

Davis, A. (2006). Placing promotional culture. In J. Curran & D. Morley (Eds.), *Media and cultural theory* (pp. 149–163). Routledge.

Davis, A. (2013). *Promotional cultures: The rise and spread of advertising, public relations, marketing and branding.* Polity Press.

de Certeau, M. (1984). *The practice of everyday life.* University of California Press.

Deuze, M., & Witschge, T. (2020). *Beyond journalism.* Polity Press.

DiMaggio, P. (1977). Market structure, the creative process, and popular culture: Toward an organizational reinterpretation of mass-culture theory. *Journal of Popular Culture, 11*(2), 436–452.

DiMaggio, P., & Hirsch, P. M. (1976). Production organizations in the arts. In R. A. Peterson (Ed.), *The production of culture* (pp. 73–90). Sage.

Du Gay, P. (Ed.). (1997). *Production of culture/cultures of production.* Sage/Open University.

Duncan, H. D. (1953). *Language and literature in society: A sociological essay on theory and method in the interpretation of linguistic symbols with a bibliographical guide to the sociology of literature.* University of Chicago Press.

Einstein, M. (2016). *Black ops advertising: Native ads, content marketing, and the covert world of the digital sell.* OR Books.

Ettema, J. S., & Whitney, D. C. (Eds.). (1982). *Individuals in mass media organizations: Creativity and constraint.* Sage Publications.

Felski, R. (2008). *Uses of literature.* Blackwell Publishing.

Gerlitz, C., & Helmond, A. (2013). The like economy: Social buttons and the data intensive web. *New Media & Society, 15*(8), 1348–1365.

Gibson, J. J. (1979). *The ecological approach to visual perception.* Houghton Mifflin.

Gillespie, T. (2019). *Custodians of the internet: Platforms, content moderation, and the decisions that shape social media.* Yale University Press.

Glynn, M. A., & Lounsbury, M. (2005). From the critics' corner: Logic blending, discursive change and authenticity in a cultural production system. *Journal of Management Studies, 42*(5), 1031–1055.

Harries, G., & Wahl-Jorgensen, K. (2007). The culture of arts journalists: Elitists, saviors or manic depressives? *Journalism: Theory, Practice and Criticism, 8*(6), 619–639.

Hartley, J. (Ed.). (2005). *Creative industries*. Blackwell Publishing.

Helmond, A. (2015). The platformization of the web: Making web data platform ready. *Social Media + Society, 1*(July–December), 1–11.

Hesmondhalgh, D. (2008). Cultural and creative industries. In T. Bennett & J. Frow (Eds.), *The Sage handbook of cultural analysis* (pp. 553–569). Sage Publications.

Hirsch, P. M. (1972). Processing fads and fashions: An organizational set analysis of cultural industry systems. *American Journal of Sociology, 77*(4), 639–659.

Hirsch, P. M. (1977). Occupational, organizational and institutional models in mass communication. In P. M. Hirsch, P. V. Miller, & F. G. Kline (Eds.), *Strategies for communication research* (pp. 13–42). Sage Publications.

Hirsch, P. M. (2000). Cultural industries revisited. *Organization Science, 11*(3), 356–361.

Hohendahl, P. U. (1982). *Institution of criticism*. Cornell University Press.

Hracs, B. J. (2015). Cultural intermediaries in the digital age: The case of independent musicians and managers in Toronto. *Regional Studies, 49*(3), 461–475. https://doi.org/10.1080/00343404.2012.750425

Hutchinson, J. (2017). *Cultural intermediaries: Audience participation in media organizations*. Palgrave Macmillan.

Johnson, R. (1986). The story so far and further transformations? In D. Punter (Ed.), *Introduction to contemporary cultural studies* (pp. 277–313). Longman.

Jones, P., Perry, B., & Long, P. (Eds.). (2019). *Cultural intermediaries connecting communities: Revisiting approaches to cultural engagement*. Policy Press.

Kammer, A. (2015). Post-industrial cultural criticism: The everyday amateur expert and the online cultural public sphere. *Journalism Practice, 9*(6), 872–889.

Kennedy, H. (2009). Going the extra mile: Emotional and commercial imperatives in new media work. *Convergence, 15*(2), 177–196. https://doi.org/10.1177/1354856508101582

Khamis, S., Ang, L., & Welling, R. (2017). Self-branding, 'micro-celebrity' and the rise of social media influencers. *Celebrity Studies, 8*(2), 191–208.

Klein, B. (2005). Dancing about architecture: Popular music criticism and the negotiation of authority. *Popular Communication, 3*(1), 1–20.

Kristensen, N. N., Hellman, H., & Riegert, K. (2019). Cultural mediators seduced by Mad Men: How cultural journalists legitimized a quality TV series in the Nordic region. *Television & New Media, 20*(3), 257–274. https://doi.org/10.1177/1527476417743574

Langley, P., & Leyshon, A. (2017). Platform capitalism: The intermediation and capitalization of digital economic circulation. *Finance and Society, 3*(1), 11–31.

Lee, H.-K. (2012). Cultural consumers as 'new cultural intermediaries': Manga scanlators. *Arts Marketing: An International Journal, 2*(2), 131–143.
McFall, L. (2010). What about the old cultural intermediaries? An historical review of advertising producers. *Cultural Studies, 16*(4), 532–552.
McGuinness, P. (2016). The people formerly known as the audience: Power shifts in the digital age. *Communication Research and Practice, 2*(4), 520–527. https://doi.org/10.1080/22041451.2016.1259974
McQuail, D. (1992). *Media performance: Mass communication and the public interest*. Sage Publications.
McVeigh-Schultz, J., & Baym, N. K. (2015). Thinking of you: Vernacular affordance in the context of the microsocial relationship app, Couple. *Social Media + Society, 1*(July). https://doi.org/10.1177/2056305115604649
Mellor, N. (2008). Arab journalists as cultural intermediaries. *The International Journal of Press/Politics, 13*(4), 465–483. https://doi.org/10.1177/1940161208322873
Moor, L. (2008). Branding consultants as cultural intermediaries. *The Sociological Review, 56*(3), 408–428. https://doi.org/10.1111/j.1467-954X.2008.00797.x
Muñiz, A. M., Jr., & O'Guinn, T. C. (2001). Brand community. *Journal of Consumer Research, 27*(4), 412–432.
Negus, K. (2002). The work of cultural intermediaries and the enduring distance between production and consumption. *Cultural Studies, 16*(4), 501–515.
Nieborg, D. B., & Poell, T. (2018). The platformization of cultural production: Theorizing the contingent cultural commodity. *New Media & Society, 20*(11), 4275–4292. https://doi.org/10.1177/1461444818769694
Nixon, S., & du Gay, P. (2002). Who needs cultural intermediaries? *Cultural Studies, 16*(4), 495–500.
Norman, D. A. (1999). Affordance, conventions, and design. *Interactions, 6*(3), 38–42.
Orlik, P. B. (2016). *Media criticism in a digital age: Professional and consumer considerations*. Taylor & Francis.
Poell, T., Nieborg, D. B., & Duffy, B. E. (2021). *Platforms and cultural production*. Polity.
Postigo, H. (2016). The socio-technical architecture of digital labour: Converting play into YouTube money. *New Media & Society, 18*(2), 332–349.
Rosen, J. (2006). *The people formerly known as the audience*. http://archive.pressthink.org/2006/06/27/ppl_frmr.html
Sandvik, K., Thorhauge, A. M., & Valtysson, B. (Eds.). (2016). *The media and the mundane: Communication across media in everyday life*. Nordicom.
Schwarzkopf, S. (2015). Cultural economy, capitalism and the logic of the public sphere. *Journal of Cultural Economy, 8*(6), 721–729. https://doi.org/10.1080/17530350.2014.949285

Simon, J. (2010). Critical proximity. *Cultural Studies Review, 16*(2), 4–23.
Smith Maguire, J. (2008). Leisure and the obligation of self-work: An examination of the fitness field. *Leisure Studies, 27*(1), 59–75. https://doi.org/10.1080/02614360701605729
Smith Maguire, J. (2010). Provenance and the liminality of production and consumption: The case of wine promoters. *Marketing Theory, 10*(3), 269–282. https://doi.org/10.1177/1470593110373190
Smith Maguire, J., & Matthews, J. (2012). Are we all cultural intermediari- es now? An introduction to cultural intermediaries in context. *European Journal of Cultural Studies, 15*(5), 551–562.
Smith Maguire, J., & Matthews, J. (Eds.). (2014). *The cultural intermediaries reader*. Sage Publications.
Srnicek, N. (2016). *Platform capitalism*. Polity Press.
Taylor, K., & Silver, L. (2019). *Smartphone ownership is growing rapidly around the world, but not always equally*. Pew Research Center. https://www.pewresearch.org/global/wp-content/uploads/sites/2/2019/02/Pew-Research-Center_Global-Technology-Use-2018_2019-02-05.pdf
Thoburn, N. (2020). Twitter, book, riot: Post-Digital publishing against race. *Theory, Culture & Society, 37*(3), 97–121. https://doi.org/10.1177/0263276419891573
Torjesen, A. (2021). The genre repertoires of Norwegian beauty and lifestyle influencers on YouTube. *Nordicom Review, 42*(2), 168–184. https://doi.org/10.2478/nor-2021-0036
van Dijck, J., & Poell, T. (2018). *The platform society: Public values in a connective world*. Oxford University Press.
Verboord, M. N. M. (2012). Exploring authority in the film blogosphere: Differences between male and female bloggers regarding blog content and structure. *Interactions: Studies in Communication & Culture, 2*(3), 243–259. https://doi.org/10.1386/iscc.2.3.243_1
Verboord, M., Kuipers, G. M. M., & Janssen, J. (2015). Institutional recognition in the transnational literary field, 1955-2005. *Cultural Sociology, 9*(3), 447–465. https://doi.org/10.1177/1749975515576939
Wenger, E. (1998). *Communities of practice: Learning, meaning, and identity*. Cambridge University Press.
Wilke, J. (2014). Art: Multiplied mediatization. In K. Lundby (Ed.), *Mediatization of communication* (Handbooks of communication science) (Vol. 21, pp. 465–482). Walter de Gruyter.
Woo, B. (2012). Alpha nerds: Cultural intermediaries in a subcultural scene. *European Journal of Cultural Studies, 15*(5), 659–676. https://doi.org/10.1177/1367549412445758

CHAPTER 4

# Reviewing in Genre and Practice Hierarchies

Remarkable for reviewing is its genre character. Reviewing follows principles of a certain type of non-fictional prose that is distinguished from other genres of non-fiction, and the reviewing activity is distinguished as a distinct *genre practice*—reviewing means following the principles of the review genre that can be applied in addressing cultural products across different forms of culture. Genre refers to established patterns in texts; genres are cultural categories that surpass the boundaries of media texts and operate within primary production, cultural mediators and audiences (Mittell, 2001). Used as a classification tool to identify the basic functional character of a given text and to differentiate it from other potential alternatives, the genre works as an essential mediating component that makes communication between the reviewer, text and audiences possible (Fowler, 1989), 'limiting the meaning-potential of a given text' (O'Sullivan et al., 1994, p. 128). The identification of a text as part of a specific genre provides potential readers with a code, or an expectation, which enables them to decide whether the text is likely to appeal to them. The alignment of a text according to a genre thus produces a tacit contract between authors and readers against which the text is produced and read, or is expected to be produced and read (Chandler, 1997).

Giltrow and Stein (2009, p. 1) note that genre typically works as a shared intuitive concept, an aggregation of linguistic patterns serving certain functions, but in the changing media landscape where different communication and publishing environments compound, it may be overly


M. Jaakkola, *Reviewing Culture Online*,
https://doi.org/10.1007/978-3-030-84848-4_4

simplistic to return a genre to textual characteristics. It seems reasonable to draw a distinction between *genres*, 'situational categories', and *text types*, 'linguistic categories' (Giltrow & Stein, 2009, p. 2). The study of text types, common in functional and pragmatist linguistics as well as rhetorical studies, aims to trace the repetitive and differing constituents of a genre and sees texts as an agglomeration of distinct linguistic features. In this respect, the form determines the function, and a certain form of a text can be distinguished from other texts according to certain textual features, which may be identified at different textual levels ranging from word choice to stylistic expression. For example, the classical organon model by Bühler (2011 [1934]) distinguishes between three alternative text types according to the primary function of a text: the representation function (describing function), the expressive function (creative function) and the conative function (appealing function). If we take the review as an example, we can note that it seeks to fulfil all these functions. However, individual texts seldom exhibit any formal common characteristics that can be returned to lexis, grammar or style. Indeed, Stegert (2001) notes that the (aesthetic) journalistic review is a very complex genre with a lot of variation in its formal and sociopragmatic features, and it cannot be fully classified according to the traditional functions. The delimitations of the genre are becoming increasingly fluid in online environments where hypertexts blur the boundaries of the entity that counts as a text, increase intertextuality, the interaction and mutual dependency of texts, and produce hybrid forms of texts such as reviewtainment (Askehave & Nielsen, 2005; Miller & Shepherd, 2009).

Genres have typically been studied in relation to each other, seeking definitions, family resemblances, prototypes or ideal types for a certain genre (Chandler, 1997). The family resemblance approach emphasizes describing similarities between texts within a genre. However, representatives of sociocultural genre theories (see, e.g., Mittell, 2001) argue, quite appropriately, that genre theories have largely defined genres in terms of their textual components, that is, being inherent in the textual features, while the processes of cultural intermediation, primary production and audience engagement have been identified as the 'context'. In the characteristically non-centralized cultural production on platforms, understandings of genres are generated within communities and their hierarchies. In the journalistic tradition it has become common to view genres as text typologies where textual features are compared to each other and distinguished from each other through searching for 'differentia specifica'.

However, even here the professional communities and their ability to accept, adopt and develop genre conventions and turn them into routines and practices play a central role.

The review genre is grouped together with opinionated genres, to be distinguished from fact-based informative texts where the neutrality of the narrator's or author's voice is a key element, and critical genres, where the central aim is to question, contest, evaluate, but also to inform and educate (Domsch, 2009). In newspapers, the basic function of a review—critically evaluating a piece of work—can be fulfilled by applying diverse genres, not only that of review, such as essays, columns, reportages and feature stories, interviews and dialogues between experts of art. In addition, both print and online newspapers develop organization-specific formats or situational subgenres (Santos Silva, 2019). As a consequence, even if the share of the text type 'review' varies, the critical function of evaluating arts may remain the same, even if it is much more difficult to measure than the number of review texts. In a similar way, cultural products can be critically evaluated in many ways across social networking and amateur review sites, making use of very different combinations of affordances that the platforms offer.

When talking about reviewing, let alone criticism or being critical, the categories of genre are contingent and fluctuating. Genres are based on 'processes of systematization' (Neale, 1980, in Chandler, 1997, p. 3), and the conventions are under constant transformation over time. This is fortified by the very concepts of criticism and reviewing that are more apt to describe an activity or a process than its outcome. Doing reviewing requires that there be a group of people that envisions a certain genre as a normative entity of rules to be applied to practice. This community of practice (Wenger, 1998) or interpretative community (Fish, 1980) identifies itself as practitioners following the genre, and is also able to develop the genre further. Even if these genre practice communities are often loose and more or less informal in their character, we can identify some major communities in the three forms of cultural critique: criticism, journalistic reviewing and online reviewing. These will be discussed next. To understand the diversity of forms of reviewing, we need to start in criticism, to then see the continuities and gradual shifts in reviewing, ending up in user-generated meanings. Reflections in previous literature tend to recognize the continuum between criticism and reviewing but stop there; my argument is that the concept of vernacular reviewing extends the scale further. First, I will address the conventional distinction between criticism and (journalistic) reviewing. Second, I will extend the discussion from the dualism of criticism and reviewing by distinguishing two types of reviewing: journalistic and online reviewing. The latter will further be categorized into two types, reviewing conducted on amateur and customer review platforms, as well as social media platforms.

## 4.1 From Criticism to Reviewing

The terms 'criticism' and 'reviewing' have been used interchangeably, but even those who see these two terms as merely semantic alternatives to each other do notice their difference at least in theory (see, e.g., Chong, 2020). The use of the two terms is not established and well defined but they seem more like fuzzy categories. Some scholars are using criticism for the forms of critique that I in my theoretical framework localize as review(ing) (see, e.g., Orlik, 2016). Despite the fluctuation of the uses, they are typically set into a framework that implies an assessment of quality, 'reviewing' being subordinated to the more serious and legitimate 'criticism' (Carroll, 2009; Hohendahl, 1982). Titchener (1998, p. 3) defines criticism as 'studied evaluation' and Carroll (2009, p. 10) as 'evaluation grounded in reasons'. In comparison, a review requires less such expertise and thus enjoys a lower status, being 'a report with opinion', characterized by a journalistic 'who-did-what-when-approach' (Titchener, 1998, p. 3). However, in the journalistic context it would be oversimplifying to call the review just 'a report with opinion', because, first, that characteristic would not distinguish it from essays, columns and other commentaries, all frequently occurring journalistic genres, and, second, reviews typically reach far beyond the allegedly descriptive 'who-did-what-when-approach' of the news reporting style. Third, as I will discuss in the next chapter regarding journalistic reviewing, reviewing is not allowed to be legitimately conducted by any other reporter but the author is expected to fulfil certain normative characteristics to be included in the symbolic community of reviewers.

Chong (2020), while using the terms reviewing and criticism interchangeably, distinguishes between journalistic, essayistic and academic forms of reviewing (and criticism, as she does not make a clear-cut distinction between these two forms). By 'journalistic reviews' she refers to 'reviews written for daily or weekly publications, that is, newspapers', while 'essayistic criticism' is, according to her, published in 'more selective and specialized journals such as monthly or quarterly literary reviews' (Chong, 2020, p. 4). I do not see the distinction between journalistic and essayistic as necessary for my purposes, as both are essentially *journalistic* forms of reviewing, only for two different types of journalistic products, newspapers and magazines, which have diverging aims and production structures but subscribe to the (very versatile and divergent) institution of (cultural) journalism. In times of media convergence, many reviewers (or critics) are actually freelancing for both types of mediums, and the professional identity of reviewers is seldom constituted according to the division between these media forms, some calling themselves 'newspaper reviewers' and others 'magazine reviewers'. Reviews in niche magazines may often be longer and more essayistic, but positioning of a reviewer as an expert of newly released art is no different. Therefore, it seems more reasonable to talk about journalistic reviewing as a grouped category and to see academic criticism and journalistic reviewing as two separate categories. Criticism carries with it academic or theoretical undercurrents and a philosophical tradition. Journalistic reviewing is methodologically and content wise less structured or disciplined, yet often adopts influences from the flows of criticism, and the genre, understood as a journalistic format distinguished from other formats such as news and columns, applied to different types of media, constitutes its core.

Semantically, criticism and reviewing point to different directions and may arouse different connotations regarding the character of the activity. The term criticism is derived via the Latin from a Greek root (Greek noun *krísis*, 'decision, event, turning point'; verb *krinein*, 'to decide'). The term has a medical background and refers to the turning point of a disease, after which the patient's state either improves or deteriorates (Koselleck, 2006). The concept thus describes the status quo of a socially constructed object as a stage in a sequence of processes, and sets it in a temporal and socio-spatial context while defining the non-anomalic or initial state of affairs. Indeed, criticism can be seen as diagnostics of a crisis, and has frequently been connected to the idea of the crisis of arts (McDonnell & Tepper, 2014). Criticism is, however, not limited to assessing a cultural object but more typically enquires into ideas and their given contexts, conditions of society, cultural phenomena and so on. The role of a critic is not an occupation or a work role, but more a floating description of a person who occasionally adopts the role of a public intellectual in a certain discussion. Gramsci (1971) pointed out two groups of intellectuals: traditional intellectuals whose function in society was based on continuance, such as teachers and priests, and organic intellectuals who compromised in their vocation (Said, 1994, p. 4). In today's digital media culture, critics have increasingly become media persons (Kristensen & Kannik, 2018; Kristensen & From, 2015).

Compared to critics, reviewers are not necessarily considered public intellectuals but more industry workers, employed to produce reviews on a continuing basis. Reviewer is also an occupational category that a communicator is more or less permanently committed to. The English word *review*, also manifest in the French *revue* and the Latin *revideo*, means looking back on something or seeing again, *re*-viewing. The act of reviewing could thus be understood as a retrospective act of reconstructing an encounter with a piece of art or culture, with a strong emphasis on reviewing a past process. The Latin word *recēnsiō* means enumeration or reassessment, from the word *recēnseō*, to count, reckon, examine, go over or revise. The proto-Indo-European word *ḱn̥seye-* refers to announcing, and recension in this respect means announcing or declaring one's opinion, which is continued in the word *anmeldelse* (Danish and Norwegian). The words *Rezension* (German), *revisión* (Spanish), *revisione* (Italian), *revisão* (Portuguese) and *recension* (Swedish) are connected to ocular inspection or reassessment, and many languages simultaneously have the equivalent word for criticism in use. In addition, it should be mentioned that the word review is in use in the academic context for literature reviews and book reviews, and in theatre for revues, entertaining and sometimes satirical productions consisting of short sketches, songs and dances. Even if these meanings have been adopted for entirely different purposes, they also bear the meanings of capturing, commenting and evaluating a sequence of topical or past events or pieces of materialized culture.

Maintaining a clear-cut line between criticism and reviewing is utopistic because the words are adopted in diverging ways to national languages, used interchangeably in academic, everyday and professional discourses, and the distinctive feature can be localized neither in the authorship (academics, traditionally referred to as critics, are also involved in journalistic reviewing) nor in semantics or stylistics (pieces of criticism and reviewing may in practice show similar textual depth). Despite these difficulties, the difference between criticism and reviewing is valid as a conceptual category. To use these terms to their fullest potential, criticism and reviewing can be seen as ends of a sliding scale in which criticism represents in-depth analysis with more requirements for argumentation and reflexivity, which is expected to be critically contested, primarily by peers, to arrive at a temporary consensus, and requires more time for its production, while reviewing denotes a more non-reflective, spontaneous act of reacting to a cultural object, not bound to a knowledge production system in the way scientific knowledge production is, and is thus more quickly forgotten. In other words, criticism and reviewing constitute a continuum, there being gradual differences in form and function.

Therefore, it can be stated that different forms of public cultural critique are differentiated from each other according to their depth, which includes the learnedness of the author in the discipline in which he or she is reviewing products, the timely embeddedness of the reviewing activity, their institutional support and embeddedness, intended audiences, and the production and publishing cycle of the review. The three forms of cultural critique are, in fact, more than just static socio-aesthetic 'forms'; they are shared structures of social relationships and thus entail a community character. They are supported by a selected group of people who have committed to conducting commonly agreed goals, retaining a common understanding of the area they engage in and developing ways for mutual communication, yet at the same time also establishing power structures that allow some to be more powerful in defining these constituents than others and leaving persons and groups seen as non-eligible outside the community. In this respect, these forms can be regarded as sociological fields (Bourdieu, 1984), structured according to an uneven distribution of symbolic capital. They can also be characterized as what Swales (1990) in the study of linguistics called discourse communities or Miller (1994) called rhetorical communities—communities that constitute a common public goal for their members, and 'own' a genre and adopt a common vocabulary to speak about it. They can also be viewed from the perspective of situated learning, or as communities of practice (Wenger, 1998), social bodies of knowledge sustained by a group of people that is established and maintained through collective learning. As in the context of online pedagogies online communities have been characterized as networked knowledge communities (Sorensen & Mara, 2014), the communities can also be aptly described as knowledge or interest communities, with a certain kind of critical activity as their common mission and object of interest. Communities of user reviewing may share a common goal and a set of practices to a lesser degree than the other forms of cultural critique, but in communities focusing on one form of art on one platform they may also find commonalities. The three community forms of cultural critique—criticism and two types of reviewing—are described in Table 4.1.

Criticism is conducted by academics and intellectuals with a specific societal mission and social responsibility (Said, 1994). Pieces of criticism

**Table 4.1** Forms of cultural critique

| *Form of cultural critique* | *Actors* | *Primary media channel* | *Range* |
|---|---|---|---|
| Criticism | Academics, intellectuals in 'critics' circles' | Scholarly, theoretical and artistic publications | From traditional to organic intellectualism |
| Journalistic reviewing | Reviewers and cultural journalists in media organizations | Journalistic publications | From intellectual/aesthetic to consumer/service/ lifestyle journalism |
| User reviewing | Online users in lifestyle communities | Digital amateur review and social media platforms | From connoisseurship to fan reviews and reviewtainment |

are often critical essays of different kinds, but critics may also be involved in producing other forms of content across media, not the least in journalistic organizations (Chong, 2020). They can be published as stand-alone books, and in arts catalogues, scientific and art-theoretical books. Criticism requires time for its production, and with regard to producing academic research output, the timeframe may be decades or even a lifetime. The outcomes are embedded in a historical framework, which means that intellectuals are expected to deliver output that makes a difference in history, advancing the intellectual resources of humanity. Critics 'uphold the eternal standards of truth and justice' (Said, 1994, p. 5), marked by their distance from practical concerns. This means that 'least of all should an intellectual be there to make his/her audiences feel good: the whole point is to be embarrassing, contrary, even unpleasant' (ibid., p. 12). The common goal for the discourse or rhetorical community of criticism is related to the shared belief of improving the conditions of arts, society or the world by practising intellectual critical public activity that can be turned into a resource of transformation.

Journalistic reviewing is conducted by persons recruited by media organizations, and recruiting can roughly be divided into two forms: first, being employed as staff personnel, either on a permanent of fixed-term contract, or, second, being commissioned for a single story on a freelance contract. All forms imply that culture desk superiors, subeditors and producers who decide what will be covered and by whom play a role in selecting and commissioning reviewers for their tasks. Reviewers can be both academic and what in Gramsci's terminology would count as traditional intellectuals, as well as practitioners of art and culture, theorists with specialization in the area they are involved in, or selected members of the 'art world' (Becker, 1982), but once they commence their activity as a reviewer they are no longer considered as lay or ordinary people; they enter the realm of institutional professionalism. In contrast to criticism and online reviewing, journalistic reviewing has a close connection to the organizations that are producing them. Journalistic organizations, for their part, have taken on a societal expectation to be as representative as possible in their monitoring of a field. If intellectuals are supposed to embed their activity in a long historical timeframe, journalistic reviewers are expected to testify to contemporary changes in the landscape. The common goal for the discourse community of journalistic reviewing is connected to journalistic aims of making journalistic coverage a public good that benefits democracy by sustaining an obligation to truth, independence and loyalty to citizens, providing a forum for public criticism and compromise (Kovach & Rosenstiel, 2007).

With a shorter publishing cycle than in criticism, journalistic reviewing is seen as a day-to-day service for audiences. In daily newspapers, broader audiences are pursued, including lay people who might occasionally become interested, while in cultural magazines the audience is more exclusive, consisting of cultural consumers with a certain amount of expertise to be considered aficionados. The perception of reviews as being an 'overnight reaction' has been overridden by only a couple of hours' time span between lived experience and published review. It is not uncommon for today's reviewer to be expected to deliver his or her review the same night that the cultural event to be reviewed takes place. In addition, live-reviewing has becoming increasingly common. The notion of accelerated time is thus true for reviewing, making the difference from criticism more notable.

User reviewing means reviewing conducted online by a heterogeneous group of people on a number of different platforms, but platforms that are not journalistic organizations. Places for user reviewing can be considered either as being connected to the formal institutions, the journalistic and academic institutions that produce reviewing and criticism, or as being more independent and not functioning in an immediate functional connection with the formal institutions. Online reviewing is considered the most ephemeral of all the forms of critique. This is notably true in the ultimate forms of 'stories' and 'updates' that may be publicly visible only for a few hours before they disappear. User reviewing is partly a heuristic term that must be seen in relation to the two other forms of cultural critique; 'users' may refer to a multitude of roles, and what these users do may not have a common goal that could be as clearly articulated as the general objectives of intellectuals and journalistic reviewers. This is partly because the objectives of intellectuals and journalistic reviewers are connected to institutional aims—for intellectuals, to those of academia and research and the intellectual discourses and practices upheld by them; and for journalistic reviewers, to the ideology of journalism that manifests in media organizations ranging from media giants to small-scale startups.

User reviewers can be professionals who are at the same time involved in review production by journalistic outlets. They can be professionals of different fields, like librarians reviewing books, or they can be professionals but not necessarily in reviewing, like a marathonist reviewing sports books. They can also be hobbyists who have acquired experience and knowledge to make informed assessments, but with no identity comparable to the professionals. Finally, they can be lay people with no extraordinary pre-knowledge about the field they are active in, but turn reviewing into entertainment or otherwise appealing content that catches audiences' attention. User reviewers may create pairs or collectives to do reviewing, and reviewing may only be one part of their communication strategy. The reviewership of online reviewing is the most varied because there are no epistemic centra, no governing key organizations or user communities exerting dominance over the others, that would set up definitions for what reviewing is and should be.

Each of the three forms of cultural critique entails internally different levels, ranging from studied evaluations to spontaneous reactions. While the intellectual enactment ideally demands time and effort from the intellectual, intellectuals are also involved in more fast-paced circles of evaluation production. Each field of cultural critique—criticism, journalistic reviewing and online reviewing—thus has its autonomous and heteronomous pole, to stick to Bourdieu's (1992) conception of fields consisting of poles that enjoy relative autonomy and poles that are subjected to heteronomy. The logics of online reviewing seem, however, to be more complex, as the hybrid economies and hybrid roles put forward reviewer roles that are not following the contrast of disinterestedness (autonomy) and commercial (heteronomy).

The distinction between criticism and reviewing is invested with emotions, romanticizing and elevating the more sublime, autonomous intellectual forms as something more preferable while envisioning the 'lower' forms targeting larger audiences as something less sophisticated. All theorists addressing the role of intellectuals in society have repeated this narrative, from Said (1994) to Gramsci (1971) and Bourdieu (1998). The established distinction is drawn between criticism as a 'higher' and, allegedly, more 'serious' form of critique, and reviewing as a more practical and down-to-earth method of conducting cultural critique. The question of whether something qualifies as criticism or reviewing is conflated with the question of whether it is good or bad criticism or reviewing. The hierarchization, both of criticism and reviewing, with their internal hierarchies between better- and worse-quality content, evokes feelings, legitimating certain forms as more sophisticated and exclusive while downplaying the others. For example, Titchener (1998, p. 3) describes the author of a review as a person who qualifies as 'an entertainment writer with a host of newspaper-based obligations'. To call a dedicated reviewer an 'entertainment writer' is something that is probably felt as derogative by the reviewer. In this line of thinking, while criticism is elevated to refer to an expert's evaluation of an event, journalistic reviewers have been alleged to compromise when writing shorter reviews, previews and other content conforming to formats that news organizations have designed for them. Last but not least, online reviewers who lie at the bottom of the hierarchy, entering commercial partnerships and becoming 'influencers', go even further than journalists in their compromised performance.

This value-imbued hierarchical structure is not surprising in any way; centra and peripheries of power and hierarchies of preference can be found in all social institutions, such as science (natural sciences vs. humanities) and journalism (political news vs. cultural news). What is important is to recognize the logics of boundary-making and avoid comparing value systems to each other. Critique takes on different forms and each of them has its own conditions of production. In examining the three levels of cultural critique it is essential to be able to identify at which level a specific act or activity of reviewing can be localized and, this way, to put reviewing into its larger context.

## 4.2 Journalistic Reviewing

Arts review is a signature genre of the specialized form of journalism called arts or cultural journalism. Arts or cultural journalism refers to coverage of culture and lifestyle issues, produced by specialized journalists within a specific organizational unit or culture desk, and placed in newspapers in a section under the vignette 'culture', 'arts and letters', 'arts and entertainment', or 'feuilleton', or published in cultural magazines with a focus on a specific form of culture such as classical music, theatre or film. Arts review is more than just an aesthetic genre practice among the genre practices available for cultural journalists. Arts review implies a specialized production structure with relative stability in professional culture (Jaakkola, 2015; Shrum, 1996) and aesthetics (Heikkilä & Gronow, 2018) not comparable to any other form of journalism. Art reviews are typically published on the major art forms of literature, music (with different genres ranging from classical to popular forms), theatre and scene art (including dance), fine arts (including photography and media arts), and popular-cultural products such as video games and comics.

Customer product reviews occur across different types of journalism, being the most prevalent in lifestyle journalism (From, 2018) and service journalism (Eide, 2017). Typically, journalistic customer product reviews are published on cars, beverages (alcohol), as well as home appliances such as home electronics and cleaning tools. Restaurant and food reviews are located between customer products and services and, being based on a sensual experience, they become close to arts reviews where the aesthetic experience lies in the foreground. While restaurant and food reviewers (Blank, 2007) and car reviewers (Dewenter & Heimeshoff, 2015) constitute the professional journalistic groups with the greatest stability and continuity in their professional identity, many less unique and replaceable products are not driven by expertise and hence their reviewing can be conducted by less profiled persons. Reviewing may also be conducted in the form of consumer product tests, and there are a number of international companies specialized in unbiased product testing and consumer-oriented research conducted in test laboratories in specific fields and selling these tests to journalistic and non-journalistic outlets to be published as reviews in the national public spheres. Examples include the German company SLG and the Italian CSI S.p.A for consumer product testing, or The Taste Lab for food testing. The American Consumer Reports, founded in 1936, belongs to the earliest organizations advocating the testing and analysis of products and services, including on hairdressers, export and import companies, jewelry designers, insurance agencies, pest control services and bedroom furniture stores. In the same fashion, the Danish company Trustpilot, launched in 2007, brings together reviews on consumer services. The company site presents reviews in 22 categories in total, ranging from 'Animals and pets' to 'Vehicles and transportation', each category organized into 6–14 subcategories. The test and review industry is complemented by news outlets' own activities within the genre of consumer and service journalism. Newspapers have, for example, developed formats of their own where consumer panels try out and compare alternative products to determine their worth.

Arts reviewing and customer product reviewing build up very different traditions and occupy different positions within the professional structures of journalism and thus they need to be discussed separately before attempting any longer-term synthesis. Arts reviews concentrate on the aesthetic dimension of works and need human evaluators, while the aesthetic dimension is often only one among the many factors in consumer products to be reviewed, which makes the reviewing of consumer reviews less dependent on the subjective profiles and opinions of human reviewers. As a consequence, arts reviewing has a more established, permanent place in the journalistic genre palette and cultural beat within the media organization, and customer reviews are more contingent, being part of the rapidly evolving structures of special sections and supplements dedicated to consumer culture. Indeed, often when talking about reviewing we only refer to aesthetic reviewing. As previously discussed, the distinction between art and consumer products, or aesthetic and ordinary consumption, is a ramification of the very definition of arts and cultural journalism where art and lifestyle are differentiated from political and local everyday life in the structure of beats. The detachment of art from life, for its part, is the consequence of the long tradition in art theory (Carroll, 2009).

Whether an art or a consumer review, journalistic reviewing is more or less an industry product. Journalism is an ideology of immediacy, the suffix '-ism' referring to an ideology and the French word 'jour' meaning 'a day'. Journalistic content production has the basic objective of informing, educating and entertaining the public, and the rise of soft news, interpretative journalism and constructive journalism has added a number of new nuances to the journalistic mission (Kovach & Rosenstiel, 2007). Journalistic production is thus based on a specific way of shared thinking by the community that practises it. The selection and addressing of topics are guided by an ideologically constructed way of perceiving the world, based on news values that stress the power elite and celebrity, surprise and magnitude (Galtung & Ruge, 1965; Harcup & O'Neill, 2017), and in arts, the quality, rarity and exclusivity (Golin & Cardoso, 2009). However, news values are an abstraction based on news journalism that has a focus on political occurrences—the area of coverage that used to be the core of journalism and journalism theory before journalism studies and education began to view journalism as 'journalisms' rather than through a single normalizing lens—and the application of news values is not entirely unproblematic in cultural journalism. Cultural journalism is seldom based on unstaged natural occurrences happening in reality without anyone anticipating them. More typically, cultural coverage is based on pseudo-events (Boorstin, 1977 [1961]), arranged events that cultural organizations have planned, such as book and album releases, concerts and exhibitions. This structure influences especially reviews that are never based on something unanticipated but always foreseeable. In fact, compared to conventional journalistic activity, reviews are one of the most formalized methods of coverage. They are based on the process of a reviewer selecting an object to be reviewed, acquainting himself or herself with it and its relevant context, and writing about it. The process is to a large extent conventionalized, pre-planned and repeatable, and thus also controllable and systematized. What is of importance is that professional reviews are an integral part of the newswork that journalists are conducting, and this bears expectations of journalistic professionalism of the review product: representativeness of the cultural product reviewed in relation to the field monitored, and representativeness of the opinion expressed in relation to a taste culture. Reviewing is conducted under the managerial control of news organizations, affected by their editorial and design policies, while imposing on them an ethical professional code that connects them to the journalistic self-regulation system that guarantees autonomy for reviewers.

Blank (2007) distinguishes between two methods of producing journalistic review: 'connoisseurial reviews' and 'procedural reviews'. The production of connoisseurial reviews is 'dependent on the ability of a person—a reviewer—who, because of unusual talents, extensive experience or special training, has developed a refined sensitivity with respect to a certain product genre' (Blank, 2007, p. 29). These kinds of reviews are opinionated texts representative of a taste community. They are based on the 'aesthetic paradigm' of cultural journalism that leans on subjectivity, opinionated, enlivening and argumentative presentation, and an individual's accumulated experience from the area being covered (Jaakkola, 2015). Procedural reviews are based on the results of empirical tests and well-defined procedures that could be conducted without human intervention (Blank, 2007, p. 8). Procedural reviews thus resemble consumer tests, and they present a method based on objective knowledge to produce reviews.

In addition, journalistic imagination in newsrooms has definitely produced a high number of hybrid forms of tasting and testing that have been published in papers as reviews (see, e.g., Jaakkola, 2015), but these typically remain experiential cases, being very context-specific and dependent on the reviewer.

In addition to the evident and at the same time contested characteristics of immediacy, the following characteristics mark the journalistic reviewsphere:

1. An argumentation-based written monologue. The tradition of journalistic reviewing is dominantly graphocentric, privileging the written word over other media forms. The ultimate output of the reviewing process has by default been a written text—short or long, varying in style, but a text. The visual conventions related to the review genre in print and, accordingly, online texts have been relatively scarce. Illustration in reviews is typically rather conventional, based on using book or album covers, or—depending on the cultural form—press material depicting scenes or author portraits, but there is only minimal visual development in general. Reviewers are typically focused on writing a text and not encouraged to come up with ideas for illustration or visualization. Experiments in visual or audiovisual storytelling are rather limited in their number compared to the extensive volume of reviews published on a regular basis. A reviewer is, in other words, expected to write down his or her experience, argue for his or her preferences, and mediate everything in words.
2. Production of a preference or rank. Critical processes are based on subjectivity, as in connoisseurial reviews, or, as in procedural reviews, the objectivization of opinion. The basic or dominant function of a review has traditionally been to define the worth of the review object. According to Carroll (2009), the critical act that applies for reviews contains the basic elements of contextualization, classification, elucidation, interpretation, analysis and evaluation, among which evaluation is a distinctive feature of the review genre (Blank, 2007, p. 7). Orlik (2016, p. 8) defines the critical process as 'knowledgeable comprehension, positive/negative ascertainment, and resulting carefully considered judgement as a means of reasonably estimating the value of the particular work under scrutiny'. Criticism seeks to 'reveal the aesthetic value of an object' ('message criticism'), to 'relate it to the structure that sustains it' ('medium criticism'), to

'relate the object to the traditions to which it belongs' ('receiver criticism'), and to 'define the intention of the artist' ('originator criticism') (Orlik, 2016, p. 78). The functions of criticism include 'guiding the audiences' (acquainting them with new cultural objects), 'building bridges' (opening up lines of communication and understanding between creator and consumer), 'suggesting new directions' (providing the audience with new interpretations), 'proposing system-cognizant change' (providing the audience with more macro-sociological analysis), 'serving as a proxy or watchdog' (discovering the concerns of citizens and cultural consumers and defining what the public needs to know), and 'entertaining the audience' (expressing ideas in a manner that captures the audience's attention) (Orlik, 2016, p. 27). All of these cognitive processes—contextualization, classification, elucidation, interpretation, analysis and evaluation—necessitate subjective knowledge from the author. A lay person ignorant of a product's context would not be able to perform these processes. However, while it would not be possible for someone to become a reviewer within a short period of time, a reviewer can be born within a relatively short period of time when a person acquires the necessary amount of knowledge to perform these critical processes based on subjectivity.

3. Boundary work through specialization. Art is a value-laden concept, and persons who are addressing art need not only to decide whether the objects they are covering are art or not, but also whether these objects represent good or bad quality. The boundaries of the review genre coincide with the sociocultural and symbolic boundaries of the artworld, and, in particular, the professional community that is conducting the review. Reviewers tend to occupy a distinct reviewer expert's identity and have traditionally not been very flexible in crossing genre boundaries, that is, unlike generalists, moving from the genre of review to other genres such as news and news feature. This is clearly reflected in an old anecdote, described by Olsen (2014), where a reviewer who came back to the newsroom after seeing that a cinema theatre was on fire, was disappointed that he could not write the review. By coming back without writing about the news event he had made the news editor very disappointed. In contrast to the review, a column has a more open production context, with less prescribed author roles that can be flexibly adopted by politicians, administrators, authorities, experts, academics, lay persons, students

or even children. Review, in contrast, cannot be adopted by any other writer with a relevant interest, but the review author has per se to be a specialist acknowledged by the art or cultural community.

4. Exclusive representativeness. Whatever the delineations between contextualization, classification, elucidation, interpretation, analysis and evaluation in the outcome of reviewing may be, the reviewer is expected to be representative of a taste culture, or the aesthetic field he or she refers to (Bourdieu, 1979). Journalistic reviewers' position-taking as reviewers is based on independence (a 'third-party' position), which, for its part, is based on the assumption that they are representing good taste. The boundaries of the authorship are thus exclusive, rather than aiming at inclusivity, and meritocratic, as the exclusive group of people who is acting as reviewers is thought of as being representative of good taste.
5. Object-dependence. Reviews are produced on new cultural products and services on the market. The products range from a book to an exhibition, from a live concert to a restaurant visit, but the ontological object of reporting is an artefact or a reified or materialized form of culture. Reviews are, in other words, by default not written on persons, institutions, processes or phenomena. In addition, in the pseudo-events of releasing these products, the products need to be accessible for the audience, or the cultural products under review need to be available on the market at the time that the review is published. Reviews thus normally do not address historical objects or events.

To sum up, journalistic reviewers are closely connected to media organizations, allocated a professional status by them, and engage within an institutional order that dictates the conditions of review production. According to content analyses spanning across decades (see, e.g., Jaakkola, 2015; Heikkilä & Gronow, 2018; Purhonen et al., 2019), journalistic reviewing has been characterized by stability, even if there has been metacritical discussion on the deterioration of the volume and quality of professional reviewing (see, e.g., Jaakkola, 2015). Only recently have the professional unions for critics loosened their membership criteria just like journalists' unions have done, now even accepting bloggers, podcasters and reviewers from the vernacular domain. Journalistic reviewing's boundaries regarding user reviewing are also becoming blurred as journalism is being produced within the structures of the non-institutional social web, or reviewers are becoming active as multipreneurs in both institutional and non-institutional contexts that both can ensure an income.

## 4.3 User Reviewing

In contrast to criticism and journalistic reviewing, user reviewing is not a structurally supported established concept or a unified tradition, practice or entity, but occurs on diverse platforms and social networking sites. Compared to the other two forms of critique, it is a young phenomenon and often borrows its ideas and models from established critical institutions, but is not restricted by their structures. User reviewing in this context refers to all non-institutional reviewing conducted by 'free' cultural citizens and consumers, and is almost without exception carried out online. It refers to activities of hobbyist reviewing, fan reviewing, nerd reviewing, fellow reviewing or peer reviewing of products that play a central role for a certain group of people who typically have a relatively high interest in that special domain. It can also be called online or internet reviewing, amateur or lay reviewing, or customer or consumer reviewing, depending on the context in which it is being discussed. User reviewing could also be referred to with the terms that I sometimes use in this book, like ordinary reviewing or mundane reviewing (cf. ordinary consumption; see Gronow & Warde, 2002). All of these terms intend to highlight the fact that this type of reviewing occurs outside the professional and institutional frame of criticism and reviewing, and that it was not enabled to its fullest until the internet came into being, as online communication provided the possibility for fans and hobbyists to create public spaces where the tasks of reviewing can be performed and become increasingly professionalized.

At a general level, user reviews occur on two types of online forum. First, there is *reviewing on user review sites*, which refers to websites, apps and services where publishing reviews from users, amateurs, customers and consumers is included in the functionality of the site. Second, there are *user reviews on the social web* that are generally referred to as 'social media', covering popular platforms using different media for communicating: services predominantly based on the written word such as blogs and microblogs, video-driven platforms, image-driven apps and audio-based podcasts. The common presumption concerning reviewing in these internet spaces of both types, even if individual professionals and organizations are also using social media in various ways, is that they are dedicated to content creation for ordinary users, that is, any one of us, who in this context count as amateurs. However, the amateur position impinges upon the users in different ways. I will refer to these spaces as user review sites and user reviews in social media.

User review sites and reviews on social media constitute opinion economies that are different from each other with regard to the creation, organization and utilization of user-generated review data. In general, the user review sites work according to an operative principle that is organized top-down, imposing on users the author and user role of reviewers and systematically collecting data from reviewers. User review sites thus include two markets: one where user reviewer data is produced and refined, and another where the data is made available for the industry that needs data on consumer behaviour to improve their products. In other words, users contribute to the production of opinion data and are involved in its structuration by measures of metarating and metareviewing. This reviewer-produced data embodies a strategic decision support for leaders and decision-makers of businesses. Users are invited to be involved in a system where their actions become a commodity for the industry, but they are not put into an immediate contact with the industry. The user reviewers are engaged on a voluntary basis and do not get any material compensation for their activities.

In comparison, reviewers who are operating on social networking sites are equally subjected to capitalization on the data they produce, but on different conditions. Unlike user review sites, reviews on social media operate bottom-up in the way that the platforms provide the users with a channel for sharing content, without limiting the possibilities of expression to reviewing. As the review content on social media is more difficult to delimit and identified as a category, the data can be used for many purposes, just like any other user-generated data on social media, and not only for the industry that would need evaluations, ratings and assessments of their products. Social media user reviewers may be involved in reviewing on a voluntary basis, but they are provided with a number of monetizing possibilities among which they themselves need to choose. They can make use of YouTube's advertising or Amazon's affiliate programmes, actively establish commercial partnerships and so on, according to their individual preferences and communication strategies. Social media user reviewers thus have more space for negotiation in terms of their relationship with the market, which comes with a heavier ethical responsibility.

On user reviewing sites, the platform or service owner has designed the processes in such a way that the role of the amateur is built into the functionalities of the platform. Users are asked to enter a platform by creating a user (reviewer) account and leaving texts on the platform that are displayed in a designed slot, labelled as amateur, user, customer or consumer review. When browsing through these texts it is evident that the content follows the expectations related to the genre of review and the authors thus act as reviewers, whoever they might be. In contrast, on social media platforms, users are free to position themselves without any preconditions, and their content may appear in a number of different contexts. Some may claim to be amateurs, others to be professionals, and many are in the process of becoming professionalized. On social media, users are owners of their own medium, or the profile (account, channel, feed or whatever you call it) in the way that they are responsible for the creation of their personal brand, rules of communication and the patterned interactions centred upon the profile. Reviewers on social media thus control their own 'micro-media' (Manovich, 2000), and amateur and professional attributes on these channels are much more relative and gradual, heterogeneous and even ambiguous, but not predefined and not necessarily contrasted to professionals. Reviewers on social media are freer to perform the reviewing functions by using the different affordances available. They can flexibly combine reviewing with other genres, or switch from reviewing to, for example, tutorials. However, this freedom should not be interpreted to mean that they are more independent or free from the mechanics of platform capitalism in which all content they create become saleable data.

The spaces of user reviewing differ from each other according to how saleable they make the user data, and how the second market cycle is organized. This affects the preformalization of the creator role on the platform—whether the user is pre-assigned a reviewer role or an open user role where he or she can flexibly define how reviewing is incorporated in his or her communication strategies on the platform. User review sites are 'closed' review spaces, specifically dedicated to reviewing, while reviews on the social web are not limited to reviewing. The readiness for saleable data also affects the structuration of internal social reward systems in the review spaces. In all spaces, an essential feature includes the ranking of users for symbolic or economic benefit. On user review sites, this is centrally structured, while on the social reviewing web, the ranking is solely based on social popularity, measured by the number of subscribers, followers or attention dedicated to the shared content. On user review sites, the data that is created through interaction between users is thus more systematized, controllable and usable. It is possible to delimit the most active and trusted reviewers and extract their data regarding a specific cultural product or cultural form.

How do user review sites and user reviews on social media look more concretely? Table 4.2 shows some examples of user review sites. User review sites designed solely for publishing user reviews under a selected theme may originate from two directions: either fans putting up a review forum by themselves, or an organization, typically with a profit interest, introducing a review function incorporated in its services. Organizations

**Table 4.2** Examples of user review platforms (2020)

| *Example* | *Review category* | *Product category* | *Visitors per month* | *Launched* | *Owner* |
|---|---|---|---|---|---|
| *Arts and culture* | | | | | |
| Goodreads | Literature reviews | Books/literature | 15 million visitors | 2006 (US) | Amazon (2013–) |
| Internet Movie Database (IMDb) | Film reviews | Films, television programmes | 250 million visitors | 1990 (UK) | Amazon (1998–) |
| LibraryThing | Literature reviews | Books/literature | 2 million visitors | 2005 (US) | Amazon (2008–) |
| Metacritic | Film reviews | Films | 12 million visitors | 1999 (US) | CBS Corporation (2008–) |
| Rotten Tomatoes | Film reviews | Films | 30 million visitors | 1998 (US) | Warner Bros. (2011–) |
| Wattpad | Literature reviews | Fan fiction texts | 45 million visitors | 2006 (CA) | Naver Corporation (2021–) |
| *Consumer products* | | | | | |
| Amazon reviews | Consumer reviews | Various consumer products | N/A | 1994 (US) | Amazon |
| Google Customer Reviews | Consumer reviews | Various consumer products | N/A | 1998 (US) | Google |
| Skytrax | Consumer reviews | Airports and airlines | 406 000 visitors | 1989 (UK) | Skytrax |
| TripAdvisor | Consumer reviews | Hotels, travel destinations, restaurants | 363 million visitors | 2000 (US) | Liberty Media Corporation |
| Yelp | Customer services | Food and restaurants | 52 million visitors (mobile) | 2004 (US) | Jeremy Stoppelman (6.1 %) |

with an interest in reviews are often directed towards selling of products and services, advocacy of specific consumer cultures, or testing of products. There are innumerable fan sites and hobby forums online, run as voluntary projects without any structured commercial ties or direct profit gains for those involved, where aficionados of certain products are allowed to submit reviews for common exchange of ideas and experiences and to create a sense of a community. These forums can be run by individual persons, informal networks or associations or can be crowdfunded. Reviews may emerge as part of the altruistic efforts to give peer feedback and collaboratively contribute to practical knowledge about the domain (while at the same time boosting the selfish aim of being seen by others as an expert). In the course of time, amateur forums may develop into more commercial enterprises or receive a more commercial character. Fan fiction writers can (peer) review each other's' texts on Wattpad or FanFiction.net in various subcategories, and fiction writers on FictionPress.com. Guitar builders and players have Thegearpage.net and Ultimate-guitar.com. Board game players can publish reviews on tabletop games at BoardGameGeek, and recipes can be reviewed on Allrecipes. Furthermore, Disney fans have TheDisInsider and ImagiNERDing to review Disney entertainment, theme parks, collectibles and more, including reviews on food and beverages at Disney theme parks only (Disney Coffee Blog, Urban Tastebud Disney, DisneyFoodBlog). Like Disney, all big brands, from Apple to Coca Cola, from Barbie to Fender, have fan communities chasing the best features and functions or the most unique experiences and uses, in which review is a central tool. Reviews on fan sites can take a slightly different form than amateur reviews on more industry-oriented sites. Fan reviews are often based on an affirmative character rather than being guided by knowledge or interest in finding out whether a product or service works, or how it works.

Many user review sites have been founded as hobby forums but turned into businesses, like the Internet Movie Database (IMDb) that originated in 1990 as a fan-operated database and became a subsidiary of Amazon in 1998, with 'entertainment fans' as the intended audience and audiovisual industry professionals as important stakeholders. At the end of 2020, IMDb presented approximately 7.5 million titles and 10.4 million personalities on its database, and had 83 million registered users. It works as an information source for films, television programmes, home videos, video games, online streaming content and related celebrity news. The site presents cast, production crew and personal biographies, plot summaries, trivia, ratings, personalized recommendations, editorial content—and reviews, which are of two types: 'user reviews' and 'external reviews'. User reviews, formerly called 'user comments', are submitted by users who are generally called 'contributors'. Submitted user reviews become the licensed property of IMDb. External reviews, also called 'critic reviews', are professionally produced reviews published outside IMDb by major media organizations. Reviewers and editors can submit links to these reviews on IMDb, and thus for professional reviewers the database offers a channel to find highly engaged readers and increase the impact of their texts. According to the guidelines for writing user reviews (IMDb, 2020), the length of a user review is between 50 and 10,000 characters, while a length of 200–500 characters is preferable. Reviewers can also add a rating ranging from 1 to 10 stars to their review. Published user reviews can be sorted according to their helpfulness, review date, number of votes and the label 'prolific reviewer'. Reviewers thus form a hierarchy based on an internal reward system and can climb up this ladder by becoming more prolific. Each reviewer gets an 'activity page' showing a collection of the user's activities on IMDb, including reviews. Users can be assigned or earn badges; for example, reviewers are automatically assigned a tenure badge showing the length of membership of IMDb, and they can earn a 'top reviewer' badge, awarded for the most frequently posting 1000 reviewers.

These user-led sites need to develop as neutral a third-party position as possible by setting up rules for transparency and unbiasedness of the reviews published. In addition to IMDb, there are two American aggregator sites for film reviews, Rotten Tomatoes, launched in 1998, and Metacritic, launched in 2001. Their ultimate aim is to rank cultural products in the hope of delivering an overview for the assistance of cultural consumers who need to make choices. Engaged hobbyists are asked to contribute, and the multitude of individual opinions and preferences becomes a collective effort of sorting pieces of art and entertainment as well as everyday products and services according to the majority's conception of good quality. A common feature of all three mentioned film sites including user reviews is that user reviews are placed side by side with professional reviews.

A number of customer review sites have an explicitly articulated objective to remain neutral and claim to be committed to improving the quality of the products and services they cover, which is more often an unarticulated aim in aesthetic or arts-oriented reviews. Amazon and Google are the multinational giants that are making extensive use of customer reviews.

Their model can be characterized as embedded reviews, because reviews are typically embedded in a context, serving other purposes than just ranking products. Amateur and customer reviews are often embedded in systems with dominant functions other than reviewing, such as shopping or supporting purchasing choices before shopping. In this context reviewing is either a by-product that has grown out of more one-directional communication, as in the case of TripAdvisor, or a subfunction designed to support another objective. Amateur reviews to an increasing extent occur in webshops and online services to support potential customers' purchasing choices.

According to Amazon (2020a), for which customer reviews can be submitted for all items listed on the site, customer reviews 'should give customers genuine product feedback from fellow shoppers, including 'both favorable and unfavorable opinions', and 'help customers to learn more about the product and decide whether it is the right product for them'. While customer reviewers are expected to follow the general community guidelines, there are also rules for specifically writing reviews. Amazon lists the types of reviews they won't allow and that will be removed as follows:

- A review by someone who has a direct or indirect financial interest in the product;
- A review by someone perceived to have a close personal relationship with the product's owner, author or artist;
- A review by the product manufacturer, posing as an unbiased shopper;
- Multiple negative reviews for the same product from one customer;
- A review in exchange for monetary reward;
- A review of a game in exchange for bonus in-game credits;
- A negative review from a seller on a competitor's product;
- A positive review from an artist on a peer's album in exchange for receiving a positive review from them.

The review platform providers make efforts to make the reviews accountable. They do not just provide an open platform for anyone to submit reviews but attempt to set up an ethical code that the users need to follow, with potential interventions and sanctions in cases where the rules are not appreciated. A review can also be labelled 'Amazon verified purchase', which means that Amazon can confirm that the reviewer has purchased the product and has not received it 'at a big discount' (Amazon, 2020b). Rules and restrictions for reviewers are important to create a body of 'trusted reviewers', as the most legitimate, productive and honest reviewers form a valuable commodity for Amazon. Amazon runs an internal promotion programme for manufacturers and publishers to receive reviews for their products, the Vine Program. Companies pay a fee to Amazon and it passes the company's products to user reviewers, who are called 'Vine voices'. 'Vine voices' are invited members of Amazon's review base who have proven to be trustworthy based on the helpfulness of their reviews and 'their demonstrated interest in the types of products that are featured in the program' (Amazon, 2020b). Helpfulness is judged by customers by clicking the button 'helpful or not'. User reviewers who consistently receive ratings for their reviews as being 'helpful' and develop a reputation for expertise in specific product categories are most likely to be invited into the programme. Amazon's reviewsphere thus forms an exclusive core that is a closed system, where the platform's owner chooses the most qualified ones to act as 'privileged' reviewers.

Customer reviewing has typically been gradually embedded in webshops and online services to refine the shopping experience and to deliver information for the sellers on the useworthiness of their goods. Review functions can form a valuable aspect of a company's strategy. Whether shopping at Amazon, Best Buy, Ikea, MediaMarkt, Walmart, Wish or Zalando, you can take a look at what consumers have written about the product before making a purchasing choice. Written customer reviews are shown in addition to recommendations ('you may also like', 'frequently bought together', 'similar products'), ratings and customer comments or quotations, and customers may be allowed to add visual material of their own and be asked to assess if the review was helpful or not by clicking a button. Accordingly, customer reviews may be sorted according to 'the most helpful positive review' and 'the most helpful negative review', to show both poles of customer assessment. The system may also automatically analyse the most frequently used words in the reviews. Users can sort reviews according to relevance, helpfulness, publishing date and rating. A high amount of customer-driven information is thus attached to the products. Consumer data is turned into information that is supposed to serve as a basis for decisions.

Skytrax, established in 1989, is a United Kingdom-based airport industry consultancy that conducts research for commercial airlines. It collects customer reviews for airports from around the world, allowing air travellers to explain their experience in written form and rate (1–5 stars) among other things queuing time, terminal cleanliness, seating and signs, as well as staff. The site has moderators and an editorial policy according to which unrelated, abusive, defamatory content or texts identifying persons, showing bad taste, including incorrect information or being too short in their aspired length (250 characters) will not be published. Besides a ranking of airlines and airports, Skytrax presents annual awards to airlines and airports, the World Airline Awards and World Airport Awards, based on votes by passengers.

Video-streaming services Netflix and HBO as well as music streaming service Spotify have incorporated viewer reviews into their video-recommendation systems. Red Ventures, the company that owns Metacritic, also runs CNET including technology and consumer electronics reviews and GameSpot for video games reviews. The American online fitness retailer Bodybuilding.com collects reviews related to dietary supplements, sports supplements and bodybuilding supplements. Open-source software development early on adopted the practice of using user reviews as part of creating knowledge on the products available. Content management systems such as WordPress and Drupal integrate reviews for their user-generated plug-ins and modules that can be downloaded for free from their sites. On top of all this, a variety of service apps make use of rating and reviewing, ranging from established service providers to young start-ups. Although not review sites at the point of their launch, some sites have increased their functional roles in reviewing along the way.

However, even non-profit cultural organizations have started embedding reviews in their operations, mostly to enhance the user experience and in this way to improve their services. For example, libraries have started incorporating interactive, participatory and collaborative features in library catalogues to enhance readers' advisory services (Tarulli & Spiteri, 2012) and to make online public access catalogues more attractive and useful, dynamic and enriched in their functionality, following the positive experiences from online bookstore catalogues (Šauperl & Saye, 2009). Even if libraries were 'late-comers' in the area of user-generated content and doubts have been expressed as to whether such small local communities as library users' can reach the critical mass of participation, the anticipated 'next-generation catalogue' (Merčun & Žumer, 2008) has become a reality within a decade, including the feature of reviewing as part of the catalogues' functionality. Together with user ratings, comments, tags and lists, reviews present a way for libraries to engage borrowers—who might no longer be just interested in borrowing books but also consumer products, as the postmodern libraries also lend DVDs, games, season tickets for musical and sports events, drilling and sewing machines, tennis rackets, ice skates and skis, earphones, health rate monitors and musical instruments—and take advantage of their contributions to generate additional metadata to enrich the catalogue. Libraries are also actively conducting public pedagogical work towards society to engage readers to participate, among other things, through writing about their reading experiences. Many book reviewing challenges circulating in the user reviewsphere are, indeed, initiated by libraries.

Based on the above, we can note that there is a wide variety of user review platforms, each employing different strategies, and different positions and functions are assigned to reviewing. However, reviewing activities on user review sites stick to some common principles:

- The texts are called reviews and are normally distinguished from 'commentaries', 'quotations', 'testimonials' and ratings.
- There is an editorial policy or a policy guidelines framework, as well as forms of active moderation (manual pre- and post-moderation, distributed moderation, automated moderation).
- There are verification methods for increasing the authenticity of the reviews and detecting fake and fraudulent reviews, such as e-mail authentication, IP location checks, as well as qualitative editorial and peer authenticity checks.
- There is typically no financial compensation for the reviewers, because the amateurs and customers are doing reviews on a voluntary basis—because they are (and should be) private persons and individuals representing themselves, not professionals.
- Reviewers may have nicknames, even if on some platforms they are also free to use their real names. Reviewers are typically encouraged to build up a review history, and the sites automatically collect all the reviews submitted by the user in one place. However, reviewers often remain faceless and impersonal, they are not expected to describe their background (educational, interest-related, professional, ethnic or similar), or expose themselves in image or video or in an embodied visual form.

The uses of online sites are prompted in social interaction in physical settings. Service providers such as restaurants and hotels, as well as cultural organizations from museums to theatres, are asking customers onsite and afterwards to submit a review, especially if the customer experience has been a positive one. The user review sites are thus utilized as part of marketing and word-of-mouth strategies as they function as publicly available depositories of customer views.

Social media, the conglomerate of websites and applications that enable users to create, publish and share content and network with other users (Fuchs, 2013, 2017), has also been able to accommodate reviews. Compared to amateur and customer reviews on specific reviewing sites, reviews on social media are harder to map and localize because reviewing can occur on almost every platform in any thinkable form, ranging from a 20,000-word essayistic piece on a blog to a one-minute video. Table 4.3 presents spaces for reviewing in popular services of social media.

Blogging, YouTubing, vlogging, instagramming, microblogging and podcasting—or, more specifically, book blogging (Driscoll, 2019; Steiner, 2010), booktubing (Tomasena, 2019; Vizcaíno-Verdú et al., 2019; de Leusse, 2017; de Lourdes López López, 2017; Sorensen & Mara, 2014), bookstagramming (Jaakkola, 2019), sharing BookToks (Merga, 2021) or booktwittering—are distinct practices of using social media, and reviewing—or, for example, reviewing books—embedded in these forms of communication. While the general methods of networked communication obviously to a great extent affect the forms of reviewing, both pragmatically and culturally, reviewing shall not be set as synonymous with the general ways of networked communication or the specific interest communities of a platform where the reviewing is conducted, such as BookTube (YouTube), Bookstagram (Instagram) or BookTok (TikTok). This needs to be noted because there seems to be a tight connection in previous

**Table 4.3** Popular social media sites and apps used for reviewing (2020)

| *Category* | *Example* | *Review communities* |
|---|---|---|
| Blogs | Technical solutions/blog hosts: WordPress (2003), Blogger (1999), Tumblr (2007), Medium (2012) | Book, music, lifestyle blogs |
| Microblogs | Twitter (2006), Weibo (2009) | Often integrated into a blog or equivalent |
| Video platforms | YouTube (2005), Vimeo (2004), TikTok/Douyin (2016) | BookTube, BookTok |
| Image platforms | Instagram (2010), Pinterest (2009) | Bookstagram, bookish communities |
| Audio platforms | Soundcloud (2007), Clubhouse (2020) | Review podcasts, social audio clips |

academic literature between BookTube, booktubing and mediation of literature online, which is seen as the same as (the loosely defined) 'literary criticism', or, simply, book reviewing. In my line of argumentation, all book reviewing on YouTube may belong to 'BookTube' and all book(ish) reviewing on Instagram to Bookstagram, but not all BookTube and Bookstagram contents are reviewing; there are numerous other subgenres that fit in these large symbolic online communities. The identification of the genre is made by using hashtags or explicitly mentioning it in the text, or, alternatively, dedicating entire channels or accounts exclusively to review content.

Blogs can be created on different blogging software, of which WordPress is the most frequently used at the time of writing; however, throughout the history of social media, there has been a versatile assortment of different hosting services available, such as Blogger, Tumblr, Medium and LiveJournal. Microblogging services such as Twitter and Weibo provide users with short-format entries. Popular blogs are often collected to blog communities according to categories (e.g. lifestyle and relevant subcategories), in which the host may take on marketing and promotion functions, acting as a management services provider. The blogosphere has developed distinct spheres according to topics, and reviewing typically occurs on book blogs, art blogs, beauty blogs, fashion blogs, lifestyle blogs, music blogs and food blogs, but it can be integrated into any type of blog, from mum blogs to splogs ('spam blogs', fake blogs created with the sole purpose of promoting affiliated websites, with the intent of 'optimizing' search results and boosting traffic).

The dominant microblog at the time of writing is Twitter, launched in 2006. However, microblogs still play a minor role for reviewing. Most often, they are used for marketing and outreach of an existing blog or review platform elsewhere but not as a place for publishing primary review content, which in the case of microblogs would be necessary to cut down to a miniformat, for example, corresponding to Twitter's word limit of 280 characters per tweet. Innovative reviewers may see potential in this concise form of expression; indeed, the emergence of Twitterature (Twitter + literature) implies that Twitter novels (twovels) and other storytelling projects in the ultra-short format, which was even shorter, 140 character, until 2017, have been realized on Twitter. Nevertheless, at the point of writing this book review communities were not strong on Twitter and the tweets hashtagged with #twitterreview were occasional, incorporating a sense of irony or humour, and they could look like this:

'The mountain between us: a film in which a golden retriever outshines two world class actors playing characters you kind of hope die. #twitter-Review' by @ashleystorrie

'I have sadly finished "You Are Loved" by @JoPlattTweets, it's a brilliant book, I can't wait to forget what happens so I can read it again 😆 ' by @Jenwizzle

Video-based platforms include YouTube, TikTok, Vimeo and Snapchat, all emphasizing different formats and attracting users from different age groups. Moreover, video is also increasingly embedded in other platforms, such as Instagram and blogs. Image-driven platforms, Instagram and Pinterest as the most popular, are based on visual storytelling, and images as their medium of expression. On both platforms, images are predominantly photographs and more seldom drawings or illustrations done using other techniques. Last but not least, audio-based podcasts have recently gained more ground as a basis for reviewing or, at least, book, music or art discussions.

Social media spaces form multi-purpose platforms, which means that the uses with regard to the intended content on these platforms are not predefined on these platforms, and neither are the communicators' roles; for reviewing, this implies that the platforms do not expect or govern users to take on the role of reviewers and reviewing is based on a 'voluntary' selection of the reviewers' role and developed in communities that have chosen to dedicate attention to the genre of reviewing. In other words, when a user starts reviewing on social media, it takes a while before it becomes clear whether the person will become a 'reviewer' and how he or she can be positioned on the map of social media reviewers. There are no detailed rules set up for particularly reviews in social media; instead, building trust and accountability follows different logics. Users are expected to follow the general policies and rules of conduct, but the socio-aesthetic rules of reviewing are set up in user communities making use of the platform affordances (see Sect. 3.4 Platformized Cultural Production).

In my analysis of the most popular 200 review video channels on YouTube (Jaakkola, 2018), I found six major categories of review videos: consumer product reviewing, game reviewing, toy reviewing, tech reviewing, cultural product reviewing and parody reviewing, and in addition a residual category that encompassed diverse channels addressing sports (mainly football play[er] reviews) and theme parks (mainly roller coasters). *Consumer product reviewing* encompassed reviews of everyday consumer products other than technological gadgets and toys, featuring a heterogeneous grouping of diverse products such as cosmetics, food and candies, cars, shoes and musical instruments. Beauty products were the most prominent topic among such reviews, often connected to other genres of beauty and fashion vlogging, such as makeup tutorials. *Game reviewing* finds its base among users who play video games and comment on them, with an intention to share their knowledge and playing tips to help other gamers. *Toy reviewing*, further discussed in Sect. 6.3 At the Playstage: Toy Reviewers on YouTube is a popular genre in which children's toys are shown in videos made for and even by young users, including infants, toddlers and pre-school children. *Tech reviewing*, which is examined on Vimeo in Sect. 6.2 Judging Gadgets: Filmmaker Reviewers on Vimeo, encompasses technology product reviews by YouTubers who typically refer to themselves as 'geeks', 'nerds' and early adopters trying to discover 'the coolest gadgets' and address product novelties or seek to determine the best consumer product in comparison to its competitors. *Cultural product reviewing* comprises videos that conform to the more traditional understandings of arts review, situated in the fields of film, music or comics. *Parody reviewing* utilizes the genre and concept of a review to explicitly make fun of certain aspects of reviewing or the product category under review. This is a mixed category when it comes to the relationship with the cultural product; instead, the focus lies on mocking the features of the genre. These review videos are addressed in more detail in Sect. 6.4 Reviewtainment: Reviews as Platformized Entertainment, under the umbrella term reviewtainment.

On social media we have to distinguish users who are using social media sites for publishing reviews as primary content and the use of the same sites for communicating about the primary content. In the communication practices of social media reviewers, using a platform as a tool for publishing reviews and using a platform as tool for spreading the word about what has been published merge with each other. My research interest is directed towards platform affordance uses and how platforms affect the form and content features of a review, which leads me to prioritize the publishing aspect of social media. A user typically has a main publishing forum for their reviews, which dictates the type of 'main product' and more or less affects the reviewer's identity—whether he or she is a blogger, bookstagrammer or podcast reviewer, and to which of these communities he or she primarily relates. Many reviewers do, however, maintain a multi-platform presence in the hope of catching a maximal number of followers' attention. This may even imply creating different versions of the single review or review topic, such as a full-text review, a shortened review, a puff, or previews (called sneak peeks in the social media vocabulary). The user, for example, establishes a blog where the reviews are placed, but they may also want to be present on Instagram, and may also occasionally or on a regular basis produce video and audio reviews, which can be embedded in the blog, and in this way spread the primary content across different platforms. In addition, the user may use Twitter and Facebook to announce the publishing of new reviews.

Social media reviews are marked by the following features:

- As the platforms are not limited to publishing reviews, reviews are not always marked clearly as 'reviews' but may be left unlabelled or embedded in another form of communication. Reviews form part of the account holder's communication strategy, and it is up to the communicator/reviewer to draw the lines (or let it be) and highlight the genre characteristics. Despite this openness, there is a common understanding of and shared rules for what counts as a 'review', embedded in the online subcultures, which makes it appropriate to talk about the genre of review.
- Review production follows the production culture of the community of practice on the specific platform, but the platform provider does not restrict or encourage any specific forms or practices concerning reviewing. Platforms pose different restrictions for the use of different media, and the extent of the output (length of text or video, size or number of images, etc.). The format of the review is significantly influenced by the platform cultures, based on conventionalized uses of affordances available.
- Reviewers are obliged to discover their own way of positioning themselves as reviewers and finding their income, which results in a high amount of variation.
- Reviewers typically have nicknames, but compared to the user review platforms, the audiovisual mode is dominant, which makes it more appropriate for reviewers to expose themselves and create an online presence that leans upon mediated embodied enactment.

On social media, reviewing is often embedded or even merged in other forms of communication. The review is limited as a format in the institutional domain, such as in newspapers and magazines as well as on amateur review platforms, in which content producers, in their pre-established reviewer roles, are expected to create a piece of work that acts as a stand-alone product called a 'review'. On social media reviewing is not as clearly defined. In vlogging, ASMR ('autonomous sensory meridian response', referring to sound-based relaxation videos giving viewers and listeners specific sensations called tingles), product presentations, testing, and the content creators may have multiple roles within the same channel or account, not being solely a reviewer; rather, the reviewer role is subordinated to the primary role of vlogger, gamer or filmmaker.

To conclude, we can state that the online environment for user reviewing is marked by two different markets and production spaces: user review sites and social media reviewing spaces. They differ from each other in their functional structures: user review sites belong to the institutional context with respect to its top-down logics of predefining the user role and subordinating the reviewer, as a consumer, citizen or, perhaps, citizen-consumer, to a user with a specific function. The controlling institution also sets up rules for reviewing, in the form of writing and style guidelines, and makes interventions to ensure proper uses, in the form of active moderation. In social media reviews, there are no specific rules for reviewing but the reviewers develop these rules in their communities, bottom-up, in relation to adopting their communication to platform affordances and community guidelines. In addition, when talking about the production environment of user reviewing, two more actors need to be taken into account: the mediating agents (or functions) and the metareviewing agents (or functions) of reviewing.

The *mediating agents* are the second-stage mediators (Sect. 3.1 Cultural Mediation) practising continuous promotion for reviewing, and they play an important role in advocating and legitimating reviewing as a societal practice that essentially belongs to all, either as receivers or producers. Some of these mediators are cornerstones of democratic society, and they are mostly institutions of education. Schools, libraries, museums, film and theatre/dance institutes and similar cultural organizations contribute to people's knowledge about cultural intermediation and may be crucial in engaging cultural consumers to be involved in processes of public reviewing by providing them with the relevant awareness, skills and channels. These institutions are apart from the production of art and consumer products, and their self-interest in promoting independent evaluating discourse is primarily related to improvement of the quality of their domain and only secondarily to their own aims. Nevertheless, commercial actors are also promoting reviewing, by enabling reviewing on their online platforms, delivering free-of-charge copies to potential reviewers. These actors have a higher self-interest, but their interest may also lie in producing more refined consumer knowledge about the products on the market, especially if this knowledge acknowledges and even prefers their own products and services. There are also services aiding industries in mediating their output, with connections to reviewing. In literature, literature agents and booksellers are working with reviewers, especially bloggers, to give them copies of new books either before or shortly after their release, to ensure their coverage in the blogosphere. The same applies for many consumer products, for example cosmetics. In literature, there are beta reader and advanced copy services, which intend to provide aspiring book reviewers with reading copies before the works have been published. There are also influencer marketing hubs collecting social influencers, mainly bloggers and vloggers, for the purposes of paid or branded content.

For companies, there is even distinct online review management software like Podium that enables organizations to send review requests to customers and collect reviews directly from them, to be analysed with automated methods.

The *metareviewing agents* are agents actively contributing to the rating and reviewing of the review products and review spaces, located outside these spaces. They can be automated or human beings, curators or specific review media. The metareviewing agents have the potential to keep the review ecosystem clean; there is also potential for detecting disinformation included in reviews, and malicious review information, or fake reviews (Sect. 7.4 Fake and Pseudo Reviews). Many metareviewing instances intend, however, to provide readers with assistance and guidance for navigating the review scene.

## References


Alba, J. W., & Hutchinson, W. (1987). Dimensions of consumer expertise. *Journal of Consumer Research, 13*(4), 411–454.

Amazon. (2020a). Customer reviews. https://www.amazon.com/gp/help/customer/display.html?nodeId=G3UA5WC5S5UUKB5G

Amazon. (2020b). What is Amazon Wine? https://www.amazon.com/gp/vine/help

Askehave, I., & Nielsen, A. E. (2005). Digital genres: A challenge to traditional genre theory. *Information Technology & People, 18*(2), 120–141.

Becker, H. S. (1982). *Art worlds*. University of California Press.
Blank, G. (2007). *Critics, ratings, and society: The sociology of reviews*. Rowman & Littlefield Publishers.
Boorstin, D. J. (1977 [1961]). *The image: A guide to pseudo-events in America* (6th ed.). Atheneum.
Bourdieu, P. (1984). *Distinction: A social critique of the judgement of taste*. Harvard University Press.
Bourdieu, P. (1998). *On television*. New Press.
Bourdieu, P. (1992). *The rules of art: Genesis and structure of the literary field*. Stanford University Press.
Bühler, K. (2011 [1934]). *Theory of language: The representational function of language*. John Benjamins Publishing Company.
Carroll, N. (2009). *On criticism: Thinking in action*. Routledge.
Chandler, D. (1997). *An introduction to genre theory*. https://faculty.washington.edu/farkas/HCDE510-Fall2012/Chandler_genre_theoryDFAnn.pdf
Chong, P. K. (2020). *Inside the critics' circle: Book reviewing on uncertain times*. Princeton University Press.
Dewenter, R., & Heimeshoff, U. (2015). Do expert reviews really drive demand? Evidence from a German car magazine. *Applied Economics Letters, 22*(14), 1150–1153. https://doi.org/10.1080/13504851.2015.1011304
Domsch, S. (2009). Critical genres: Generic changes of literary criticism in computer-mediated communication. In J. Giltrow & D. Stein (Eds.), *Genres in the Internet* (pp. 221–238). John Benjamins Publishing Company.
Driscoll, B. (2019). Book blogs as tastemakers. *Participations: Journal of Audience and Reception Studies, 16*(1), 280–305.
Eide, M. (2017). The culture of service journalism. In N. N. Kristensen & K. Riegert (Eds.), *Cultural journalism in the Nordic countries* (pp. 195–204). Nordicom.
Fish, S. (1980). *Is there a text in this class? The authority of interpretative communities*. Harvard University Press.
Fowler, A. (1989). Genre. In E. Barnouw (Ed.), *International Encyclopedia of Communications* (Vol. 2, pp. 215–217). Oxford University Press.
From, U. (2018, September 26). Lifestyle journalism. *Oxford Research Encyclopedia of Communication*. Retrieved December 23, 2020, from https://oxfordre.com/communication/view/10.1093/acrefore/9780190228613.001.0001/acrefore-9780190228613-e-835
Fuchs, C. (2013). Social media and capitalism. In T. Olsson (Ed.), *Producing the Internet: Critical perspectives of social media* (pp. 25–44). Nordicom.
Fuchs, C. (2017). *Social media: A critical introduction*. Sage.
Galtung, J., & Ruge, M. (1965). The structure of foreign news: The presentation of the Congo, Cuba and Cyprus crises in four Norwegian newspapers. *Journal*

*of International Peace Research, 2*, 64–90. https://doi.org/10.1177/002234336500200104

Giltrow, J., & Stein, D. (2009). Genres in the Internet: Innovation, evolution, and genre theory. In J. Giltrow & D. Stein (Eds.), *Genres in the Internet: Issues in the theory of genre* (pp. 1–26). John Benjamins Publishing Company.

Golin, C., & Cardoso, E. (2009). Cultural journalists in Brazil: Academic research, discursive change, visibility, mediation and news values. *Journalism, 10*(1), 69–89.

Gramsci, A. (1971). *The prison notebooks: Selections*. International Publishers.

Gronow, J., & Warde, A. (2002). *Ordinary consumption*. Routledge.

Harcup, T., & O'Neill, D. (2017). What is news? News values revisited (again). *Journalism Studies, 18*(12), 1470–1488. https://doi.org/10.1080/1461670X.2016.1150193

Heikkilä, R., & Gronow, J. (2018). Stability and change in the style and standards of European newspapers' arts reviews, 1960–2010. *Journalism Practice, 12*(5), 624–639.

Hohendahl, P. U. (1982). *Institution of criticism*. Cornell University Press.

IMDb, Internet Movie Database. (2020). User review guidelines. https://help.imdb.com/article/contribution/contribution-information/user-review-guidelines/GABTWSNLDNFLPRRH?ref_=helpart_nav_9#

Jaakkola, M. (2015). *The contested autonomy of arts and journalism: Change and continuity of the dual professionalism of cultural journalism*. Doctoral dissertation, Tampere University Press.

Jaakkola, M. (2018). Vernacular reviews as a form of co-consumption: User-generated review videos on YouTube. *MedieKultur – Journal of Media and Communication Research, 34*(65), 10–30.

Jaakkola, M. (2019). From re-viewers to me-viewers: The #Bookstagram review sphere on Instagram and the perceived uses of the platform and genre affordances. *Interactions: Studies in Communication and Culture, 10*(1–2), 91–110.

Koselleck, R. (2006). Crisis. *Journal of the History of Ideas, 67*(2), 357–400.

Kovach, B., & Rosenstiel, T. (2007). *The elements of journalism: What newspeople should know and the public should expect*. Three Rivers Press.

Kristensen, N. N., & From, U. (2015). From ivory tower to cross-media personas. *Journalism Practice, 9*(6), 853–871. https://doi.org/10.1080/17512786.2015.1051370

Kristensen, N. N., & Kannik, H. K. (2018). Cultural critique: Re-negotiating cultural authority in digital media culture. *MedieKultur: Journal of Media and Communication Research, 65*, 3–9.

de Leusse, S. (2017). Les booktubers, nouveaux critiques? [Booktubers, new critics?]. *Strenæ: Recherches sur les livres et objets culturels de l'enfance, 12*(1). https://doi.org/10.4000/strenae.1719

de Lourdes López López, M. (2017). Booktubers y literatura [Booktubers and literature]. *Revista Publicando, 4*(13), 963–974.
Manovich, L. (2000). Macro-media and micro-media. http://manovich.net/index.php/projects/macro-media-and-micro-media
McDonnell, T., & Tepper, S. J. (2014). Culture in crisis: Deploying metaphor in defense of art. *Poetics, 43*(1), 20–42.
Merčun, T., & Žumer, M. (2008). New generation of catalogues for the new generation of users: A comparison of six library catalogues. *Program: Electronic Library and Information Systems, 42*(3), 243–261. https://doi.org/10.1108/00330330810892668
Merga, M. K. (2021). How can Booktok on TikTok inform readers' advisory services for young people? *Library & Information Science Research, 43*(2). https://doi.org/10.1016/j.lisr.2021.101091.
Miller, C. R. (1994). Rhetorical community: The cultural basis of genre. In A. Freedman & P. Medway (Eds.), *Genre and the new rhetoric* (pp. 67–78). Taylor & Francis.
Miller, C. R., & Shepherd, D. (2009). Questions for genre theory from the blogosphere. In J. Giltrow & D. Stein (Eds.), *Genres in the Internet: Issues in the theory of genre* (pp. 163–290). John Benjamins Publishing Company.
Mittell, J. (2001). A cultural approach to television genre theory. *Cinema Journal, 40*(3), 3–24.
O'Sullivan, T., Hartley, J., Saunders, D., Montgomery, M., & Fiske, J. (1994). *Key concepts in communication and cultural studies.* Routledge.
Olsen, T. A. (2014). *Kritisk kulturjournalistikk* [Critical cultural journalism]. Cappelen Damm.
Orlik, P. B. (2016). *Media criticism in a digital age: Professional and consumer considerations.* Taylor & Francis.
Purhonen, S., Heikkilä, R., Karademir Hazir, I., Lauronen, T., Rodríguez, C. J. F., & Gronow, J. (2019). *Enter culture, exit arts? The transformation of cultural hierarchies in European newspaper culture sections, 1960–2010.* Routledge.
Said, E. W. (1994). *Representations of the intellectual: The 1993 Reith lectures.* Vintage Books.
Santos Silva, D. (2019). Digitally empowered: New patterns of sourcing and expertise in cultural journalism and criticism. *Journalism Practice, 13*(5), 592–601. https://doi.org/10.1080/17512786.2018.1507682
Šauperl, A., & Saye, J. D. (2009). Have we made any progress? Catalogues of the future revisited. *Journal of Documentation, 65*(3), 500–514. https://doi.org/10.1108/00220410910952447
Shrum, W. M., Jr. (1996). *Fringe and fortune: The role of critics in high and popular art.* Princeton University Press.
Sorensen, K., & Mara, A. (2014). BookTubers as a networked knowledge community. In M. Limbu & B. Gurung (Eds.), *Emerging pedagogies in the net-*

*worked knowledge society: Practices integrating social media and globalization* (pp. 87–99). IGI Global. https://doi.org/10.4018/978-1-4666-4757-2.ch004

Stegert, G. (2001). Kommunikative Funktionen der Zeitungsrezensionen [Communicative functions of newspaper reviews]. In J.-F. Leonhard, H.-W. Ludwig, D. Schwarze, & E. Strabner (Eds.), *Medienwissenschaft: Ein Handbuch zur Entwicklung der Medien- und Kommunikationsform* (pp. 1725–1729). Walter de Gruyter.

Steiner, A. (2010). Personal readings and public texts: Book blogs and online writing about literature. *Culture Unbound: Journal of Current Cultural Research, 2*(2), 471–494.

Swales, J. M. (1990). *Genre analysis: English in academic and research settings.* Cambridge University Press.

Tarulli, L., & Spiteri, L. F. (2012). Library catalogues of the future: A social space and collaborative tool? *Library Trends, 61*(1), 107–131. https://doi.org/10.1353/lib.2012.0032

Titchener, C. B. (1998). *Reviewing the arts* (3rd ed.). Lawrence Erlbaum.

Tomasena, J. M. (2019). Negotiating collaborations: BookTubers, the publishing industry, and YouTube's ecosystem. *Social Media + Society, 5*(4), n.p. https://doi.org/10.1177/2056305119894004

Vizcaíno-Verdú, A., Contreras-Pulido, P., & Guzmán-Franco, M.-D. (2019). Lectura y aprendizaje informal en YouTube: El booktuber [Reading and informal learning trends on YouTube: The booktuber]. *Comunicar, 59*(17), 95–104. https://doi.org/10.3916/C59-2019-09

Wenger, E. (1998). *Communities of practice: Learning, meaning, and identity.* Cambridge University Press.

CHAPTER 5

# Post-Professional Reviewers

In the previous chapter I distinguished between three overarching forms of cultural critique—criticism, journalistic reviewing and user reviewing—and discussed them as specific discursive communities, or communities of practice. The focus was on the diverging environments where reviewers operate, or the structural conditions that form the basis of different types of cultural critique. As for user reviewing, I examined it in specific online environments. In this chapter I will go further and cast more light on reviewers in the context of digital labour. Digital, online, platform, unpaid or free labour (see, e.g., Burston et al., 2010; Terranova, 2000; Hesmondhalgh, 2010, 2015) forms an intensively discussed framework within studies of online cultures where working life has entered a 'new normal' and people's boundaries between work and life are breaking down (Taylor & Luckman, 2018; Ashton & Patel, 2018). In general, the terms intend to describe the communication individuals are conducting, and focal interest varies in concepts such as relational labour (Baym, 2015), aspirational labour (Duffy, 2017), visibility labour (Abidin, 2016) or affective labour (Gregg, 2009; Terranova, 2000). These attributes describe the unpaid, performative, self-centred, emotional and sacrificial character of the online production cultures and the work within them. The study of reviewing prioritizes the inspection of everyday expertise, and how it is constituted in varying degrees in the continuum between professional and amateur.

For reviewers to be engaged in media production and meaning making on platforms they need to build up a certain kind of agency. Agency can in


M. Jaakkola, *Reviewing Culture Online*,
https://doi.org/10.1007/978-3-030-84848-4_5

general be defined as the capacity of individuals to act independently and to make their own free choices (Barker, 2005, p. 448), and, more particularly, in the context of digital labour, to be able to self-author their own reviewership (Holland et al., 2001). Being a reviewer implies the establishment of a creatorship of a certain kind, enforced by audience or peer user attention such as likes, dislikes, follows, subscriptions, commentaries and mentions (van Dijck, 2009). The question of this kind of creatorship and how it is constituted in the reviewsphere boils down to matters of expertise in cultural substance and media production, whether the reviewers are considered amateurs or professionals. Rather than simply being a question of individual identity, the different degrees of professionalism have ramifications that I will discuss as post-professionalism, with regard to the changing field of criticism and reviewing.

Conceptions of professionals and, accordingly, amateurs have been developed in the context of industrial society. The era of linear mass media and mass industrial production emphasized specialization and qualification. The concept of profession is defined by characteristics that can be achieved through gradual development and social closure. Professions are the outcome of professionalization, and they underlie certain professionalism. Professionalism, in practices used in the same fashion as and even interchangeably with 'professional cultures' (Hanitzsch et al., 2019) and 'professional identities' (Deuze, 2005), refers to the conduct of being a professional according to a certain set of standards and the efforts of improving the quality and standards of this practice (Hargreaves, 2000). Professionalization is the attempt at the status and standing of professionals or aspiring professionals. According to the classical Durkheimian differentiation theory, professions have emerged through societal differentiation and functional division of labour, with specialization and transferability of skills as an outcome. Professionalization aims at construction of autonomy to avoid intrusion from external factors, which entails the proliferation of objective standards of work, a theoretical body of knowledge, education and training, and the establishment of professional rules and entry criteria for supporting autonomous expertise and the service ideal (Freidson, 2001; Larson, 1977). Professionalization is, however, never a completed project but rather implies a constant struggle in which professionals continually negotiate and try to maintain their position with an ultimate aim to uphold the autonomy which is a precondition for functioning independently. Professional claims thus serve to settle boundaries between those on the inside and outside of the profession (Waisbord, 2013).

Nevertheless, the discourses on professionalization and professionalism often assume internal coherency of a profession, which may not be the case even in classical professions. Especially in journalism, let alone criticism, entries into the professional activity are numerous, and different professional subgroups show varying places in the internal professional hierarchy. In the cultural beat, staff writers and freelancers, writers of different cultural forms and reviewers employed and used with varying contracts enjoy different positionings within the organizational environment. Cultural journalism, like its partner in crime in evaluative pseudo-event reporting, sports journalism, has been regarded as the 'toy department' of news media organizations (Rowe, 2007), with cultural journalists cherishing a certain kind of art exceptionalism that lets them see themselves as better journalists than the average news journalists (Harries & Wahl-Jorgensen, 2007). The professionalism of critics and reviewers employed by journalistic media seeks to maintain a distinction between professionals and non-professionals. Not surprisingly, the employment of lay reviewers or residence critics has aroused indignation among professional reviewers, and as in any other professional field, the professional unions of reviewers work for the recognition of professionals at both national and transnational level.

In essence, the post-professional framework implies two parallel tracks of professionalization and successive professionalism(s). At the same time, we see a development of non-professionals becoming more professional, that is, showing increased professionalism in their conduct. These non-professionals' activities become more rationalized, more patterned, and they succeed in achieving a stability and autonomy that can be compared to the old professionals' professionalized condition. These 'neo-professionals' may show different professionalism from the original professionals, but they ensure themselves a continued existence through building up economic and sociocultural structures. The new processes of professionalization contest the boundaries between professional and amateur media, the amateur media becoming professionalized and the professional media de-professionalized, both forms challenging each other, and not only in the sense that would threaten the other's existential stability but also in a fruitful way, spurring innovation and creativity for renewal.

Postmodern professionalism has been enabled and facilitated by changes in the postmodern society, in which the industrial order, with its linear mass production (Bell, 1973), centrality of newsrooms (Deuze & Witschge, 2020) and privilege of professionals and intellectuals as opinion- and tastemakers (Kristensen & Kannik, 2018), is being contested. Expert systems dissembled individuals from their local experiential world where knowledge is produced as commonsense knowledge related to everyday experiences (Giddens, 2013). Postmodern culture, conceptualized by Bauman (2011) as liquid culture, is marked by the fluidity of cultural categories such as expertise (Eräsaari, 2009). Accordingly, post-professionalism has been characterized by the loss of exclusivity, an increase in segmentation (or specialization) and an increased role of the use of technologies. As a theoretical framework, post-professionalism has been discussed in terms of more traditional professions, such as law (Kritzer, 1999), teaching (Hargreaves, 2000) and architecture (Sadri, 2018), while—as previously discussed—journalism, and in particular cultural journalism, has never been strictly defined as a profession with a social closure and an open entry into the trade and extensive use of freelancers as critics, but rather as a semi-profession (Aldridge & Evetts, 2003; see, e.g., Fletcher & Lobato, 2013). User reviewing, across the user review sites and reviewing on social media platforms, is based on inclusiveness and openness of participation…, and a gliding scale between amateur and professional code of conduct (Bruns, 2013). All these reviewing communities require and foster a specific kind of agency, which is the topic of the next sections, in which I will present a typology of institutional and non-institutional reviewers. 'Post-Professional' is thus an institutional attribute that implies that the contemporaneity, the historical present in which we are living, enables the existence of parallel alternative professionalisms that should not be seen in opposition to each other.

## 5.1 Typology of Post-Professional Reviewers

In the post-professional landscape, a focal question is how communicators who were previously termed amateurs have become professionalized to different degrees (van Driel & Dumitrica, 2021). In general terms, there is a relative consensus that there is a difference between professional and amateur reviewers, but simultaneously it is unclear how the line between these two should be drawn, as the shift from amateur to semi-professional is a gradual one. I argued in the previous chapter for a distinction between two user reviewer groups: user reviewers on user, 'amateur' or customer platforms on one hand, and user reviewers on social media on the other. Based on this distinction, we can state that user review platforms without an exception invite and inhabit amateur reviewers; the fact that even professional products may be published on these sites side by side with user-generated content underlines the status of users' content as amateur review content. On the social web, however, the role of the reviewer is not predefined in terms of their expert status, but users are able to construct a profile that potentially turns them into a more professionalized player. I will thus further differentiate between two categories of reviewers on social media: the ideal types of professionalized social media reviewers and amateur or lay social media reviewers.

Institutionalization of social media platforms refers to the general trend where an increasing number of homegrown celebrities are turning into professional content creators (Burgess, 2012; Hou, 2018; Kim, 2012). Becoming a professional on the social web depends upon fame, or popularity, which, for its part requires entrepreneurial calculation in the user reviewer's strategies and presentation, which reaches far beyond the amateur reviewing practices on user review platforms. In terms of institutionalization, we may, however, distinguish between formalization of the production environment and the expertise or agency within it. In other words, institutionalization refers to the centralization of the operating principles of a product environment or to the increased formalization and structure of the communication activity. Media organizations and user review sites are venues of high institutionalization. The production environment in this institutional domain of reviewing is formalized by organizations that set the production roles and the equivalent rules of conduct, regulating the critical authority and autonomy of the reviewers. In contrast to media organizations, social media platforms let formalization occur through the politics of visibility that direct the users' micro-media.

In cultural theory, 'vernacular' has come to refer to non-institutional cultural forms and practices (Blank, 2007; Brownlie & Hewer, 2011; Howard, 2005, 2008a, 2008b, 2010). Vernacular uses of discourses emerge 'from discussions between self-identified smaller communities' within larger communities, and have been conceptualized as an expression of alterity to institutional power (Conti, 2013; Howard, 2010). Being in a dialectical relationship with the institutionalized forms of discourse, vernacular discourses emerge through the appropriation of dominant discourses in ways that are better suited to the vernacular community (Conti, 2013; Howard, 2008a). Theorists of vernacularity have thus viewed the institutional and the vernacular as fundamentally inseparable, with the vernacular establishing its meaning by asserting itself against the institutional, and in this respect situating the institutional as 'institutionally prior' (Howard, 2008b, 2010). Vernacularity allows the contestation of institutional normativity, which emerges from the creativity within a community and differs from the professional normativity of institutionalized reviewing. Reviewing, embedded in the ordinary, commonplace, mundane or everyday practices, is a space for 'vernacular creativity', which Burgess (2006, p. 206) defines as 'the process by which available cultural resources—are recombined in novel ways, so that they are both recognizable because of their familiar elements, and create affective impact through the innovative process of this recombination'. Vernacular creativity is thus 'a productive articulation of consumer practices and knowledges—with older popular traditions and communicative practices' (ibid., p. 207). Gibbs et al. (2015) extend this notion of cultural participation and self-representation by introducing the concept of the 'platform vernacular' to include the style, grammar and logical specificities that delimit modes of expression or action on the communication platform. 'Platform vernaculars' are 'shared (but not static) conventions and grammars of communication, which emerge from the ongoing interactions between platforms and users' (ibid., p. 257).

In Fig. 5.1, the x axis describes the agency and the y axis the production environment, both of which can possess different degrees of institutionalization. According to degrees of institutionalization in these dimensions, we can distinguish four ideal types: (1) institutionalized professional reviewers, (2) institutionalized amateur reviewers, (3) vernacular

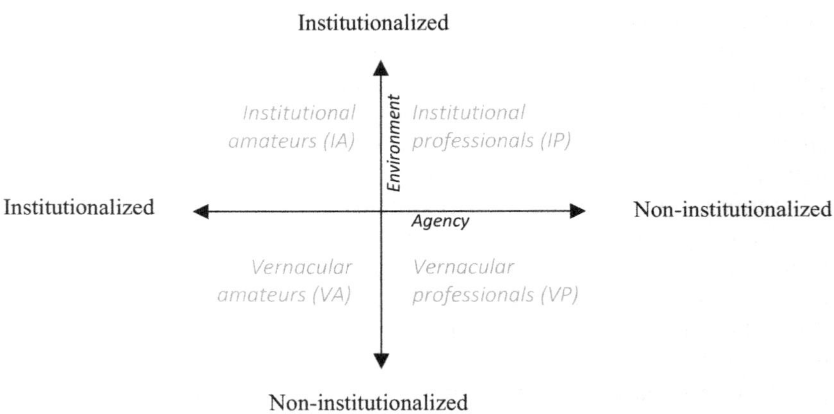


**Fig. 5.1** A typology of reviewers

professional reviewers and (4) vernacular amateur reviewers. I will refer to these as *institutional professionals* (IP), *institutional amateurs* (IA), *vernacular professionals* (VP) and *vernacular amateurs* (VA), respectively.

When discussing user reviewing, the focal interest lies in the non-institutional or vernacular domain, in vernacular amateurs and professionals who distinguish through a low degree of institutionalization in their production environment but a high degree of institutionalization in their media production agency. However, as all ideal types of reviewers are mutually connected and to some extent influence each other, and in order to continue syntethisizing the different professionalisms of reviewing, it is appropriate to briefly discuss the institutional professionals and amateurs before proceeding to vernacular creatorship. I will pay attention to the internal power structures and positionings in terms of building review expertise. In other words, how are internal hierarchies within the community constituted and how can members develop to gain a higher status in the community? How are the genre-essential features of critical authority and critical autonomy constructed, or, possibly dismissed and re-defined? Next, I will describe the four categories of institutional professionals, institutional amateurs, vernacular professionals and vernacular amateurs separately.

## 5.2 Institutional Professionals

The institutional professional (IP) reviewer is the type of reviewer that one usually refers to in everyday discourse when talking about critics or reviewers. Traditionally, IP reviewers are well-known public figures with a distinguished profile. IP reviews are most often written texts, published in cultural magazines, cultural sections of daily newspapers or culture supplements of newspapers. There is a long list of professional reviewers, often characterized as critics as well, including Harold Bloom (1930–2019) in literature; Arthur Danto (1924–2013), John Berger (1926–2017), Rosalind Krauss (b. 1941), Jerry Saltz (b. 1951) in visual arts, Pauline Kael (1919–2001), Leonard Maltin (b. 1950) and Peter Bradshaw (b. 1962) in film; Howard Rosenberg (b. 1942), James Poniewozik (b. 1968) and Emily Nussbaum (b. 1966) in television; Harold C. Schonberg (1915–2003) in music; Robert Gottlieb (b. 1931), Jack Anderson (b. 1935), Joan Acocella (b. 1943) and Sarah Kaufman (b. 1963) in dance; and Michael Sorkin (1948–2020), Paul Goldberger (b. 1950), Justin Davidson (b. 1966) and Alexandra Lange (b. 1973) in architecture, to name but a few—the list is long and depends on the preferences of who you is asking. Moreover, national cultural public spheres and subcultures host their own stars who have significantly contributed to the formation of their field. Typically, IP reviewers are writing for major publications such as *The Guardian*, *The New Yorker*, *Rolling Stone* or *Slate*. The early reviewers for the modern mass media were also public intellectuals, academics and theorists defining the core concepts of their field—more critics than journalistic reviewers as they are defined in this book.

Although the tradition to a large extent relies upon written cultures and reviewers typically even call themselves 'writers', for example 'theatre writers' or 'music writers', IP reviews have traditionally occurred, and continue to do so, even in audiovisual and audio media. In television, there is a tradition of television magazines where reviews are inserted, or complete programmes dedicated to reviewing. Anglo-American television history involves a number of film review shows, such as Gene Siskel (1946–1999) and Roger Ebert's (1942–2013) *At the Movies* in 1986–2010; the *Sneak Previews* in 1975–1996 by the aforementioned critics and their colleagues Neal Gabler (1982–1985), Jeffrey Lyons (1982–1996) and Michael Medved (1985–1996) and *The Review Show* on the BBC, run under several titles in 1994–2014 by Mark Lawson (1994–2005), Kirsty Wark (2002–2014) and Martha Kearney (2006–2014). The German literary critic Marcel Reich-Ranicki (1920–2013), who earned the nickname *Literaturpapst* ('pope of literature'), hosted a literary talk show, *Literarisches Quartet*, on German public television in 1988–2001 and became a public reviewer figure.

Furthermore, reviews have been sent into the radio but with perhaps less focus on pieces of work than on reviewing cultural events in a more general way. For example, on *Saturday Review* on BBC Radio 4, host Tom Sutcliffe has since 1999 invited guests, according to their webpage, to 'offer sharp, critical discussion of the week's cultural events'. The audio tradition is continued by an increasing number of literature, film, music and lifestyle podcasts with a focus on reviewing, such as *The Book Review* podcast by *The New York Times*. New apps employing the possibilities of audio, such as Clubhouse, launched in 2020, may contribute to the diversity of audio review forms. In any case, audiovisual forms have constantly gained legitimacy within reviewing, and one sign of this is that in 2020 podcasts and audio reporting were for the first time eligible for the Pulitzer Prize for Criticism.

The professional tradition of IP reviewers is centred around high-cultural products, as the high arts constitute the core of the cultural journalistic canon of cultural forms (see, e.g., Kristensen, 2019). Consumer reviews sustain a less coherent tradition that would assign a symbolic value to it. News outlets typically host reviewers of video games, cars, beauty products, food and beverage. The IP reviewers conducting consumer reviews are, however, and if possible, less 'stars' and more similar to news workers in service of delivering assessment of new products for an interested audience. In consumer reviewing, there are also independent companies dedicated to consumer product reviewing of a certain kind. For example, the review site Coffee Review (www.coffeereview.com), founded by Kenneth Davids and Ron Walters in 1997, is a small media company that publishes coffee tasting reports and blog posts. According to their website, they host over one million unique visitors per year. Kenneth Davids is the editor-in-chief and chief cupper, there are associated editors, active as professionals in the businesses of food, wine and travel, and Ron Walters manages marketing and social media. They developed a 100-point scale rating for evaluating coffee that has been adopted by other actors in the business. They regard themselves as representative of a global coffee community's values and assumptions, as well as being dedicated to developing the standards of tasting, assumably with a demonstrated impact.

Some IP reviewers may also be active on social networking sites, even if it is less common that they use social media as their primary publishing platform. Despite the diversification of the production contexts of journalism and journalistic practice, as more and more journalists endorse an entrepreneurial approach and start doing journalism beyond the traditional institutional context (Deuze & Witschge, 2020), IP reviewers' production environment is culturally and *symbolically* still primarily dictated by legacy media organizations. Being an IP reviewer thus strongly co-exists with journalistic reviewing discussed in Sect. 4.1 Journalistic Reviewing, IP reviewers being highly marked by the modern tradition established by the mass media critics of the twentieth century. To put it differently, the typical understanding of what is meant by a 'review' is drawn from the institutionalized professional (IP) form of reviewing, particularly its journalistic form that is subordinated to criticism.

Yet what makes a reviewer professional? In the animated series *The Critic*, the main character, a New York-based film reviewer called Jay Prescott Sherman, is described as a cold, socially incompetent, mean-spirited and elitist person whose signature line for film reviews is 'It stinks!'

In a similar fashion, in his influential essay *Confessions of a Book Reviewer* (1968), George Orwell describes an archetypical reviewer as a 'man of thirty-five, but looks fifty'—'bald', with 'varicose veins', wearing 'spectacles, or would wear them if his only pair were not chronically lost':

> In a cold but stuffy bed-sitting room littered with cigarette ends and half-empty cups of tea, a man in a moth-eaten dressing-grown sits at a rickety table, trying to find room for his typewriter among the piles of dusty papers that surround it. He cannot throw the papers away because the wastepaper basket is already overflowing, and besides, somewhere among the unanswered letters and unpaid bills it is possible that there is a cheque for two guineas which he is nearly certain he forgot to pay into the bank. There are also letters with addresses which ought to be entered in his address book. He has lost this address book, and the thought of looking for it, or indeed of looking for anything, afflicts him with acute suicidal impulses.

*New York Times* film reviewer Anthony O. Scott (2016, p. 13) writes, on a personal note: 'If you ask around,—you will learn that a critic (a professional reviewer) is, above all, a failed artist, unloading long-simmering, envious resentments on those who had the luck, talent, or discipline to succeed'. Indeed, a prevalent feature of the IP reviewer in the metadiscourse describing these professionals is the pejorative way of characterizing their institutional authority and power, supported by the subaltern character of journalistic reviewing being 'lower-rank' criticism, as discussed in Chap. 4 Reviewing in Genre and Practice Hierarchies. Contesting and making fun of the institutional professional, to the point of creating an inverse image or counter-discourse of it, is also a prominent vernacular feature, frequently encountered in reviewtainment (Sect. 6.4 Reviewtainment: Reviews as Platformized Entertainment).

Professionals become legitimate by being selected by professional media organizations, and institutional professionals are media industry workers. However, review professionals occupy a vaguer position within the institutional landscape than journalists. In my studies on cultural journalism in daily newspapers, I have identified the professionalism of cultural journalism as consisting of two dominant dimensions, the journalistic and the aesthetic paradigm (Hellman & Jaakkola, 2012; Jaakkola, 2015). While the journalistic paradigm presents the news orientation, underlining the competences and values connected to fact-basedness and unbiased presentation, immediacy and newsworthiness, the aesthetic paradigm is based on subjectivity, opinionated, enlivening and argumentative presentation, and accumulated experience from the area being covered. These traditions have always been inherent in modern cultural journalism, constituting both a dynamic dualism in reporting and tensions that have complicated the internal dialogue between different subgroups of cultural journalism. Moreover, their mutual relationship has been configured across decades. While news journalism, the traditional core of 'hard news', has been 'softened' and become more interpretative and narrative in its orientation (Esser & Umbricht, 2014), core news areas such as political journalism have become closer to cultural journalism. At the same time, the journalistic paradigm in cultural journalism has been strengthened in cultural newsrooms that have through a number of various re-designs and development projects become more under managerial control in news organizations—a development that could be interpreted as professionalization but is often also perceived as deprivation of the special character, exceptionalism or autonomy of arts journalism. The aesthetic paradigm, with reviewers as key protagonists, has a less stable position within the professionalist framework, as it is more likely to be outsourced or seen as excessive in terms of the core mission of journalism of delivering news. The review, in other words, is settled into the journalistic genre hierarchy but holds an ambiguous rank, being highly appreciated but confronted by economic necessities and easily seen as excessive, or at least outsourcable material (see, e.g., Jaakkola, 2015). In today's media, the number of reviewers who are privileged enough to have a long career in one media organization is decreasing.

In addition, while journalists are staff writers employed within the news organization, reviewing leans upon freelancing and has been a full-time occupation to a few only. The vast majority of reviewers have needed to search for income in related occupations, being artists, educators or cultural intermediary professionals of another type. Multipreneurialism has not, however, been a problem but rather the contrary, as reviewers have typically occupied a double identity between the art world and journalism (Dickstein, 1992). Being a multiprofessional in kinship occupations has thus to a great extent supported the reviewer's occupation and given added legitimacy for the reviewer, while the media organization has been the guarantee for the critical autonomy that the reviewer needs to adopt while reviewing on an ethical basis.

IP reviewers are expected to show a considerable, extraordinary body of knowledge in the area they are covering, compared to non- or semi-professionals. IP reviewers are thought to have a privileged position in the art world; they are part of the art community, have access to sources and information, they are *living* with and in the arts. If scientific expertise has been based, in Robert K. Merton's wording, on cognitive authority (Turner, 2014a), critics and reviewers in arts have been held to possess a judgemental authority. The high amount of knowledge is typically acquired and honed through accumulated experience, or the iterative process of inspecting art and reviewing it, but the qualifications may also be acquired through formal education, such as in university programmes and art education, or by informal education and by accumulated practice, which all contribute to the institutionalization of the reviewer's agency. There are no formal criteria for education, but cultural journalists tend to have more formal education than other journalists (Hovden & Kristensen, 2018). There are professional structures such as professional unions and academic recognition of the field, supporting aesthetic professionalism, as well as academic education. However, reviewing is only occasionally integrated into formal curricula of arts education, ranging from studies in literature to architecture, and often combined with aspects of curation or arts journalism in general, but study programmes solely focusing on criticism and reviewing remain scarce. As one of the few exceptions, the journalism school at Columbia University in New York hosts an MA programme on arts writing, including training in reviewing and criticism (CU, 2021). Educational efforts are often individual specialization courses or projects driven by associations and non-governmental organizations. In 2017, there was an educational programme established for architecture reviewers, the NAW (New Architecture Writers), initiated by Phineas Harper and Tom Wilkinson in London to counteract the underrepresentation of black and minority ethnic writers in architecture and design criticism and curation. The free programme aims to develop the 'journalistic skill, editorial connections and critical voice of its participants' (NAW, 2020). It is supported by institutional actors: *The Architectural Review*, The Architecture Foundation, the Royal College of Art and the *RIBA Journal*.

Because of the central role of the media organization as a regulator of activities, professionals are paid for reviewing. Because IP reviewers are paid for their work, they need to remain careful about crossing the line between compensated and non-compensated activity. For many freelancers this means that they should not give their expertise for free; voluntary work may pay off in the long run but it is more often dismissed as a less preferred alternative, as reviewers are already professionals, unlike the aspiring professionals in the vernacular domain. In the theory and practice of the classical intellectual expert field, lay perspectives are typically defined in an inversive manner: not knowing is ignorance, dilettantism or philistinism, which functions as marking and maintaining the boundaries of the sphere of professionalism. The antipathy towards the amateur is part of the strategic boundary work of the reviewers, as much as their sympathy with the public-intellectual critics as defined in previous chapters.

In its most institutionalized form, the review is written for a restricted audience that has a relatively high knowledge of the topic. During recent decades, IP reviews have received criticism regarding their unnegotiable authority, top-down character, compromised or non-transparent autonomy, and elitist distance towards their audiences (see, e.g., Elkins, 2003; Elkins & Newman, 2008; Frey, 2014, Berger, 1998; McDonald, 2007; Pool, 2007). However, these are precisely the dimensions that are being re-negotiated and re-adjusted in other forms of reviews, or in user reviewing. More and more reviewers are also starting their own start-ups, financing their work through crowdfunding, and becoming active on the social web, either doing self-promotional activities, complementing their reviewing activity by adding background to the professional conduct by, for example, keeping a journal-like blog, or even re-publishing original reviews online. Uncertainty, a post-professional feature, has become a characteristic of the IP professional's work.

## 5.3 Institutional Amateurs

Institutional amateurs (IA) live up to the basic expectation of what is typically identified as amateurs: A reviewer is invited to participate on a voluntary basis. He or she is not typically paid by conventional means and does not make any claims for being anything other than an 'ordinary person' but draws on his or her everyday expertise of the subject. However, their voluntary participation is shaped and controlled by an institution (i.e. a media organization or platform provider) that predefines the reviewer's role, using terms such as 'amateur', 'customer' or 'fan', regulates their activities, and sometimes even contributes to their hierarchization for the sake of easier access to the audience.

Prominent examples of IA forums include Amazon (e.g. the invitation-only Vine Programme that gathers 'trusted reviewers' to 'post opinions to fellow customers'; see Amazon, 2020) and its affiliate Goodreads, Google (Google Reviews), as well as a number of review platforms, such as Rotten

Tomatoes, Metacritic and the Internet Movie Database (IMDb). A number of service platforms such as TripAdvisor and Yelp include reviews, coupling them with the latest updates and service information. Even online shops and onsite warehouses want people to leave their comments on a review forum, and, as discussed earlier, there are companies organized around the idea of pledging reviews from customers, such as Trustpilot. Further, in literature there are partially paid book review services set up for new and self-published authors for marketing, the so-called ARC (Advance Review/Reading Copy) services or e-galley services. Examples of these include, among many others, Candid Book Reviews, Hidden Gems Books and NetGalley. In these services, the pre-publication proofs are given to readers in advance of the book launch with the hope that they choose to review the book as soon as it is released.

A reviewer on IMDb describes himself in the following way:

> I am an individual who is extremely passionate about films and everything they stand for. I appreciate a good film when I see one, and get emotionally involved in the films I watch. I will also dismantle the bad apples as well, the ones that make me upset just thinking about them. I enjoy being involved in the world of cinema and can't wait for the next great film. I hope one day I can have a career in the film industry, but for now, this is good enough.

This is how a book reviewer on Goodreads presents herself in a public discussion thread:

> I'm a book nerd and reading enthusiast alike, as well as an honest reviewer. I'll call myself a writer because I do write…have written many many poems, and have started many "novels" but finished none…but I will continue to try and finish at least one my books in my lifetime. I run/own BeautifulBargainista.com, which is where you can find my book review blog cleverly titled The Bargainsta Book Review. FYI—I have taken a bit of a "break" in reviewing/reading for the moment as I have been working 2 jobs, and having a hard time find time to really give it my all. I look forward to picking up the pace again soon!

In the same fashion, amateur Instagram reviewers (see Sect. 6.1 Prettifying Books: Book Reviewers on Instagram) define themselves as 'ordinary readers', typically targeting 'persons like me', other engaged readers such as members of book clubs and social reading communities, active readers of a designated genre or literary omnivores with a high reading frequency. The books selected for review are representative of the individual, and—even if somewhat idealized—idiosyncratic tastes of one reader. One Instagram survey respondent (see Sect. 1.4 Methodological Background) explained:

> I review what I read. I read what I am interested in. I'm interested in exciting new releases, classics, beautiful books, books I read with my book club, books I discover in the publishers [sic] catalogues, books I see recommended on IG and in the *Guardian* literary newsletter etc. I get offers for review copies only seldomly. I haven't set up proper blogger relations with publishers since I can get many books I want for free through my job as a bookseller. I'm not a professional reviewer.

This marks a difference from the traditional reviews that aim at representativeness with regard to a certain genre and its canon, trying to monitor all or the most important new pieces of work in a specific domain (Chong, 2020). Indeed, the reviewers tended to pinpoint that their position was that of an amateur and that they were not professional reviewers.

The type of IA imposed by democratic institutions is strongly influenced by the frame of cultural or literary citizenship, but the embeddedness of the activity in economic profit varies. The lacking financial incentive and, accordingly, ambition to gain profit is a prevalent characteristic of the IA reviewer. Being an amateur is 'good enough', as the film reviewer above describes his situation. Unlike the vernacular professional reviewers, the activities of IA reviewers are not based on self-celebrification but, quite the other way round, on the possibility to remain anonymous, or just an ordinary person. The IA reviewers typically use nicknames or first names and do not disclose any personal data.

Many IA reviewers take the opportunity to educate themselves and see the reviewing activity not as an aspirational work but rather as an educational one, a path into becoming an autodidact in the field of reviewing, which adds another layer to being a cineaste or a bookworm, without any serious attempts to boost a more professionally oriented career. Reviewing cultural products such as books constitutes one component in the leisure-time activity, yet making the following of literature more systematic and, when recognized by others, rewarding. The affordances of user review platforms enable the tracking and quantification of one's own reading activity, making it through measurability more visible, comprehensible, cumulative and comparable to others' profiles. Content wise, the strength of IA is typically found in the powerful combination of authenticity and persuasiveness, utilizing the word-of-mouth principle and the assessments of a product that come 'directly' from consumers and ordinary people. Therefore, the performed non-professionalism is frequently (mis)interpreted as being synonymous with honesty and a lack of agenda. Nevertheless, IA reviewers are less involved in the strategic games of calibrated amateurism or mimicking of ordinary authenticity that to a great extent characterizes the vernacular professionals.

Moreover, cultural institutions mobilize citizens as cultural consumers and citizens online within their pre-structured frames, such as reading promotions, which encourage library users to read and review books (Asselin & Doiron, 2016), audience development, where museum visitors are asked to create presentations on their experiences (Runnel & Pruulmann-Vengerfeldt, 2014), or in journalism, employing principles of citizen, public or participatory journalism (Wall, 2020). In many cases, these campaigns are aimed at increasing the outreach of the organizations' output and are thus lineated to audience engagement, implying audience education, taste cultivation, extended marketing and cultural inclusion (Jaakkola, 2020).

## 5.4 Vernacular Professionals

Vernacular professionals (VP) are similar to the users who are most often the focus of discussions on content creators and platform celebrities. VP reviewers operate in the non-institutionalized domain of the social web (Sect. 4.2 User Reviewing), which leaves the option for reviewing open. In accordance with the features of the social review web, vernacular or non-institutionalized reviews are neither controlled nor regulated by an intermediary institution or organization in a centralized manner, but the users are freer to adjust their communication in terms of the choice of their platform, production form, form of organization and application of the traits of the genre, thus affecting the degree of their critical autonomy and authority. Indeed, being or becoming a reviewer is only one possible identity attached to the online engagement of culturally active users. Reviewing is also typically merged into other communication strategies within a platform profile. What makes vernacular reviewers 'professional', even if the reviewers themselves might not call themselves 'professionals', is their relatively serious intention to standardize and structure their product and conduct in order to create autonomy or integrity in production, which, again, allows the users to take a more intermediary position in the cultural production chain. In a way, VPs are self-made reviewers: by starting to regularly review a sphere of culture, they label themselves as reviewers and enter the open process of public legitimatization, which eventually indicates whether they are accepted and acknowledged by their audience or not. In order to ensure this, they have to apply advanced and versatile strategies of audience engagement and dialogue.

The participatory culture of content creators similar to VP reviewers has often been attributed community-seeking features such as low barriers to artistic expression and civic engagement, strong mutual support and informal mentorship between users, or transfer of knowledge from the more experienced to newbies, and a feeling among the members that their contributions matter (Jenkins, 2007). User reviewers are typically said to build collaborative organizations, including learning from coaches and peers, through which skills are passed on and accredited, 'through clubs, networks, events, competitions and performances' (Leadbeater, 2007, n.p.). However, in accordance with the disbelief in the wisdom of crowds à la Keen (2007), scholars have remarked that the idea of a user involved in participatory culture indicates a certain mythology of a creative worker that does not do justice to the reality of online labour. A number of scholars (see, e.g., Duffy, 2015; Duffy & Wissinger, 2017; Geff, 2012; Kaitajärvi-Tiekso, 2020) have stressed that the narratives of a creative cultural worker contradict the individualized self-branding practices undertaken by cultural workers in an unstable and precarious economy. They argue that the deployment of narratives of authenticity, creative autonomy and collaboration are strategic, and effectively conceals the ways that digitally enabled forms of creative production emulate traditional industry structures and logics. The organization of aspirational work is self-promotional and, as such, hierarchical, market-driven and competitive, as well as fully immersed in neoliberal capitalism and consumer culture.

Indeed, the reviewsphere of VP reviewers is individually centred and based on the logics of self-promotional practices to make a person-centred profile of a film pundit, music expert or a cultural online personality. As for IP reviewers, they manage distinct personal profiles that create expectations of a certain taste and who audiences start following, thus investing personal trust in them. The film reviewer is the brand and the object of admiration among the viewers who develop a parasocial relationship with their trusted figure. Users need to employ self-celebrification practices to become 'micro-celebrities' as proposed by Senft (2008) and Graeme

Turner (2014b), or social media influencers (see also Khamis et al., 2017). The size of the audience is no criterion for becoming a micro- or even a nano-celebrity; instead, users who succeed in sustaining enough credibility though appropriate self-presentation to affect consumer purchase decisions count as such. Source credibility is based upon three main dimensions: trustworthiness, attractiveness and expertise (Djafarova & Trofimenko, 2018; Ohanian, 1990), which all make up essential features of a review.

Examples of vernacular professionals include the most subscribed-to YouTube film reviewers Jeremy Jahns, Chris Stuckmann and Anthony Fantano. These VP reviewers have been active via video on YouTube more than a decade, and they started at about the same time, towards the end of the 2000s. Jeremy Jahns (b. 1981) joined YouTube in 2007 and started reviewing films in 2009 after the release of *Transformers 2: Revenge of the Fallen*—a film that he despised. At the time of writing, he has 1.8 million subscribers on YouTube, 89,000 followers on Instagram and 155,000 followers on Twitter. On YouTube, he has uploaded almost 1800 videos that have received 717 million views, and he continues to make weekly reviews on the latest film releases. Jahns' review production includes film reviews, as well as occasional game, trailer and television reviews. His typical setup includes speaking to camera against a red background. He has a 6-grade film rating scale: 'awesometacular'—that is also his tagline—'would buy on Blu-Ray', 'good time no alcohol required', 'good time… if you're drunk', 'will forget in T-minus…' and 'dogshit'.

Christopher Stuckmann (b. 1988) published his first film review the same year as Jahns, having 1.9 million subscribers as of the beginning of 2021. A writer on IMDb describes Stuckmann as having 'a very similar setup as Jeremy Jahns, but Chris is more precise, and pays attention to detail more'. He continues: 'If you are a movie lover who also pays attention to things like camera work, directing, camera shots, and other technical stuff, then he is the critic for you. However, he's not boring, he has passion for films, and he shows it in his reviews'. Mocking low-quality films, similar to the popular gamer PewDiePie—Swedish Felix Kjellberg (b. 1989) who started his YouTube video production by reviewing terrible games—Stuckmann runs a series of 'Hilariocity review' videos for movies that he describes as 'such an atrocity that it's hilarious'. He also runs a series of 'Overlooked movies' on films that were so overrated that they have not drawn much attention among audiences. A number of vlog-oriented formats with comments rather than evaluations complement Stuckmann's review output.

Antony Fantano (b. 1985) created a YouTube music review channel called The Needle Drop in 2009, focusing on a variety of genres such as rock, pop, electronic, metal, hip hop and experimental music. Calling himself 'the Internet's busiest music nerd', he has run multiple channels. With his 2.3 million subscribers, *New York Times* writer Joe Coscarelli (2020) described him as the most important music reviewer for young generations and 'probably the most popular music critic left standing'. According to Coscarelli, by building up 'a legion of followers and imitators', Fantano has 'helped to push a notoriously insular and endangered art form—the record review—toward a new default medium and younger audience'. He goes further and describes Fantano's business as an 'independent one-man empire' built 'from his suburban Connecticut home, with merchandise, a paying pool of Patreon subscribers and (pre-Covid-19) live appearances, plus fervent message-board chatter, social-media hate, meta-memes and endless videos about his videos. He concludes that Fantano's 'D.I.Y. bedroom model feels increasingly like the future'.

Indeed, the 'D.I.Y. bedroom model' is characteristic of VP reviewers, who, unlike amateurs and institutional professionals, have to figure out methods of monetization for their review business. Typically, reviewers start doing reviews with no income, but gradually they must develop revenue streams to ensure the continuity of their reviewing activities. A sustainable existence can be safeguarded by making use of the platform's monetizing affordances; for example, YouTube pays content creators with a sufficient number of subscribers based on the number of views and ad displays. Also, income can be generated by leaning upon crowdfunding, making sponsored videos, selling merchandise or doing affiliate marketing (a brand or product pays the content creator a percentage of their sales when users buy their product). Similarly, the Amazon Services LLC Associates Program is an affiliate advertising programme designed to provide a means to earn fees by linking to Amazon.com and affiliated websites. Typically, VP reviewers collect their funding from multiple sources.

In contrast to professional institutional reviewers, these YouTube reviewers actively work towards their audience, trying to meet their audiences' needs and wishes, and in order to do this they cultivate a regular dialogue with audience members. This feature distinguishes VP reviewers most significantly from vernacular amateurs who are self-centric in another way, without stressing the presence of an audience as a separate entity but rather merging into this fan community. Making efforts for the sake of audiences—in order to construct and maintain them—is thus another distinct professional endeavour, along with personification and self-celebrification. These efforts include making choices that are likely to please the audience such as choosing topics recommended by fans and followers, using a style that is appealing to audiences, and regularly collecting and utilizing feedback for upcoming productions. VP reviewers develop recognizable aesthetics and idiomatic expression, as well as iterative formats that become their own signature reviewing style.

VP reviewers are new media professionals, just as IP reviewers are industry workers. They have frequently been described as professional amateurs (pro-ams) or semi-professionals (Leadbeater & Miller, 2004), which are descriptions based on substantial expertise from the area of coverage. According to Leadbeater (2007, n.p.), pro-ams refers to 'people who engage in activity for the love of it, but perform to very high standards'. Their 'motivations are avowedly amateur but the standards they set themselves are comparable to those of professionals'. In addition, they perform their work in their leisure time. Following this line of thought, VP reviewers would have amateur conduct but produce products that fulfil professional criteria. However, the definition of professional and amateur, although a gradual and sliding one, cannot be left to subjective assessment of the level of standards. Some VP reviewers are as much professionals as the institutional professionals; for example, Chris Stuckmann is a member of the Critics' Choice Association (CCA), the association of television, radio and online critics in the United States and Canada. The factor that categorizes him as a VP reviewer within the framework of this book is that he is operating within the non-institutional structures of media, namely making use of platformized production.

However, in the post-professional reviewsphere substance expertise is relative; an institutional amateur on a film user review site or even a vernacular amateur running an Instagram account on books may have considerable expertise in the specific subgenre of his or her interest. The feature that distinguishes VP reviewers from amateurs and institutional professionals is thus their new media expertise. They need to master the processes related to platformized production in order to construct sustainable reviewership. In their role as micro-media managers, they own the entire communication chain from idea work to production and further to distribution, adjusting their communication strategies to the platform affordances. This is the most significant difference from the institutional review professionals who are typically incorporated into pre-made editorial processes without any additional responsibility for planning, editing, publishing and distribution of their output.

As for their expertise concerning the substance area they are covering, VP reviewers adopt diverging strategies. Among these, connoisseurship is not the only viable one, and, as shown later in the chapters presenting case studies of reviewing communities (Chap. 6 Vernacular Reviewers' Communities: Case Studies), other strategies include reflexive consumption and self-management, promotion and entertainment. One interesting example of a unique approach to reviewing driven by vernacular professionals is The Subway Book Review (@subwaybookreview), a social media project by German-born culture writer Uli Beutter Cohen. The main idea in the project is asking strangers in public places what they were reading; this format has been followed on social media in other domains of arts and culture as well, for example Your Soundtracks (@yoursoundtracks) in music, as well as in the human-interest story-based form of listening to people's life destinies in Humans of New York (@humansofny). In November 2018, the project introduced a subproject for children, the Subway Book Review for Kids (@subwaybookreviewforkids). Started in 2013 in the New York City subway, the project had contributors in, for example, Washington DC, Mexico City, London, Berlin, Milan, Barcelona and Sydney. It operated through crowdfunding and had also developed into a blog-based online presence (Bausells, 2015). In these social media reviews, interviews with strangers produce a novel form of coverage that could perhaps be subsumed under 'review feature', a more journalistic approach to covering literature while still intensively drawing on the genre of review. Through a presumedly spontaneous encounter on the street, a basic journalistic interview is conducted, to listen to the person, and based on this interview the literary voice of the stranger is reconstructed and the reading experience narrated by a facilitator, who is someone other than the actual reader of the book. Reviews based on such voice-giving practice could also be called facilitated reviews. They produce another type of coverage that has never become a permanent part of the institutional journalistic review and feature coverage that have been much more focused on institutional sources rather than the man on the street. Amateur voices and preferences have been the most typically presented in listings of best-selling and top borrowed books, while a review driven by an ordinary cultural consumer has been a format only occasionally employed, and even in that case it has more often been an interview than a 'facilitated review'.

Indeed, VP reviewers may feature areas that are not systematically covered by legacy media and even introduce completely new ways of producing reviews. One prominent example of this is the introduction of children into the reviewsphere. This is aptly exemplified by two child YouTube reviewers, Ryan from the YouTube channel Ryan's World (formerly Ryan's ToysReview) and Iain, the star of the channel Iain Loves Theatre. Ryan has become the figure behind the entire genre of toy reviews (see Sect. 6.3 At the Playstage: Toy Reviewers on YouTube). In 2018, the family behind Ryan ToysReview reached the top of the highest-earning content creators' list, with 22 million dollars in income (Robehmet & Berg, 2018). In 2017, the channel, with 18 million subscribers, has partnered with a start-up for marketing, including collectables, merchandise and a mobile application. In the wake of Ryan's success, toy reviewing has become an established way of communicating new toys to an audience, and several toy review channels have emerged (see Sect. 6.3 At the Playstage: Toy Reviewers on YouTube). Iain Armitage operates the channel Iain Loves Theatre. Iain , a 12-year year boy active since he was 4, delivers oral assessments of shows he has seen, mostly Broadway shows. Ryan's professionalism lies in commercial partnerships with the toy industry and constructing a brand of his own, while Iain's professionalism is more similar to the connoisseur criticism in which professionalism is based on the objectification of opinion.

Another example is the review of products that do not typically undergo systematic reviewing in general interest journalistic outlets. This might apply for perfume reviews, conducted, for example, by the German beauty vlogger and perfume reviewer Tommelise for 15,000 subscribers, or female sex toys reviews, produced by Tawney Seren for 141,000 subscribers. In addition, the boundaries with institutional professionalism are porous. Professional vernacular reviewers are also most likely to be invited to enter institutionalized professionalism, in the same way that vernacular amateurs may flexibly visit the institutional domain. The postmodern dream, cherished by diverse talent-seeking television programmes, is that a vernacular amateur suddenly becomes an institutionalized professional.

## 5.5 Vernacular Amateurs

Vernacular amateurs (VA) are private citizens-customers in public action. VA reviewers can be regarded as the social web counterpart of institutional amateurs, but, as they are part of the social web review platforms, their activities are, like VPs', not controlled by an intermediary organization directing their content focus on reviewing and trying to organize and structure this activity. VA reviewers are ordinary people who become extraordinary—public readers (Steiner, 2010)—through the communication they provide, becoming user reviewers enabled by online technology, but, as in the IA domain, without any claims for being a professional, or at least not being there yet.

The VA reviewer's role is often underpinned by both platform providers and themselves and by the emotional vocabulary of the community, declaring reviewers to be enthusiasts, aficionados, hobbyists, culture lovers, bookworms, nerds, geeks or other committed members of a cultural community. The participants do not possess any formal characteristics of reviewers but rather act—also using this as a conscious strategy for producing authenticity—as members of the audience, and thus as lay reviewers—'lay' referring to 'non-ordained' or 'secular' in contrast to the professionalized priesthood. In contrast to vernacular institutionalized reviewers embedded in the production paradigm, vernacular amateurs' knowledge is based on the reception or consumption paradigm and an intermediary function within their community. Some researchers (Kristensen & From, 2015; Kammer, 2015) use the term 'everyday amateur experts' to refer to amateurs in general—'everyday' underscoring the ordinary, mundane and commonplace contexts of cultural production in delivering the review. Indeed, the role of home and family as an intimate production context is strongly present in vernacular amateurism (Barbour & Heise, 2019; Gibbs et al., 2015). Connoisseurial expertise, in contrast, is not as essential a component among vernacular amateurs as it is among vernacular professionals.

Vernacular amateur reviewers differ from professional vernacular reviewers in that they do not typically seek critical autonomy as vernacular professionals do. Their attitudes towards professional enforcement range from being entirely ignorant to conscious anti-professionalism. Instead, many of the most successful vernacular amateur reviewers—successful, above all, in terms of the size of their audiences and, depending on this, their financial success—base their operating principles on commercial partnerships with the primary producers or industry that delivers the products and services that they review.

The VA reviewer's context is mundane, placing the reception of a cultural product in the everyday settings of consumption. For example, public readers (especially on Goodreads and Instagram's #Bookstore communities) are engaged readers who track their reading activity and encourage other similar-minded people, participate in book reading challenges and feel that through mediated reading experiences they receive something that adds to their reading hobby. 'Reviewing' in this category is often also connected to testing something, which, in concrete terms, refers to making personal contact with the product (or similar), proving it, feeling it and delivering some immediate reactions to an audience who has not yet experienced the product first-hand. The consumptive encounters with the cultural product are coupled with performative acts of unboxing, tutorials, play-throughs (in-game reviews) or pretend plays (in toy reviews). Alternatively, the form of participation that engages a vast majority of amateur vernacular users is reviewing campaigns, for example in the case of book reading, readathons and book challenges.

In the VA category, more often than in the other categories the review genre does not live up to the definition of the review—in the way it is typically defined in genre theory—and is in this respect exploited or misinterpreted, or even misused and hijacked, up to becoming covert and even generating fake reviews (see Sect. 7.4 Fake and Pseudo Reviews). Furthermore, postmodern irony and lack of seriousness may make it difficult to decipher a 'reviewer's' statements, and they may position themselves rather as promotional intermediaries, producing entertainment disguised as review. Cultural intramediaries who partner with distributors, sales agents and strategic communicators without trying to create critical distance from them function as extended marketers of the primary production. The work of such mediators who in the context of cultural intermediation rather appear as pseudo-intermediaries needs to be detached from the work of cultural intermediaries, as the former are part of the promotional culture of capitalist democracy, while the latter take a more disinterested position and make claims for independence (see also Freberg et al., 2011). On the other hand, from the perspective of consumption, promotional intermediaries may also possess critical potential in inventing new forms of consumption and lifestyles, even if they do not contribute to added knowledge concerning the cultural product in terms of its aesthetic and symbolic worth in the production history.

## References


Abidin, C. (2016). Visibility labour: Engaging with influencers' fashion brands and #OOTD advertorial campaigns on Instagram. *Media International Australia, 161*(1), 86–100.

Aldridge, M., & Evetts, J. (2003). Rethinking the concept of professionalism: The case of journalism. *The British Journal of Sociology, 54*(4), 547–564.

Amazon (2020). *What is Amazon Wine?* https://www.amazon.com/gp/vine/help

Ashton, D., & Patel, K. (2018). Vlogging careers: Everyday expertise, collaboration and authenticity. In S. Taylor & S. Luckman (Eds.), *The new normal of working lives: Dynamics of virtual work* (pp. 147–169). Palgrave Macmillan. https://doi.org/10.1007/978-3-319-66038-7_8

Asselin, M., & Doiron, R. (2016). *Linking literacy and libraries in global communities.* Routledge.

Barbour, K., & Heise, L. (2019). Sharing #home on Instagram. *Media International Australia, 172*(1), 35–47.

Barker, C. (2005). *Cultural studies: Theory and practice.* Sage.

Bauman, Z. (2011). *Culture in a liquid modern world.* Polity.

Bausells, M. (2015, October 5). Subway book review glimpses the lives of New Yorkers via the books they read. *The Guardian.* https://www.theguardian.com/books/2015/oct/05/subway-book-review-glimpses-the-lives-of-new-yorkers-via-the-books-they-read

Baym, N. K. (2015). Connect with your audience! The relational labor of connection. *The Communication Review, 18*(1), 14–22. https://doi.org/10.1080/10714421.2015.996401

Bell, D. (1973). *The coming of post-industrial society: A venture in social forecasting.* Basic Books.

Berger, M. (Ed.). (1998). *The crisis of criticism.* New York Press.

Blank, G. (2007). *Critics, ratings, and society: The sociology of reviews.* Rowman & Littlefield Publishers.

Brownlie, D., & Hewer, P. (2011). Articulating consumers through practices of vernacular creativity. *Scandinavian Journal of Management, 2*, 243–253.

Bruns, A. (2013). Exploring the pro-am interface between production and produsage. In F. L. F. Lee, L. Leung, J. L. Qiu, & D. S. C. Chu (Eds.), *Frontiers in new media research* (pp. 241–258). Routledge.

Burgess, J. (2006). Hearing ordinary voices: Cultural studies, vernacular creativity and digital storytelling. *Continuum: Journal of Media & Cultural Studies, 20*(2), 201–214. https://doi.org/10.1080/10304310600641737

Burgess, J. (2012). YouTube and the formalisation of amateur media. In D. Hunter, R. Lobato, M. Richardson, & J. Thomas (Eds.), *Amateur media: Social, cultural and legal perspectives* (pp. 53–58). Routledge.

Burston, J., Dyer-Witheford, N., & Hearn, A. (2010). Digital labour: Workers, authors, citizens. *Ephemera: Theory and Politics in Organization, 10*(3–4), 214–221.

Chong, P. K. (2020). *Inside the critics' circle: Book reviewing on uncertain times.* Princeton University Press.

CU, Columbia University. (2021). *Arts and culture.* https://journalism.columbia.edu/arts-and-culture#What_We_Offer

Conti, O. (2013). Disciplining the vernacular: Fair use, YouTube, and remixer agency. *M/C Journal, 16*(4), n.p.

Coscarelli, J. (2020, September 30). The only music critic who matters (if you're under 25). *The New York Times.* https://www.nytimes.com/2020/09/30/arts/music/anthony-fantano-the-needle-drop.html

Deuze, M. (2005). What is journalism? Professional identity and ideology of journalists reconsidered. *Journalism, 6*(4), 442–464.

Deuze, M., & Witschge, T. (2020). *Beyond journalism.* Polity Press.

Dickstein, M. (1992). *Double agent: The critic and society.* Oxford University Press.

van Dijck, J. (2009). Users like you? Theorizing agency in user-generated content. *Media, Culture and Society, 31*(1), 41–58.

Djafarova, E., & Trofimenko, O. (2018). 'Instafamous' – Credibility and self-presentation of micro-celebrities on social media. *Information, Communication & Society, 22*(10), 1432–1446.

van Driel, L., & Dumitrica, D. (2021). Selling brands while staying 'authentic': The professionalization of Instagram influencers. *Convergence, 27*(1), 66–84. https://doi.org/10.1177/1354856520902136

Duffy, B. E. (2015). Amateur, autonomous, and collaborative: Myths of aspiring female cultural producers in web 2.0. *Critical Studies in Media Communication, 32*(1), 48–64.

Duffy, B. E. (2017). *(Not) getting paid to do what you love: Gender, social media, and aspirational work.* Yale University Press.

Duffy, B. E., & Wissinger, E. (2017). Mythologies of creative work in the social media age: Fun, free and 'Just Being Me'. *International Journal of Communication, 11*(1), 4652–4671.

Elkins, J. (2003). *What happened to arts criticism?* Prickly Paradigm Bristol University Presses.

Elkins, J., & Newman, M. (Eds.). (2008). *The state of art criticism.* Routledge.

Eräsaari, R. (2009). Open-context expertise. In M. A. Peters, T. Besley, M. Olssen, S. Maurer, & S. Weber (Eds.), *Governmentality studies in education* (pp. 55–76). Brill. https://doi.org/10.1163/9789087909857_005

Esser, F., & Umbricht, A. (2014). The evolution of objective and interpretative journalism in the Western press: Comparing six news systems since the 1960s. *Journalism & Mass Communication Quarterly, 91*(2), 229–249.

Fletcher, L., & Lobato, R. (2013). Living and labouring as a music writer. *Cultural Studies Review, 19*(1), 155–176.

Freberg, K., Graham, K., McGaughey, K., & Freberg, L. A. (2011). Who are the social media influencers? A study of public perceptions of personality. *Public Relations Review, 37*(1), 90–92. https://doi.org/10.1016/j.pubrev.2010.11.001

Freidson, E. (2001). *Professionalism: The third logic.* Polity Press.

Frey, M. (2014). *The permanent crisis of film criticism: The anxiety of authority.* Amsterdam University Press.

Geff, G. (2012). *Venture labor: Work and the burden of risk in innovative industries.* The MIT Press

Gibbs, M., Meese, J., Arnold, M., Nansen, B., & Carter, M. (2015). #Funeral and Instagram: Death, social media, and platform vernacular. *Information, Communication & Society, 18*(3), 255–268.

Giddens, A. (2013). *The consequences of modernity.* John Wiley & Sons.

Gregg, M. (2009). Learning to (love) labour: Production cultures and the affective turn. *Communication and Critical/Cultural Studies, 6*(2), 209–214. https://doi.org/10.1080/14791420902868045

Hanitzsch, T., Hanusch, F., Ramaprasad, J., & de Beer, A. S. (Eds.). (2019). *Worlds of journalism: Journalistic cultures around the globe.* Columbia University Press.

Hargreaves, A. (2000). Four ages of professionalism and professional learning. *Teachers and Teaching, 6*(2), 151–182. https://doi.org/10.1080/713698714

Harries, G., & Wahl-Jorgensen, K. (2007). The culture of arts journalists: Elitists, saviors or manic depressives? *Journalism: Theory, Practice and Criticism, 8*(6), 619–639.

Hellman, H., & Jaakkola, M. (2012). From aesthetes to reporters: The paradigm shift in arts journalism in Finland. *Journalism, 13*(8), 1–19.

Hesmondhalgh, D. (2010). User-generated content, free labour and the cultural industries. *Ephemera: Theory and Politics in Organization, 10*(3/4), 267–284.

Hesmondhalgh, D. (2015). Exploitation and media labor. In Maxwell, R. (Ed.), *The Routledge companion to labor and media*(30–39). New York: Routledge.

Holland, D., Lachicotte, W. S., Jr., Skinner, D., & Cain, C. (2001). *Identity and agency in cultural worlds.* Harvard University Press.

Hou, M. (2018). Social media celebrity and the institutionalization of YouTube. *Convergence: The International Research Journal into New Media Technologies,* Online First: 1–20.

Hovden, J. F., & Kristensen, N. N. (2018). The cultural journalist around the globe: A comparative study of characteristics, role perceptions, and perceived influences. *Journalism,* 1–20. https://doi.org/10.1177/1464884918791224

Howard, R. G. (2005). Toward a theory of the World Wide Web vernacular: The case for pet cloning. *Journal of Folklore Research, 42*(3), 323–360.

Howard, R. G. (2008a). Electronic hybridity: The persistent processes of the vernacular web. *Journal of American Folklore, 121*(480), 192–218.

Howard, R. G. (2008b). The vernacular web of participatory media. *Critical Studies in Media Communication, 25*(5), 490–513.

Howard, R. G. (2010). The vernacular mode: Locating the non-institutional in the practice of citizenship. In D. C. Brouwer & R. Asen (Eds.), *Public modalities: Rhetoric, culture, media, and the shape of public life* (pp. 240–262). University of Alabama Press.

Jaakkola, M. (2015). *The contested autonomy of arts and journalism: Change and continuity of the dual professionalism of cultural journalism.* Doctoral dissertation, Tampere University Press.

Jaakkola, M. (2020). Oman lukukokemuksensa visualisoijat: käyttäjälähtöiset kirjallisuusarvostelut Instagramissa [Visualizers of their own reading experience: The user-generated literature reviews on Instagram]. *Kulttuurintutkimus, 36*(3–4), 31–44.

Jenkins, H. (2007). Confronting the challenges of participatory culture: Media education for the 21st century (part one). *Nordic Journal of Digital Literacy, 2*, 23–33.

Kaitajärvi-Tiekso, J. T. (2020). Monetizing amateurs: Artistic critique, new online record production and neoliberal conjuncture. *Culture Unbound: Journal of Current Cultural Research, 12*(2), 412–435. https://doi.org/10.3384/cu.v12i2.894

Kammer, A. (2015). Post-industrial cultural criticism: The everyday amateur expert and the online cultural public sphere. *Journalism Practice, 9*(6), 872–889. https://doi.org/10.1080/17512786.2015.1051371

Keen, A. (2007). *The cult of the amateur: How blogs, Myspace, YouTube and the rest of today's user generated media are killing our culture and economy.* Doubleday.

Khamis, S., Ang, L., & Welling, R. (2017). Self-branding, 'micro-celebrity' and the rise of social media influencers. *Celebrity Studies, 8*(2), 191–208.

Kim, J. (2012). The institutionalization of YouTube: From user-generated content to professionally generated content. *Media, Culture & Society, 34*(1), 53–67.

Kristensen, N. N. (2019). Arts, culture and entertainment coverage. In T. P. Vos & F. Hanusch (Eds.), *The international encyclopedia of journalism studies.* Wiley-Blackwell. https://doi.org/10.1002/9781118841570.iejs0195

Kristensen, N. N., & From, U. (2015). From ivory tower to cross-media personas. *Journalism Practice, 9*(6), 853–871. https://doi.org/10.1080/17512786.2015.1051370

Kristensen, N. N., & Kannik, H. K. (2018). Cultural critique: Re-negotiating cultural authority in digital media culture. *MedieKultur: Journal of Media and Communication Research, 65*, 3–9.

Kritzer, H. M. (1999). The professions are dead, long live the professions: Legal practice in a postprofessional world. *Law & Society Review, 33*(3), 713–759.

Larson, M. S. (1977). *The rise of professionalism: A sociological analysis.* University of California Press.

Leadbeater, C. (2007). *We think: Why mass creativity is the next big thing.* http://charlesleadbeater.net/wp-content/uploads/2010/01/We-Think-charles-full-draft.pdf

Leadbeater, C., & Miller, P. (2004). *The pro-am revolution: How enthusiasts are changing our society and economy*. Demos.

McDonald, R. (2007). *The death of the critic*. Continuum.

NAW, the New Architecture Writers. (2020). *About*. http://newarchitecturewriters.org/about/

Ohanian, R. (1990). Construction and validation of a scale to measure celebrity endorsers' perceived expertise, trustworthiness, and attractiveness. *Journal of Advertising, 19*(3), 39–52.

Orwell, G. (1968). Confessions of a book reviewer. In S. Orwell & I. Angus (Eds.), *The collected essays, journalism and letters of George Orwell. Volume 4: In front of your nose, 1945–1950* (pp. 181–184). Mariner Books.

Pool, G. (2007). *Faint praise: The plight of book reviewing in America*. University of Missouri Press.

Robehmet, N., & Berg, M. (2018, December 3). Highest-paid YouTube stars 2018: Markiplier, Jake Paul, PewDiePie and more. *Forbes*. https://www.forbes.com/sites/natalierobehmed/2018/12/03/highest-paid-youtube-stars-2018-markiplier-jake-paul-pewdiepie-and-more/#6e3606ba909a

Rowe, D. (2007). Sports journalism: Still the 'toy department' of the news media? *Journalism, 8*(4), 385–405.

Runnel, P., & Pruulmann-Vengerfeldt, P. (Eds.). (2014). *Democratising the Museum: Reflections on participatory technologies*. Peter Lang.

Sadri, H. (Ed.). (2018). *Neo-liberalism and the architecture of the post professional era*. Springer.

Scott, A. O. (2016). *Better living through criticism: How to think about art, pleasure, beauty and truth*. Jonathan Cape.

Senft, T. M. (2008). *Camgirls: Celebrity and community in the age of social networks*. Peter Lang.

Steiner, A. (2010). Personal readings and public texts: Book blogs and online writing about literature. *Culture Unbound: Journal of Current Cultural Research, 2*(2), 471–494.

Taylor, S., & Luckman, S. (2018). Collection introduction: The 'new normal' of working lives. In S. Taylor & S. Luckman (Eds.), *The new normal of working lives: Dynamics of virtual work* (pp. 1–15). Palgrave Macmillan. https://doi.org/10.1007/978-3-319-66038-7

Terranova, T. (2000). Free labor: Producing culture for the digital economy. *Social Text, 18*(2), 33–58.

Turner, S. P. (2014a). *The politics of expertise*. Routledge.

Turner, G. (2014b). *Understanding celebrity*. Sage.

Waisbord, S. (2013). *Reinventing professionalism: Journalism and news in global perspective*. Polity Press.

Wall, M. (2020). *Mapping citizen and participatory journalism in newsrooms, classrooms and beyond*. Routledge.

CHAPTER 6

# Vernacular Reviewers' Communities: Case Studies

Reviews encompass different online lifestyle cultures and sustain a number of different production cultures. To highlight the special character of vernacular reviewing, which is an implication of platformized production, this chapter is dedicated to different case studies on communities focused on various types of reviewing and maintained by diverse groups of reviewers on the social web, that is, vernacular amateurs and vernacular professionals.

First, I will discuss book reviewers on Instagram, which has during the first decade of its existence become a home for user-generated book coverage. As a visual mobile app, it alters the forms of reviewing in the most significant way, inserting visuals, which has probably been the most foreign element to the tradition of reviewing, into the conventions of reading. I am thus interested in how the creation of diverse visual styles has become a method of expression and a reviewing practice for the users in the imagined community of Bookstagram. Second, I will cast more light on the male-dominated vernacular professional reviewer community on the video-sharing platform Vimeo, which is presented as different from YouTube, hosting professionals and professional amateurs passionate about testing filmmaking equipment. Third, I will examine how reviewing is embedded in the popular children's and family content on YouTube, attracting vast audiences and turning children into co-creators of content, yet being entirely immersed in the commercial and consumerist structures of the digital economy. Last but not least, I will explore the massive and


M. Jaakkola, *Reviewing Culture Online*,
https://doi.org/10.1007/978-3-030-84848-4_6

heterogeneous type of entertainment reviewing or *reviewtainment*, which, in contrast to the other cases in this chapter, is less a separate community and more like an overarching category to host a number of different approaches related to humour, but largely affected by YouTube's production culture.

All the sections showcase platform-specific practices of reviewing generally spread across various platforms, and to a great extent occurring on blogs and user review sites for institutional amateur reviewing. As new and emerging venues for vernacular review production, they significantly affect how user reviewing is shaped in its various forms. Case studies on reviews may add to our knowledge of vernacular reviewing as a platform-specific online creativity, related to the digital-native understandings of the genre of non-professional review. Nevertheless, at the point of their documentation towards the end of the 2010s, the online-native genre of review was still very young. In the advent of the blogosphere, weblogs were typically characterized as reading journals or online diaries (Steiner, 2010). Since then, they have shown degrees of institutionalization or professionalization (Kim, 2012; Leadbeater & Miller, 2004). It might be that at the point in time of the analysis, some review communities have not yet developed into a fully independent form of expression but live through the co-existence with other platforms, discourses and genres. It is also likely that new development will unfold rapidly.

## 6.1 Prettifying Books: Book Reviewers on Instagram

Among the younger major social networking sites, the visual medium Instagram, launched in 2010, has become one of the most prolific social platforms for readers to connect with books. Instagram has rapidly developed into a social media platform that is the most popular image-based communication tool, with 800 million active users and almost 40 billion photos posted (WordStream, 2017). Designed for mobile media, it appeals in particular to 18–29 year olds and, therefore, offers insights into reviews and reviewing among younger audiences. Instagram is used multiple times per day by 71 per cent of Americans between the ages of 18 and 24 (Smith & Anderson, 2018). The popularity of the subject of books on Instagram is reflected in frequently used hashtags such as #book, which at the beginning of 2021 had almost 54 million entries, and #bookstagram, which had over 58 million entries. According to Faroukh Naseem, the Bookstagrammer of the Year at the London Book Fair 2018, the Bookstagram community is 'an online space on Instagram where people post pictures and videos of books and talk all things bookish' (Naseem, 2018). As part of these 'bookish' discourses and practices, users are also reviewing books. At the beginning of 2021, the hashtag #bookreview was found by manual search in more than 3 million posts.

The top-rated definition for Bookstagram in the user-generated *Urban Dictionary* was the following, which describes it as an inclusive community based on Instagram, with numerous positive attributes:

> A kick-ass social platform for professional booknerds—and by "professional", I mean even those who sit in their pjs under comfy blankets in a cozy place with a good book. It's main base is on Instagram and you can see it by using #bookstagram and trust me, you'll find a HUMONGOUS amount of booklovers who share your taste and welcome you into the bookstagram community with open arms. (Bookishstarlight, 2017)

As a visual medium, Instagram suggests an entirely novel dimension for reviewing. Images are the platform-specific characteristic of Instagram reviews. The visual tradition of reviewing has historically been scarce, and in this respect a platform that is image-driven paves the way for new means of expression. On Instagram, central affordances for producing a post are the possibilities and restrictions related to using images, written text, user interaction and cross-platform communication. User reviewers must thus make a choice between still images and videos, select the manner of visualization, make more or less informed choices regarding the text content, structure and length, and choose how to use Instagram posts as part of their communication on social media in general. Review authors are, above all, making use of the perceived visual affordances of Instagram's interface and the patterns of the review genre, and by doing this they are to some extent re-inventing the review genre in the specific visually imbued online environment of Instagram. By examining how the Instagram review or the 'IG review' (#igreview) is conceived and applied, we can increase our understandings of the emerging phenomenon of vernacular reviewing beyond the textual practices, that is, using written language, which is still the dominant or sole mode on user reviewing sites (Sect. 4.2 User Reviewing in Chap. 4), as well as on blogs and fan forums. For Instagram reviewers, to establish a review authority, it is less important to argue on a textual basis and more important to create an appropriate visual style that would qualify as their signature style.

Instagram reviewers are mostly vernacular amateurs, even if vernacular and institutional professionals also engage on the platform. Instagram reviewing is thus, above all, peer-to-peer activity, and a prominent example of cultural intramediation (Sect. 3.3 Cultural Intramediation in Chap. 3). As such, it is to a great extent centred upon the individual reviewer, who identifies himself or herself as being part of the community he or she is directing the review messages to. As an implication of this, a large amount of Instagram reviewing is self-presentational and self-monitorial work. In fact, this does not deviate much from the majority of produsage of literary citizens on blogs where digital self-representation has become a prominent feature (see, e.g., Driscoll, 2019; Steiner, 2008, 2010). However, a large number of Instagram book reviewers, different from bloggers, are more likely to dwell in their amateur and ordinary reader role, which makes it appropriate to ask how the me-centric lifestyle work is conducted by respective positionings and how book reviewers' self-perceptions look. I define user reviewers as *me-reviewers*, a concept anchored in the idea of cultural intramediation, and ask what kind of visual reviewing work these me-reviewers are engaged in.

I will first take a look at the book reviewers' use of perceived affordances on Instagram, to capture the practices related to the creation of visual styles that play a key role in conducting reviewing. As Instagram is primarily a visual medium, I want to ask how review posts typically make use of the visual affordances of the platform. Subordinated to this question, I will also to some extent enquire into the written texts, asking how review posts typically make use of the textual affordances and apply the textual conventions of the review genre, even if this element appears as a question of less importance when creating reviews as part of Bookstagram. Thereafter, I will focus on the reviewers' self-perceptions and positionings by looking at self-presentations and drawing on survey results (see Sect. 1.4 Methodological Background in Chap. 1). This question is related to the communication strategies of vernacular amateurs, underlining book readers' primary intentions for engaging in cultural prosumption and envisioning reviewing as a vernacular lay practice.

Instagram being a visual medium designed for mobile use, the space for written text is limited. The written text is clearly designed to be captions to assist the visual images, and its maximal length is limited to 2200 characters. In the public display mode, text is additionally truncated after 125 characters, and the reader needs to click 'more' to see the rest of the text. There are also other features that make the writing of text far from user friendly. The interface for writing text is limited, occupying less than half of the mobile screen in the edit mode. Paragraphs must be separated with the help of punctuation marks or symbols. Instagram also restricts outbound traffic by not allowing in-text links. This means that as links are not supported in the body text, they need to be limited to one and attached to the bio, or completely omitted or placed elsewhere.

Despite these major restrictions for written text, many of the Instagram reviews had a focus on text, while the image typically presented the book cover, possibly with carefully designed accessories, but often in a very simple manner. Indeed, with regard to the fact that Instagram is designed for visual representations, it is striking that the reviews are for the most part relatively conventional in their visual imagery, putting more emphasis on their textual content than the visual innovation of expression. Despite restrictions for writing, the written text continues to play a central role, the atmosphere, featured in very structured and similar ways, being the most central input and added value of the images. However, the feature that applies especially for review cultures is the fact that the literary review has always to a great extent leant on written communication, where the focus is on verbal expression of an aesthetic encounter and its interpretation and elucidation, with a pronunciation of an aesthetic judgement and an argument for this judgement (Orlik, 2016; see Chap. 4). Paying attention to written argumentation is thus the very essence of the review, and in this respect it is not surprising that many reviews seemed to resist the platform policy by intentionally misinterpreting the caption norm and turning the written text into the primary mode of communication. Nevertheless, the micro-format written discourse also allows fruitful micro-format experimentation, such as in the account @7wordbookreview that was drawing on Instagram's short format and producing aphorism-like seven-word judgements, rounded off with a numeric rating. Within the texts, some reviewers were using a star rating or numeric system, which they even clarified in a specific entry, delivering a written description for every level of assessment. In addition to numbers (1–5 or 1–10), some used emojis, such as stars, flowers or animal faces.

The restrictions related to links organically direct Instagram reviewers to use other platforms to extend their argumentation. A manual content analysis of a small sample ($N = 160$ posts) of a local book review community from Finland, with posts tagged with #kirjaarvostelu (equivalent to

#bookreview) (Jaakkola, 2020), indicated that more than a third of the review content was classified as metacoverage, referring to original content that is published beyond the app. In total, 36 per cent ($N$ = 57) of the sample was categorized as metacoverage, referring to a book review published somewhere other than on Instagram. In particular, the following forms of metacoverage were identified:

- *Mentions of reviews published elsewhere* ($N$ = 40, 70 per cent): references to content published, for example, on Goodreads, or on individual book blogs, podcasts or vlogs.
- *Shortened reviews* ($N$ = 9, 16 per cent): truncated or short versions of full reviews that were published elsewhere. Most of the producers added metatext or appropriate hashtags to signal that the full version of the review is in the primary publication venue, but some did not, relying on the reader being knowledgeable about the YouTube channel or book blog, the link to which was attached to the bio.
- *Teasers* ($N$ = 4, 7 per cent): descriptions or sneak peeks of upcoming reviews that may be published on Instagram or other platforms.
- *Contextual posts* ($N$ = 4, 7 per cent): accounts concerning the production of reviews; clarification of the evaluation criteria; glimpses into the process of reading and initial thoughts about a book under process; description of reading goals; and wrap-ups of reading activities within a certain period, usually monthly or annually.

According to a strict definition, the authors of these posts were not original-content creators, placing their primary content in blogs or vlogs and using Instagram posts only to connect to potential audiences or peers. In this respect, it can be stated that a considerable amount of book review material on Instagram is actually supportive material rather than original reviews. For many users, and this applies especially to vernacular professionals, the primary motivation for using Instagram for review coverage is to drive traffic to the original content. Users intend to use Instagram for increased visibility and connectivity, or to drive traffic to original content, rather than producing original content within the app. Rather than pushing the genre conventions by more powerfully using the possibilities of new media within the app, Instagram appears to be a mixed-media or crossroads platform that endorses close ties with other platforms. The bounce or junction function supports (textual) presentation and argumentation in the long format of blogs and vlogs. Even here, it can be noted that the uses of affordances counteract the intended strategic platform mission (to produce original content).

In the visual storytelling among Instagram reviewers, the creation of a certain atmosphere and, through some repetitive and individual elements in the feed, of the signature style plays a key role (see also Leaver et al., 2020). The dominant function of review images seems to be to mediate an atmosphere related to the act of reading. With distinct visual styles, reviewers are largely creating atmospheres that connect to the ideas of literature and the experience of reading and residing in a fantasy world, in a physical and mundane context. Rather than striving to visualize the content of a specific book, Instagram reviewers intend to conform to the imaginary of affectivity to manifest their love for reading. According to Kolehmainen and Mäkinen (2021), this kind of affective labour is collective, intercorporeal and trans-subjective, and they characterize it as co-production, highlighting the community-based dimension of the work that they discuss in the context of audience production.

Atmospheres are expressed through styles that include elements of both shared connectivity between users and an attempt to distinguish from each other. An old saying says that style is the dress of thoughts; in this respect, creating a style is a matter of choosing a dress for aesthetic purposes to capture a certain feeling attributed to the reading experience and reader's mental state, and further, the reader's mentality. The term 'style' is an ambiguous category and has been used interchangeably with other terms, such as register, code, form, format, mode, voice, tone and scheme, or conflated in broader concepts such as genre, discourse, ideology, representation and narration (Jaakkola, 2018). According to the *Oxford English Dictionary*, the word 'style' derives from the fourteenth-century Latin word *stylus*, which describes a sharp-pointed writing tool used to incise letters on wax tablets. Over time, its meaning has expanded to describe patterning in language, or, in this context, in visual language, and especially the *choices* that an author makes to ensure that the form of language adopted for a particular context is appropriate.

There are three basic dimensions in creating a visual style in book reviewing images. First and foremost, the most basic choice is to focus on the book as a material artefact. Books are photographed in a number of ways: up front by placing the book on a surface and photographing it from above, holding a book in front of a selected backdrop, showing the spine of the book or a number of books piled on top of each other, or making a constellation of books that may be colour-coded, similar to a figure or abstract art. Some images attached to book reviewing showed the reviewer reading or walking and holding an open book. In these images, the exposure of the book cover was rejected and the reviewer chose to focus on the process of reading in a more general way instead, showing an open book.

Second, what is common for book and book cover photos is that there is an environment that may convey meaning, in particular anchoring the book-reading experience in its reception context. The book is often placed on a surface or inserted into a more three-dimensional environment or background. Two contrastive environments alternate in this respect: the private space of home, most often a living room (with bookshelves, sofas and coffee table) or a bedroom (with beds or other cosy corners), and a selected public place, which could be, among other things, a street, park, beach, swimming pool, café, library or any other place where people tend to spend their leisure time. The environment could thus be a staged one, just for the sake of creating an image of a private time or luxury, or bear witness to the authentic milieu of reading, the space where the reviewer has been when reading the actual book.

Third, while the text presented a description of the book with a rating, the images focused on quite a limited number of carefully selected details, or props, such as coffee or teacups, food, flowers, rocks and shells. Alternatively, bed linen, blankets, rugs, carpets, earphones, laptops and home decorations were used as atmosphere-creating props. Besides, the props could be related to the topic of the book; for example, cookbooks were accompanied by a relevant food display. The props were arranged into constellations with proportions, resembling the still-life tradition in the long history of painting that depicts inanimate commonplace objects such as household utensils, fruit and flowers. Instead of a bowl of fruit, a vase or a water jug, there is the man-made object of a book that is placed like a sacred object on an altar. Indeed, early still-life paintings that were created in the seventeenth century often contained religious and allegorical symbolism related to the objects depicted. The still-life elements reproduce a slice of modern life, as a *vanitas* motive, an eternalization of a passing moment within the hectic everyday. Painters in the still-life genre, less appreciated as part of the artistic genre canon but popular among the art-buying audiences, also used the form to make self-portraits, for example Vincent van Gogh depicting items of his personal life, including his pipe, onions, an inspirational book and a letter from his brother, all laid out on his table without his own presence. The still-life tradition also included the special variant of depicting books as part of the compositions

(Schneider, 2003). The Instagram review still-life pictures also highlight the slowness of reading, contributing to a reconstitution of the present (Thrift, 2000) in the lives of readers.

The book review images are indexical in their nature; they provide hints of a human presence but very rarely expose the reviewer in the pictures or show physical spaces in their entirety. Posts focusing on the reviewer instead of the book reviewed were typically separated from the review content by hashtags such as #meetthebookstagrammer or #currentlyreadingselfie. This disembodied form of reviewing is essentially a continuation of the classical review tradition, in which the reviewer builds a profile through textual representations. In the selfie-saturated culture, it is, however, noteworthy that one form of expression in such a systematic way avoids the representation of persons. The systematic dissolvement of the reviewer's person highlights the focus on book content.

When it comes to combinations of these three choices of presenting the book as a material artefact in an environment with associated props, four basic styles can be identified. In Fig. 6.1, four typical topoi in the signature styles are presented (beyond the very basic form where only the book cover is displayed, with barely anything else being seen in the picture). As these images mostly stem from vernacular amateurs, the accounts in question are anonymized. Row A presents a *composition style*, with one book surrounded by carefully selected decorations, props that function as symbols or hints of private meanings. Row B shows examples of images that develop the composition further into *arranged still lifes* in which a number of books form a figure or a composition, almost making the artefacts into abstract figures. Row C contains examples of images with *environment-focused styles* where the book is captured half-casually in a selected environment, for example on the street, at the beach, at a summer cottage or at home, often with a hand holding it against a given backdrop, without the addition of any props. Finally, row D includes photos with *bodies* included, often only partly disclosed, to preserve the reviewer's privacy. These four typical stylistic choices imply re-creation by always sticking to the same topos, yet varying the content according to personal accentuations, constantly inventing new nuances of showing a book within the selected stylistic framework. By re-creating this visual universe that resides in the common understanding of bookstagrammers, the user reviewers intend to connect with the community, following the common internal grammar, a certain platform vernacular (Gibbs et al., 2015) related to book reviewing.

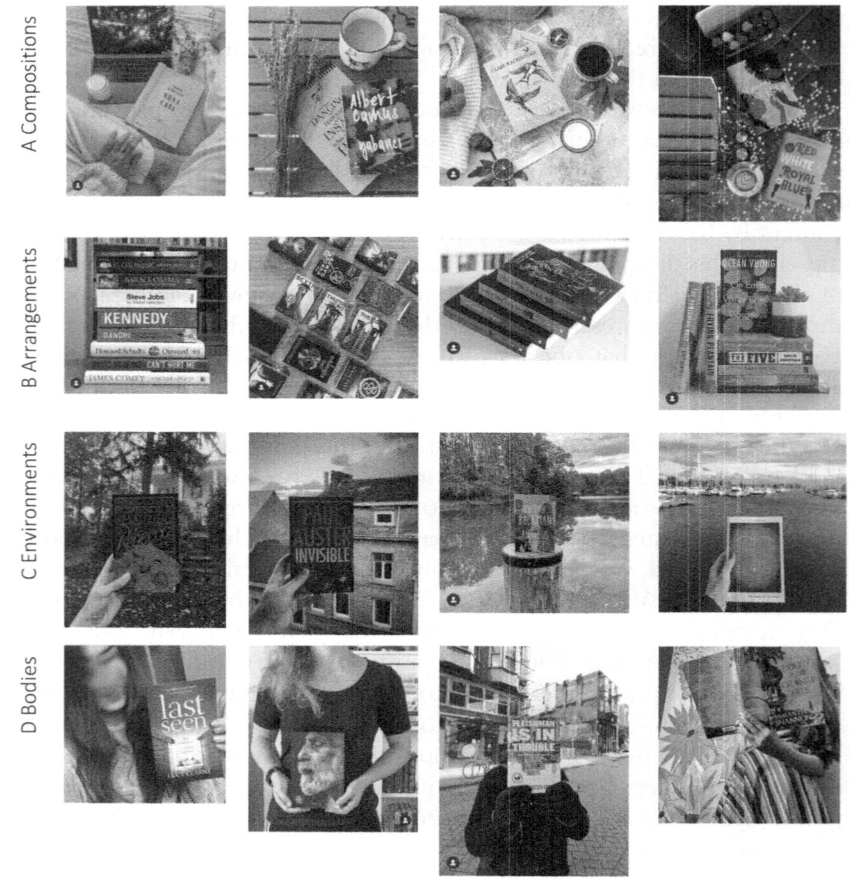


**Fig. 6.1** Four signature styles among book reviewers

The imagery in Instagram book reviews seems to be to a high degree photography-centric, as the mobile app encourages users to take mobile photos instead of creating graphical illustrations. However, some reviewers did further develop the visual dimension of the reviews. The account Book Reviews Sketches (@bookreviewsketches), launched in May 2018 to address one book a day, with an initial goal to read and review 100 books, featured as attachments to short written reviews book covers drawn with the finger on a mobile app by a UK-based reviewer. Attached to the written reviews, the user also took up questions of the day (QOTD), addressing her book-reading habits and preferences beyond the actual book reviews. Like many other Bookstagrammers, this user had previously been tracking her reading activity on Goodreads, and, in her own words, 'I had considered starting a blog, but that seemed like a lot of work to set up so I started an Instagram account to keep it separate from my personal one' (personal communication, 10 January 2019).

Instagram not only allows the use of still images but also launched video sharing in June 2013. In the beginning, the length was restricted to fifteen seconds but in 2016 this was extended to 60 seconds. Since the review format typically requires in-depth analysis and argumentation and leans upon a logocentric tradition, the application of the moving image, the very limited length, requires innovative solutions to be used. A typical example is The One Minute Book Review (@oneminutebookreview), an account driven by Aun Abdi, a vlogger who describes himself as a 'level 2 personal trainer and wannabe accountant'. He started his Instagram video reviews in March 2018, simultaneously running a YouTube channel. Another example of uses of video was Kaitlyn Walker (@ktxx22), who used a hashtag of her own to tag the video reviews, #ktxx22reviews, and published her first Instagram book-review video in March 2017. She called the one-minute reviews 'book bursts', inspired by a vlogger called Family Food Dude who had developed a format on YouTube for reviewing ice cream and junk food. Both these video-review examples make use of the vlogging format, in which a talking head looks straight into the camera. Other options in video reviews included browsing through the book, showing the book in movement or in special lighting, or showing video on the original review text being scrolled on the screen, assisted by an accompanying text.

Moving on from the matter of content, another relevant question is for whom the reviewers are creating the content. As for the review genre, the creation of the legitimate authority is paramount. By positioning himself or herself consciously as a reviewer, or constituting a reviewer's voice that is eventually legitimized, rejected or ignored by the audiences, the reviewer in some way produces itself through review texts. Adapting a reviewer's role is thus a reciprocal act of proclaiming oneself to be a reviewer while possibly gaining confirmation and legitimacy from the audiences. In the case of online audiences, the legitimization occurs through the accumulation of followers and user feedback (likes, commentaries, re-posts). Given that book reviewers form a vast and heterogeneous community, of which the majority are vernacular amateurs, we can outline this community by first looking at the most popular and visible reviewers and second the general patterns in labelling oneself as a 'bookworm'. The first question deals with vernacular professionals on the platform and the other with vernacular amateurs. Congruent with this division, the manual content analysis of the limited sample of Finnish book reviewers (Jaakkola, 2020) indicated that the review content originated from three main types of profiles: online content creators ($N = 33$ posts, 21 per cent), hobbyists or experts reviewing books ($N = 23$, 14 per cent), and book enthusiasts or 'ordinary readers' ($N = 104$, 65 per cent). Online content creators (e.g. book bloggers and podcasters) used Instagram as one of their platforms to spread messages and connect with like-minded users. Hobbyists were anchored in a special area of interest (e.g. cooking, knitting, sports), accidentally applying the genre of review. The core of the original Instagram reviewers were the book enthusiasts, who set goals for themselves to read a certain number of books and used Instagram as their reading journal. The phenomenon of book reviewing can be seen to comprise a population with a wide age range. Although the majority are adults from 25 to 35, reviewing also engages individuals who are younger and older.

When examined in terms of one single variable (number of posts, followed users, following users and most-liked posts), the lists of 'top book reviewers' may look very different. While posting frequency does not indicate relevance or influence, and a high number of comments is typically a sign of a campaign or competition organized for the followers (e.g. giveaways), the number of followers and likes indicates attention. Tables 6.1 and 6.2 present a multivariable list of 20 Instagram book reviewers in terms of their attention and influence. Table 6.1 is a production-driven presentation, featuring the most frequently posting users, while Table 6.2 puts forward an audience-driven presentation, showing the user reviewers with the largest audiences (the highest number of followers) and the most intensive audience interaction (the highest number of likes and comments).

As indicated in the tables, many of the top reviewers appear to be book bloggers or vloggers, engaged public readers or online book communities with a review function. The reviewing activity was typically accompanied by other book-related community markers, such as #bookworm, #booklove, #bookaholic, #bookobsessed and #igbooks, and a number of linguistic derivatives.

**Table 6.1** The 20 book reviewers on Instagram with the highest review posting frequency

| *Username* | *Category* | *Country* | *N of reviews* | *N of posts in total* | *N of followers* | *Average N of comments on reviews* | *Average N of likes for reviews* |
|---|---|---|---|---|---|---|---|
| New Adult E Dintorni @newadultedintorniblog | Blogger | Italy | 885 (35%) | 2501 | 1557 | 0.3 | 36.8 |
| Baker Street Shelves@ bakerstshelves | Reader | UK | 859 (39%) | 2181 | 816 | 1.1 | 43.5 |
| Ari Stone@candidbreviews | Community | USA | 649 (25%) | 2614 | 157 | 0.2 | 8.4 |
| Ana's Attic Book Blog@ anasatticblog | Blogger | USA | 624 (26%) | 2415 | 8739 | 2.4 | 40.0 |
| EDGy Reviews@edgyreviews | Community | USA | 521 (49%) | 1062 | 682 | 0.8 | 19.2 |
| Minx@thegenreminxbookreviews | Blogger | USA | 403 (57%) | 710 | 247 | 0.7 | 10.9 |
| Rizky Mirgawati @rizkymirgawati | Blogger | Indonesia | 400 (17%) | 2383 | 7,100 | 3.7 | 65.4 |
| Hidden Gems Books@hgbooks | Community | USA | 380 (31%) | 1216 | 514 | 1.0 | 8.3 |
| Deborah Stevenson@runningrara | Blogger | USA | 380 (10%) | 3917 | 1,129 | 5.4 | 94.1 |
| Bambi Unbridled @bambi_unbridled | Blogger | USA | 375 (43%) | 866 | 390 | 0.6 | 10.9 |
| Lulu's Vintage@lulualamode | Blogger | USA | 349 (57%) | 609 | 263 | 0.8 | 14.7 |
| Búho @buhosbookreview | Blogger | Nicaragua | 345 (44%) | 779 | 495 | 0.7 | 33.0 |

(*continued*)

**Table 6.1** (continued)

| *Username* | *Category* | *Country* | *N of reviews* | *N of posts in total* | *N of followers* | *Average N of comments on reviews* | *Average N of likes for reviews* |
|---|---|---|---|---|---|---|---|
| Just A Girl & Her Books@lauras_book_addiction | Reader | UK | 335 (3%) | 10,000 | 6223 | 2.7 | 45.3 |
| Books&Sweets @books_sweets | Blogger | Croatia | 315 (45%) | 707 | 1606 | 2.7 | 112.6 |
| Kim B.@kimberlyfayereads | Reader | USA | 294 (10%) | 3274 | 2939 | 2.6 | 44.8 |
| Helen@whathelsreadnext | Reader | Sweden/ UK | 290 (67%) | 436 | 240 | 0.8 | 15.4 |
| Rae@rae.reads.books | Reader | NA | 284 (52%) | 541 | 93 | 0.2 | 10.7 |
| Geramie Kate Barker@ gemsbooknook | Blogger | Australia | 269 (40%) | 676 | 129 | 2.8 | 53.4 |
| Barbara Pitanti@barpit | Blogger | Italy | 265 (36%) | 734 | 311 | 0.8 | 19.9 |
| Juliette Frye@bookish.juju | Reader | USA/ France | 247 (55%) | 451 | 370 | 0.7 | 35.2 |

**Table 6.2** The 20 book reviewers on Instagram with the most followers and most likes per individual review posts

| *Username* | *Category* | *Country* | *N of reviews in data* | *N of posts in total* | *N of followers* | *Average N of comments on reviews* | *Average N of likes for reviews* |
|---|---|---|---|---|---|---|---|
| Bill@kenyan_library | Blogger | Kenya | 22 (4%) | 555 | 13,817 | 4.3 | 85.4 |
| Coconut Books@coconutbooks | Blogger | Indonesia | 13 (1%) | 2069 | 77,246 | 40.0 | 1549.0 |
| Reading Women@thereadingwomen | Podcaster | USA | 64 (7%) | 873 | 102,413 | 5.0 | 100.2 |
| Nel @bookish_nel | Reader | USA | 5 (2%) | 240 | 13,567 | 8.7 | 200.6 |
| Folded Pages Distillery @foldedpagesdistillery | Blogger | USA | 29 (2%) | 1268 | 125.147 | 54.7 | 2511.1 |
| Abbie@ab_reads | Reader | USA | 78 (5%) | 1733 | 39,169 | 5.0 | 100.9 |
| Read the Write Act@readthewriteact | Reader | Australia | 88 (10%) | 877 | 17,429 | 3.3 | 62.5 |
| Sally@whatsallyreadnext | Blogger | UK | 26 (5%) | 575 | 16,143 | 4.3 | 84.6 |
| Abura @lookingforabura | Blogger | United Arab Emirates | 21 (1%) | 1517 | 55,229 | 30.0 | 947.9 |
| Amena@theclubofbooks | Reader | UK | 60 (5%) | 1128 | 14,286 | 3.8 | 73.5 |
| Silke Wadskjær Mølgaard @silkreads | Reader | Denmark | 42 (4%) | 1169 | 50,821 | 7.3 | 160.4 |
| Kath @kath_reads | Blogger | Germany | 6 (0%) | 1392 | 42,974 | 29.3 | 915.7 |
| Christine @weereader | Reader | UK | 52 (4%) | 1206 | 32,006 | 12.0 | 293.8 |
| Meredith Mara@meredith.mara | Reader | South Africa | 13 (1%) | 1691 | 40,283 | 34.0 | 1301.6 |
| Jeana @hotcocoareads | Reader | USA | 7 (1%) | 574 | 17,407 | 28.4 | 726.8 |
| Renée@somekindofalibrary | Blogger | USA | 35 (4%) | 793 | 27,233 | 4.1 | 80.2 |
| Lisa@lifeinlit | Blogger | USA | 6 (0%) | 3217 | 81,965 | 35.2 | 1470.7 |

(*continued*)

**Table 6.2** (continued)

| *Username* | *Category* | *Country* | *N of reviews in data* | *N of posts in total* | *N of followers* | *Average N of comments on reviews* | *Average N of likes for reviews* |
|---|---|---|---|---|---|---|---|
| Zoe & Charli@ thestiffs | Blogger | UK | 18 (1%) | 1689 | 43,191 | 5.3 | 103.2 |
| Jenna@ jennareadsbooks | Blogger | USA | 6 (1%) | 432 | 21,356 | 30.5 | 1068.4 |
| Rivka@readbyred | Reader | NA | 155 (8%) | 2027 | 7503 | 3.9 | 74.1 |

The answers to the survey suggest that initially many book reviewers had had an external incitement to start: they had been involved in a book club, had attended a course where Instagram was introduced or had been engaged by a reading campaign or a similar initiative. Alternatively, they had an entry point into the sphere of literature in another book-related occupation, being booksellers, librarians or teachers. Many respondents had a book blog or a reader profile available beyond Instagram, and their motivation was to drive traffic to this external content or make reading engagement more visible and livelier through the appealing images that can accompany such reviews on Instagram. The visual feed seemed to make the accumulated efforts more tangible. A common reason for book reviewing on Instagram seemed to be that the users didn't have the energy to create a real blog. Also, rather than aspiring to establish a 'micro-medium' for reviewing, many of the reviewers were involved in book-reading challenges, and the reviews marked the break points in the process of this personal engagement.

In the profile descriptions of their accounts, in the so-called handles (see below), the most frequently occurring self-assigned producer roles, other than reviewers, included cultural professionals ('author', 'writer', 'blogger', 'artist', 'student', 'teacher', 'founder', 'editor', 'coach', 'speaker', 'creator'), hobbyists or afficionados ('lover', 'reader', 'addict', 'person', 'bookworm', 'enthusiast', 'bibliophile', 'ravenclaw', 'nerd', 'fanatic') or family members ('mom'/'mum'/'mother'/'mama', 'wife', 'girl', 'friend'). These roles, whether professional or private, obviously provided reviewers with personal-life entry points to literature, while enabling the amateur reviewers to remain amateurs. Instead of professionalism, the 'me-viewers' employ a discourse of affectivity that can be observed at many levels. The most frequently occurring English words in all Instagram handles ($N = 727$ individual users) are shown in a word cloud in Fig. 6.2. Among the 100 most frequent words—beyond the most obvious 'book' (28,203 occurrences)—were 'read' (9535), 'author' (9019), 'love' (7263), 'writer' (7234), 'review' (7080), 'lover' (6451) and 'blogger' (6054). Frequent self-descriptions were connected to traditionally female-dominated areas, such as design, fashion, beauty and home decoration, as well as family functions (mother, wife, child, girl).

The self-descriptive vocabulary reinforces affective features; words that occur often include 'dream', 'passion', 'heart', 'obsess', 'fun', 'wine', 'enjoy' and 'happy'. Individual user names are detached as much as possible to restore the users' anonymity. It can be seen that book love is reflected in attributes of oneself as a book lover; common descriptions include 'bookworm', 'book dragon', 'ravenclaw', 'book nerd', 'book geek', 'bibliophile', 'book muncher', 'bookie' and 'bookbum', or 'book addict/addicted to books', 'hooked on books', 'book hoarder', 'book obsessed' and 'fanatic'. Reviewers may also identify themselves with fantasy figures either created by themselves or borrowed from public

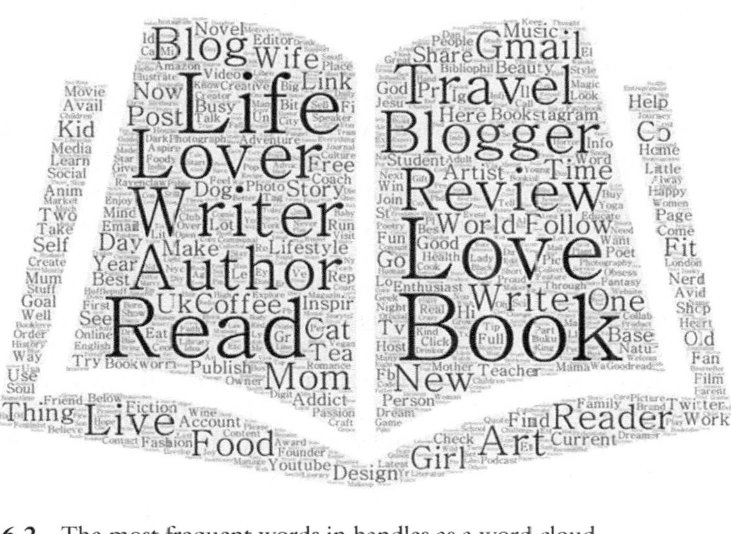


**Fig. 6.2** The most frequent words in handles as a word cloud

imaginary, or call their virtual spaces, for example, 'Gryffindor' or 'Hufflepuff', referring to the school houses in the Harry Potter books by JK Rowling. It is also reinforced in word choices that describe the places where book lovers reside: 'book attic', 'book nook', 'bookshelf', 'book café', 'fictional realm', 'literary world', 'fantasy world'. 'Bookish' and 'nook' are fetish words that are especially widely circulated in account names, e-mail addresses and descriptions. Book attics and nooks describe the blissful solitude connected with reading: it is just me and my books or reading, writing and me—a 'single member book club', as one reviewer put it. Furthermore, it is seen in metaphors for reading and reviewing activities, such as 'breathing in books', 'armchair adventures', 'sleep-walking dreams' and 'page travels'. The book reviewers are 'living the nerd dream', a 'bookish life' or 'the literary dream', making this silent activity into something more material. The love of reading is sometimes exaggerated to the extent that it becomes a 'mania', a 'disease' or (preferably) a 'deviation'. Characterizations like 'obsession', 'addiction' and 'bookaholism', or the Japanese term *tsundoku*, which means the hoarding of books without reading them, refer to an incurable love.

These choices underline a shared passion or love that is articulated as a central common community feature. The same tone was effectively highlighted in survey responses where informants frequently talked about loving books and sharing their book love. Affective work and intimate publics (Dobson et al., 2018) are present in the existing discourse on *book love* or the *love of reading*, which has become a concept fostered in literacy research (Cramer & Castle, 1994; Ferris, 2009). In reading promotion, this kind of affectionate relationship with books has been envisioned to lay the basis for a lifelong reading habit (Layne, 2009). In this respect, book love is connected to the very essence of being an amateur (French: lover), an art lover. 'It started as a hobby, became a passion', as one survey respondent declared.

With regard to Instagram reviewers' love of books, their deep attachment to books, literature and reading is displayed by them showing books as sacred cultural goods, or, as Olave (2020) puts it, as iconic cultural objects, which has long been a prevalent feature of bibliomania among book collectors (Holzenberg, 2019) and to which the literary life shown in Instagram images bears similarities. Showing these icons does not necessarily mean that the books have been read, interpreted and analysed, but the aesthetic immersion of their materiality has a high symbolic value. Books have historically been used and valued non-textually, manifesting a material value as talismans and agents of divine will (Watson, 2019). As part of the postmodern obsession with screening the material objects of books, reviewing, especially on a photo-driven app like Instagram, becomes synonymous with showing 'shelfies' as a sign of 'bookishness', which has even been characterized as 'book porn' (Rodger, 2019). The term 'bookish' allows a loose relationship with books and literature, reflecting on book culture on a very general level, incorporating aspects of lifestyles where books play a role, such as in home decoration; however, it can be noted that among all bookstagrammers, book reviewers can be presupposed to be closest to the content of the books they are showing, or reviewing, and thus to literature. In more particular cases, self-descriptions suggest that what is central to manifesting a love of reading and literature is creating a literary-fantastical, or maybe a slightly escapist, space to live in with the literature one is fond of.

Because of the individually centred character of reading and reviewing activities, reviewers do not adopt moral superiority regarding their audiences in attempting to educate them about good taste. Immersed in their own bibliomania, they are more directed to sharing and explaining their personal lifestyle experiences in an emotionally engaged way. By opening up their reading processes online, users intend to help others in choosing and evaluating literature. In Instagram reviews, the judgemental character of the review is softened or downplayed by using related hashtags, such as #booksuggestion and #bookrecommendation. In this respect, as textual representations, the Instagram reviews are to be understood as contingent manifestations of relatively long-lasting participatory practices (see also Bruns, 2008) or part of an ongoing process of participation in the social life of fan communities or scenes (see also Ito, 2010) rather than as media or literary works designed to stand on their own, apart from their social and cultural context.

The analysis conforms to the basic feature of cultural intramediation according to which vernacular amateurs on Instagram are closer to the reading audiences than are institutionalized reviewers. While institutionalized reviewers position themselves in between the primary production of literature and the audience, vernacular reviewers declare themselves part of the audience, benefiting from the primary production and giving direct feedback to it but not seeking an independent position between these two. The reviewing is, therefore, not attached to a framework inbuilt in professional reviewing, which dedicates special attention to localizing a specific work in a history and tradition, or to its production context (Orlik, 2016). Vernacular Instagram reviewers are not so much re-viewers, retrospectively looking back at a carefully selected published piece of work to place it in a larger sociocultural and historical context, as me-viewers, individualized experts in their own reading experience, mediating their intellectual, emotional and aesthetic ephemeral experience regarding the book product they happen to have received or stumbled upon. While the context for re-viewers is (the production of) literature, the context for me-reviewers is book culture, or reading culture. Both groups of producers are public receivers of literature, but re-viewers relate this public reception to the production and me-viewers to the consumption paradigm.

One aspect that needs to be recognized in institutional amateurs' engagement is the influential role of mediators (see Sect. 3.1 Cultural Mediation in Chap. 3). Not only on Instagram but also on other platforms of social reading such as NetGalley, LibraryThing, Reedsy Discovery, LoveReading, BookBub, SFBook Review, The Millions and Fantasy Book Review, there are structures that urge reviewers to continue in their activities. As mentioned earlier in Sect. 4.2 User Reviewing in Chap. 4, the most structured communities are the paid book-review services set up for new and self-publishing authors for marketing, the so-called ARC (Advance Review/Reading Copy) services. Examples include Candid Book Reviews (@candidbreviews) and Hidden Gems Books (@hgbooks). ARCs are given to readers in advance of the book launch with the hope that they will choose to review the book as soon as it is released. The review services often collaborate with Amazon, and Instagram was yet another channel for them to reach audiences.

When it comes to the perceived affordances of platform and genre, a number of observations are worth emphasizing. Instagram reviews present a short format for individualized participation that aims at addressing one's reading experiences concerning a specific book. Reviews are more typically to be considered as recommendations or suggestions based on a reading experience that is alleged to be individual, idiosyncratic and unique, instead of in-depth analyses with generalizable observations concerning a specific (sub)field of literature. Reviewing is connected to self-improvement rather than improvement of literature. Reviews are thus equally, if not more, important for their creators, and making personal reading engagement visible is the key. As reflected in the sports-inspired term 'readathons', reviews often function as break points of a reading marathon, with personal goals set, typically measured by the number of books to be read within a period of a year or a month. Review entries can thus be understood as book-reading accomplishments, where a central objective is to create a public image of oneself as a reading person. This creation of a 'reading self' (Goffman, 1959) is based on systematically performing cultural engagement online and taking care of its impression management in a public space, and is intended to be seen as such by others. Reporting the accumulated results of this 'reading sport' makes it more meaningful and helps assess one's identity and capabilities as a cultural consumer or citizen.

## 6.2 Judging Gadgets: Filmmaker Reviewers on Vimeo

A great extent of reviewing in video occurs on YouTube, but there are also review videos published on other platforms, affecting the production culture by imposing different 'grammars' penetrating the genre, such as the video-sharing service Vimeo. In general, Vimeo is less driven by entertainment goals than the more mainstream and popular video platform YouTube, which makes it to an apt platform for vernacular professionals to both showcase and comment on their work. Vimeo was founded three months before YouTube, in October 2004, by two American entrepreneurs, Jake Lodwick and Zach Klein. Vimeo became known for its early technological advancements, as it established a video-on-demand service (VOD) and supported HD earlier than YouTube. Vimeo is, indeed, often seen as an alternative or opposite to YouTube, which has, as one of the most frequently used social media platforms in the world, received more of a mass audience and popular character. As a smaller and more limited community, Vimeo is regarded as more 'indie', more 'mature' and 'tasteful', more 'supportive', and more 'professional' or 'academic' (see, e.g., Quora, 2018). Unlike YouTube, Vimeo does not run advertisements, but is based on a premium model that allows users to upgrade their free accounts to Plus or Pro level. In its corporate narrative, Vimeo presents itself as 'a supportive community covering a wide range of interests' and 'a community of real, amazing humans' (Vimeo, 2018b).

Explicit commercial content is more seldom seen on Vimeo, as promotional videos (e.g. product demos) and videos focused on short-term sales (e.g. real estate walk-throughs) are advised to be kept private on Vimeo (Vimeo, 2018b). However, commercial content is allowed: 'As long as you make it clear in the description that you are sharing the video as an example of your creative work and not as an actual advertisement, you can upload videos with commercial content even if you are not a PRO user. To qualify for this exception, you must be an independent artist or a production company or a non-profit organization' (Vimeo, 2018b). Vimeo may also attract producers who do not strive for the widest possible audiences and highest grade of visibility with a strategic plan of becoming influencers or otherwise making their activities economically beneficial, but initially just want a platform on which to share their work. In this way, the platform also creates a horizon of expectations regarding the form and style of the content.

On Vimeo, films and filmmaking form a normative centre against which the content is typically mirrored. Indeed, the name Vimeo is an anagram of the word 'movie'—as well as a combination of 'video' and 'me'—and thus the focus is expected to be on films. However, as can also be seen in the sample, many users do not necessarily make an exclusive choice between Vimeo and YouTube but have accounts on both, perhaps in the hope of reaching different audiences or temporarily testing out which platform functions better, or to gain practical knowledge of them both as a publisher. Vimeo has adopted the term 'Vimeans', a counterpart to 'Youtubers', to refer to the members of the community, thus implying a sense of affinity and exclusivity. Vimeo calls the video publishers 'creators', in the same fashion as YouTube has established the term 'content creators' to denote the users producing, publishing and sharing videos.

Using the hashtag #review for retrieval and an individual video as a unit of analysis, there were 1661 videos available on Vimeo in 2017. As depicted in Table 6.3 that lists the identifiable product groups reviewed in the videos, it can be seen that the overwhelming majority of these review videos were focused on technical equipment ($N = 1004$), which made up 79 per cent of all the review videos in the sample. The majority of this technical equipment was related to filmmaking; gadgets reviewed were cameras and filming equipment such as lenses, handles, sliders, dollies, tripods and software plug-ins. These technical film equipment reviews were thus tech or gadget reviews related to the overarching topic of the Vimeo community: film and filmmaking.

Film reviews included heterogeneous approaches to film content. A major producer, with 40 videos in the sample, was a user focused on reviewing niche cultural products, namely aesthetic products of LGBTQ+ culture such as LGBTQ+ films and television programmes, but even comic books and toys. In general, the films reviewed were not blockbusters but often works by other professionals of an 'indie' nature, technically analysed in order to learn from them for an improved performance. Game

**Table 6.3** The cultural areas reviewed on Vimeo

| *Category* | *N videos* | *%* | *N producers* | *%* | *Av. N likes per video* | *Av. N followers per producer* | *Examples* |
|---|---|---|---|---|---|---|---|
| Technical film equipment | 1004 | 79 | 476 | 78 | 70 | 2.1 | Cameras and filming equipment |
| Film | 98 | 8 | 48 | 8 | 68 | 2.0 | Films |
| Clothes | 56 | 4 | 13 | 2 | 72 | 4.3 | Underwear, sportswear |
| Games | 36 | 3 | 11 | 2 | 40 | 3.3 | Video games |
| Other consumer products | 19 | 1 | 16 | 3 | 20 | 1.0 | Cars, sports gear |
| Events | 15 | 1 | 14 | 2 | 76 | 1.1 | Festivals, shows, fairs |
| Food | 11 | 1 | 3 | 0 | 36 | 3.7 | Restaurants, pizza |
| Music | 9 | 0 | 9 | 1 | 134 | 1.0 | Albums |
| Other | 25 | 2 | 19 | 3 | 155 | 1.3 | Miscellaneous |
| *Total/*average* | *1273* | *100* | *609* | *100* | **533* | **2.2* | - |

reviews featured a rather minor group of videos, which is perhaps not surprising as in 2008–2014, gameplay videos were not allowed on Vimeo because they did not comply with the quality requirements of creative expression. The rest of the video review types included quite a few items, showing a great diversity in approaches and styles and stemming from a limited number of producers following the review format. For example, there were a handful of review videos on pizza, music festivals, cars, bikes, skates, kiteboards, flysurfers, skimboards and rollercoasters.

However, the majority of user reviewers who have chosen Vimeo are clearly filmmakers and filming enthusiasts from the field of film and media production. Video reviewers on Vimeo thus make up a distinct group of prosumers who are professional customers in the area of consumption they represent (filmmaking). More specifically, the core of the reviewers is formed by film gadget reviewers ($N = 27$) who are mostly professional (or semi-professional) filmmakers testing equipment in their leisure time. Many of the film reviewers also add to this group of filmmakers or hands-on practitioners, focusing on the technical aspects of image quality or the creation of special effects in films. What these reviewers share in common is that they position themselves vis-à-vis the producers of cultural content rather than being part of film audiences, or they can at least be regarded as the DIY enthusiasts of the film or video scene. They are practitioners, and are using their expertise and practical knowledge from the technical production of videos to test and evaluate new products. As a by-product of their primary expertise, they are producing knowledge to assist other media makers in their choices of camera equipment. This dimension of being in service for others is distinctively characteristic of the review videos. This anchors the Vimeo review videos powerfully in the digital labour of vernacular professionals, especially professional amateurs (pro-ams), in which the aspects of 'venture labour' (Geff, 2012), 'relational labour' (Baym, 2015) and 'aspirational work' (Duffy, 2017) are featured. Venture labour refers to work characterized by precariousness, insecurity and high instability of work that digital workers need take up for the lack of better alternatives (Geff, 2012). Relational labour is, according to Baym (2015, p. 20), part of 'ongoing communicative practices and skills of building and maintaining interpersonal and group relationships central to maintaining many careers'. Duffy (2017) relates aspirational work to career goals and entrepreneurial dreams, arguing that aspirational users regard unpaid work online as investment in a future self that will hopefully be able to 'do what they love' for a living. Out of these epithets, relational work may be the most powerful account of the character of work that the film gadget reviewers are doing to maintain their careers in the film industry (and beyond). While it is evident that the film gadget reviewers are seeking to maintain and develop their careers in filmmaking by investing in relationship-building, possibility-enhancing communication, when it comes to reviewing it is particularly interesting to ask how they are building their reviewer position while doing this. As what kind of venture, relational and aspirational work, worth engaging in, does reviewing appear to them?

Venture, relational and aspirational labour have been frequently discussed in the context of female workers, seeing the social, non-monetary and affective value building as exploitation of workers, by workers internalizing the logics (and, above all, the risks) of entrepreneurialism (Duffy, 2016, 2017; Luckman, 2015; Nakamura, 2015). What is striking is that the reviewsphere of film gadget reviewers on Vimeo was an all-male community: nearly all the producers of Vimeo reviews in the sample were males. Among the almost 30 most frequent reviewers, there were no females (alphabetical order): Safwan Ahmedmia, Matthew Allard, Johnnie Behiri, Cinema5D, Dave Dugdale, emmagination, Gay Comic Geek, Rod

Guadajardo, Philip Bloom, Stefan Czech, Mark, Martin Foerster, Gizmodo, Tom Guilmette, John Hope, Philip Johnston, Gordon Laing, Nino Leitner, Erik Naso, OSWreview, Daniel Peters, Caleb Pike, Andrew Reid, Ron Risman, ShutUpShow, UNB Blog and Chris Weatherly. Surely the range of interests concerning products to be reviewed—technology, cars, extreme sports—reflects activities typically favoured by males. The male dominance of the reviewing sector is thus not an exception to the gender gap found among filmmakers (Lauzen, 2018a), or to the fact that issues in popular culture are more likely to be covered by male journalists (Jaakkola, 2015), and film reviewers more often tend to be men (Lauzen, 2018b).

The film gadget reviewers are active filmmakers, generally pursuing a career and related continuance and permanency by producing videos of metadiscourse (these are not original film creations but the reviewers comment on these and their production context). The review videos deal with the production context: the techniques, tools, competences and other approaches to media production. For the primary production of filmmaking equipment, they also form a niche market of customers with a serious interest and high expectations with regard to the quality of the products. For the film industry, these media producers constitute a potential pool of employees. As public testers of products, with a high degree of accumulated experience as well as the capability and willingness to share the outcome of their tests, they can be considered potential promotional intermediaries. However, many film gadget reviewers attempt to sustain integrity in order to become legitimate reviewers, detached from the immediate circulation of goods. By seeking to create a discourse independent from the immediate consumption of technical equipment and technology, they also create mediation expertise and authority in the metadiscourse that shapes reviewing. For them, reviewing represents portfolio work that takes on the form of competence development and professional learning, which play an important role for indie and freelancer filmmakers who are typically working separately from a physical and even social workplace community.

In the case of film equipment reviews, the 'articulated opinion' judgement ('Is something good or bad?') may take a variety of forms—for example, testing or putting something into practice in comparison to something else, such as different versions of a gadget. Some of the videos hashtagged with #review were short shots—typically called 'test films'—marking the result of a filming and a simultaneous reviewing process, perhaps featuring some tests or alternative scenes at the end of the video. Alternatively, for example, the video could include deconstructing and analysing well-known pieces of cinema. The professional vernacular reviews can thus be characterized as both connoisseurial and procedural reviews on consumer products, as defined by Blank (2007) in the institutionalized domain.

Produced by an engaged group of users, they demonstrate, or at least aim to demonstrate, a high level of knowledge and experience upon which the assessments are based, showing parallels to the institutionalized forms of reviewing. Yet the overarching question is 'Is this useful or not?' rather than 'Is this good or bad?', putting the use value of the object in the foreground, instead of the aesthetic or symbolic value.

The film gadget reviewers are not necessarily marketing the original content while addressing the contextual features of production; they are not comparable to artists who must produce, distribute and market their work as well as shoulder community and business management, but they are solely focusing on reviewing a delimited aspect of production and creating a reviewer profile separate from the filmmaker profile, even if drawing on filmmaking competences. However, reviewing may efficiently work as an extension of marketing of the self as a filmmaker. Individual Vimeo videos that had gained over 1000 likes were a slow-motion video test showing liquids and motions (3879 likes), a comparison video on shooting in dark and at daylight (2149 likes), a review of the career of the film director Emmanuel Lubezki, a tribute similar to a video essay (1982 likes) and a technical review of the BlackMagic Cinema Camera (1754 likes). They point to the fact that, particularly in audiovisual works, the poetics of a particular piece become an important feature; they are not only watched as reviews or tests of something, but also for their aesthetic and poetic accomplishment, as artworks in their own right. In particular, these skillful pieces demonstrate the ability of their producers to make films of high technical and aesthetic quality, and enforce their positioning as professionals or professional amateurs in the field of film production. In other words, the review videos are manifestations of production and consumption processes that are essential to a free-time activity, hobby, part-time occupation or even full-time profession of the video producer.

Despite the marketing aspect, reviews in the film gadget reviewer community are, above all, produced in an endeavour to help others and in order to be able to share one's own experiences. Like many reviewers on YouTube, especially those with reviewtainmental aims (see Sect. 6.4

Reviewtainment: Reviews as Platformized Entertainment), the reviewers on Vimeo are seemingly not primarily led by the logics of attention to aspire to the widest possible number of views in order to get their activities financed and/or to get commercial partnerships and, in this way, to make their content production more economically profitable. Film gadget reviewers typically envisage themselves as experienced seniors in some kind of a tutor role; their pedagogical mission is to teach people with similar interests and goals to use tools better, but what is important is that they simultaneously conceive of themselves as part of that community.

Shared interests can be seen in the somewhat childish enthusiasm the reviewers allow themselves, even on the most professionally oriented site, such as in using the word 'killer', and by using the pronoun 'we' as a community marker. Indeed, a central intention in all the review videos is the mediation of an opinion or experience concerning a newly launched product to a peer audience. This is in many cases a highly exclusive and limited audience. For example, often the professional vernacular reviews concerned the new version of the model and included a comparison to the previous version. These differences may appear quite tiny to many consumers, and they would hardly interest anyone other than nerds and enthusiasts—people who are regularly using the gadgets and software and need to know how to improve their performance through better tools. This impression is also supported by language use, which includes the regular use of vocabulary that ordinary people have no idea about, such as M43 mount, S-gamut or AVCHD codec, which were not typically explained.

However, it would be naïve to presume that they only have altruistic goals. Quite obviously, reviewing provides filmmakers with a boost to their personal brand and establishes them as authorities in the field of video or film production, while at the same time making their own professional or amateur activity meaningful and more structured. Reviewing can thus also be allotted to the context of career development and personal brand building. Here, though, it is interesting that the gadget reviewers' reviewing is characterized by negotiations between two, partially contradictory, positionings. First, in the usefulness to others, the reviewing activity juggles between negotiations between promotion of products and creating distance from the industry. Reviewers are part of the circulation of goods, adding to the symbolic value of products on the market by making intermediary interventions in the form of reviews and thus being positioned to the value chain originating from the industry. Indeed, some of the most sophisticated review videos appeared like commercials for the products, trying to show off, for example, a camera in perfect studio conditions. Simultaneously, Vimeo reviewers attempt to resist the selling function and create integrity by establishing an ethical code to boast of autonomy and professionalism.

A central dimension in creating a convincing professional image and communicating usefulness is the trustworthiness of the producers' output. In the traditional review, independence was guaranteed by the intermediary organization that commissioned the reviewer and stood for his or her professional integrity and third-party position. To create trustworthiness, the vernacular reviewers produce a great deal of metadiscourse around the review. In the sample, they dedicated space to explaining the specific choices or occurrences that led to certain decisions concerning the review that was published by the media for which they were working. One of the most frequent professional reviewers, Philip Bloom—who also declared in one of his videos that 'without my ethics, my opinion is pointless' (Bloom, 2013)—explained in an attached blog (Bloom, 2014):

> I am extremely choosy about which cameras I review. I have to be interested in them to put the huge amount of time and effort it takes to make them. If I have no interest in a camera, then I simply won't make a review. They are occasionally subsidized by a dealer, never the company who makes them due to my ethics (this one CVP are subsidizing) but even then they're 90% self-funded. I am not sure they could stomach the actual cost of all the time I put into making them!

However, the vernacular reviewers' critical authority is not a simple and unproblematic issue, and this still distinguishes them from institutionalized reviewers, for whom the intermediary organization that commissions the review serves as a guarantor. Even if the vernacular reviewers act in good faith, a 'good consumer bias' may occur, similar to the 'good citizen bias' identified among survey respondents, who for the sake of social desirability or other causes tend to self-report about themselves more positively than what they are in reality. The social desirability bias may make the reviewers present their products in a more positive light, and the economic bound may result in reinforcing the popularity of certain brands in the community: Having made a decision to spend your money on something, which may be relatively pricey, as is the case for a good deal of camera equipment, you may not want your choice to appear as a complete failure.

Second, reviewing being part of the politics of creating the professional self, the usefulness to self is divided into the altruistic ambitions of helping others to learn and develop and the efforts of promoting self on the employment market. The first dimension is manifest in the practices of peer pedagogies of putting things into practice, the latter in the narrative of a ready-to-be-employed experienced and creative filmmaker. As peers—specialized amateurs—the reviewers see themselves as part of a community willing to share the newest home-made test results. Indeed, in the commentary field many users reinforced the pedagogical aspect; for example, for test footage, users could ask if they were any new findings regarding some specific technical features of the gadget reviewed, and the reviewer could provide the audience with more hands-on experience. The other side of helping others was the effort of self-branding—standing out as an expert, or being seen as an expert, referring to professional traits, such as naming a client, mentioning the reviewer's name or using a logo of one's own.

Content wise, the useful creativity on Vimeo is not homogeneous: it can be characterized as something that ranges from a serious enthusiast's laboratory to an arena of shared impressions and co-consumption.

The film gadget reviewers depart and derive from the pro-am community, but also direct their messages to this exclusive community, without any claims of being too inclusive. In this respect, they are similar to the vernacular book reviewers who often act in amateur roles but, in an equal way, because they are an integral part of the community to which they communicate, can be described as cultural intramediaries (Sect. 6.1 Prettifying Books: Book Reviewers on Instagram). The film gadget reviewers on Vimeo are professionally oriented cultural intramediaries, acting like professionals but not aspiring to an intermediary positioning between the primary industry and audience; rather, they merge with their audience. This kind of specialized or niche intermediation qualifies as another type of cultural intramediation than discussed in the context of Instagram book reviewers.

## 6.3 At the Playstage: Toy Reviewers on YouTube

Family has become one of the most popular content categories on YouTube (Lange, 2014; Strangelove, 2010) and it saw immense growth in popularity during the 2010s. Children are a large and growing audience because they start using YouTube at a very early age. For example, in Sweden, half of children under five years of age use (48 per cent) the internet on a daily basis, mostly for watching videos and mostly on a tablet, and their internet use has been consistently increasing (Alexanderson, 2019). At the same time, toys, and other material artefacts, have continued to be central to children's play in the digital era (Johansen, 2018). In today's cultural economy, children have aesthetic agency (von Bonsdorff, 2018; de la Ville et al., 2021; Holland et al., 2001) that in the era of mediatization is being seen and heard, at least potentially, by more and more people (see also UN, 2021). Among different genres with exposure of toys, reviewing of toys has recently gained popularity and toy reviewing now constitutes an established category. While the classical review has almost exclusively been based on adult-to-adult communication, vernacular reviews frequently include children as (co-)producers, and this alterity makes toy reviews a special case worth looking at. The online toy reviewing culture has emerged gradually on YouTube since the early 2000s. It is now widespread and connected to other forms of play and action.

Since 2018, the highest-earning content creator in the world has been the family behind the channel Ryan's World that had its origins as a toy review channel, Ryan ToysReview—Ryan Kaji (b. 2011), his mother Loann Kaji, father Shion Kaji and twin sisters Emma and Kate, living in California in the United States—with earnings of 22 million dollars in 2018 (Robehmet & Berg, 2018) and almost 30 million dollars in mid-2021 (Statista, 2021). Since 2017, the channel, with almost 30 million subscribers in May 2021, has partnered with a Los Angeles-based start-up, Pocket.watch, for merchandise and marketing, including collectibles, merchandise and a mobile application, Tag with Ryan (Pocket.watch, 2018). In the wake of Ryan's success, toy reviewing has become an established way of communicating about new toys to an audience, and a number of toy (review) channels have emerged, such as Fun Toys Collector Disney Toys Review (11.3 million subscribers in January 2021, launched in 2011), Blu Toys Club Surprise (7 million subscribers, launched in 2010), Sandaroo Kids (6.2 million subscribers, launched in 2012), PS Toy Reviews (1.8 million subscribers, launched in 2013) and TTPM Toy Reviews (465,000 subscribers, launched in 2008). All of these channels have far greater audiences than traditional children's television programmes. In addition, general toy channels employing a variety of different formats on a regular basis, such as CookieSwirlC (15 million subscribers) and Kinder Spielzeug Kanal (14 million subscribers), as well as children's and family vlogs with global reach such as Like Nastya (72 million subscribers) and Vlad and Niki (65 million subscribers), occasionally incorporate toy reviews in their repertoire.

Toy reviewing is a phenomenon driven by US creators, which is largely based on the popularity and global reach of English-language videos. However, local scenes with similar profiles and agendas have emerged during the second decade of the twenty-first century. For example, there were similar toy (review) channels active in the Nordic countries at the beginning of 2019: Family Playlab (4.2 million subscribers in January 2021, launched in 2006) and Lek med oss in Sweden (143,000 subscribers, launched in 2017); Henrik & Andrea (15,900 subscribers, launched in 2015) and aBABYc ToysReview (81,417 subscribers, launched in 2015) in Norway; and WooBooTV in Finland (56,400 subscribers, launched in 2011). These channels deliver content in their national languages, combining descriptions of toys with English to reach a more global audience, and some of the producers ranked high on the national list of earnings (see, e.g., Karlsten, 2017).

Marketing and advertising have increasingly infiltrated children's everyday lives: not only have licensing-based merchandise and explicit promotion become part of traditional mass media such as film and broadcasting (Bainbridge, 2017), but also children's use of technology and new media has increased and children's play has been mediatized (see, e.g., Johansen, 2018; Hjarvard, 2004). Advertisers and industry have discovered ways of directly targeting children instead of addressing them through adults (Hjarvard, 2004; Schor, 2004), and children's influence on purchasing choices in families, 'kidsfluence', has increased (Schor, 2004). While persuasion and hidden advertisements targeting children are not a new phenomenon (see, e.g., Buckingham, 1995), the promotional dimension has become a more inseparable part of children's media cultures in an era of 'content confusion' where the boundaries between democratic and commercial communication have been blurred (Einstein, 2016). Simultaneously, commercial or promotional content has become a naturalized and acceptable component in even those communication environments where younger people spend their time.

In the past few years, as family accounts have become more popular on social media, featuring children's everyday lives and cultural engagement, pre-teens, toddlers and even infants have more and more often become public co-producers of content. Family accounts are driven by adults and motivated by performing maternity online and sharing parenting experiences, typically referred to as sharenting, mommy blogging and family influencing (Blum-Ross & Livingstone, 2017; Abidin, 2017). As vernacular spaces become perpetuated by commercial interests of platform providers, marketers and industry, family content producers have become powerful mediators of commercial messages, that is, promotional intermediaries often referred to as family influencers (Hunter, 2016; Abidin, 2017). However, instead of emphasizing the character of branded entertainment as a word-of-mouth method of persuasion and means of monetization, prevalent in digital networks (Hudson & Hudson, 2006; Hunter, 2016; Wiedmann et al., 2010), the endorsing processes are often presented—not the least by the users themselves—as expressions of enthusiasm, related to creativity, fandom, amateurism or everyday expertise, or as altruism and aspirations to help others by sharing this experience-based expertise (Edensor et al., 2009). Still, indeed, the inclusion of children in the cultural public online sphere may also be connected to listening to children's authentic voice and promoting their participation, thus diversifying the variety of voices in cultural mediation (Oswell, 2013; UN, 2021).

As commercial content targeting children (e.g. Buckingham, 2007; Schor, 2004), exposure to targeted advertising and embedded marketing on social media has been identified as potentially harmful to young people (Livingstone, 2013; Livingstone et al., 2018). It is a practice that is accelerating due to the uncontrolled dynamics of user-generated content. Discussions around family-oriented videos, child-friendly content and child safety on YouTube have been extensive, especially after Elsagate—a controversy related to the discovery of content inappropriate for children camouflaged as Disney characters. Elsagate, named after a character from Disney's animated film *Frozen*, appeared on the Toy Freaks channel (2012–2017) and depicted members of the family that ran the channel (the father and his children) in disturbing situations. Since then, Google has adopted stricter guidelines regarding children's content on its platform and developed an app for parents to monitor their children's content consumption, YouTube Kids, which released in 2015 (for an analysis, see Burroughs, 2017). Discussions have centered around explicitly inappropriate content, such as violence, abuse and sexual content, whereas the appropriateness of other, perhaps softer and more nuanced content qualities has remained beyond the scope of these public discussions, including the roles of mediated societal values, educational affordances of the content, and the line between communication and marketing.

User-generated content plays an ever-increasing role in children's online video use, embedded in everyday routines at home. Nine out of 10 of the most subscribed-to child-oriented YouTube channels worldwide in January 2019 were user-generated (Statista, 2019). A mother blogger illustratively described the typical way these channels are discovered and their appeal—the parental need for child-free time in order to take care of everyday tasks, as well as children's recognition of and attraction to popular brands of media culture:

> My son was obsessed with Paw Patrol. So, when I needed to take a shower or cook a meal, I'd go to YouTube on the iPad and find Paw Patrol-related videos for him to watch. He fell in love with the Kinder Surprise Egg videos, where some chick with long fingernails and a squeaky, condescending voice opens plastic eggs (sometimes covered in Play-Doh, which is gross and makes little sense to me), and reveals a Paw Patrol toy, a Peppa Pig winder, or something similar. (Wisner, 2016, n.p.)

The mother concluded by calling the toy videos, which include the category of toy reviews, 'toddler crack' and 'plastic bullshit', remarking that '[t]hese videos are basically like creepy commercials for toys, except for some godforsaken reason, they are much more interesting and addictive to kids than actual commercials' (ibid.). Indeed, according to adult quality standards, the repetitive, attention-grabbing 'review' content does not seem to strive for quality as conventionally understood in reviewing, with the informed argument at the centre. While content the main purpose of which is to attract attention and make a viewer click on a hyperlink is called clickbait, the attention-seeking video material that aims at exploiting young viewers' media consumption patterns can be called kidbait. However, as clickbait, the term kidbait is slightly value-laden, referring to the speaker's assessment of the content rather than to actual conditions, and it is sometimes questionable what is exploitation and what is not.

Toy (review) videos are not the only type of videos in the exploitation genre of kidbait but they are powerful among their child audiences. Kidbait videos are a result of the algorithmic recommendation system employed by platforms like YouTube (Airoldi et al., 2016). The more attention—views and subscribers—a video receives, the more likely it is that the video will be recommended to viewers. For a toddler audience, the recommendations that are displayed as still thumbnail images in the side menu play the most significant role in the selection of video content. Thumbnails typically make use of strong colours, as well as identifiable merchandise and persons. Infants and toddlers, the majority of which are illiterate, cannot change their search strategies by entering new words into the search field but navigate only by selecting these algorithm-based recommendations shown on the screen. As long as toy videos are frequently watched content, it is probable that children end up watching the most popular videos if an adult does not intervene in the video watching process.

An internet user (VanDeGraph, 2016) discovered that toy videos on YouTube have a different viewing pattern than other videos. Usually, people watch shorter videos for longer than they do long videos; the total time watched is usually about half the video length. However, VanDeGraph found that toy videos were watched for the same amount of time on average, no matter how long the video was. For example, some of the videos are probably watched on autoplay and, as noted by VanDeGraph (2016), toy videos are also 'English optional', meaning that children are not hindered by language barriers in their binge-watching. These factors may partly contribute to the high viewing numbers that toy videos tend to attain.

The toy review channels have a relatively high number of subscriptions and a very high number of views on average. In the sample of toy reviews, entertainment was the most common self-designated category of the YouTube channels ($N = 25$, 71 per cent). The average age of the channels at the point of the analysis in 2018 was five years, with an average launch date of 2013. Not surprisingly, the most viewed and subscribed-to channels were based in the United States ($N = 22$, 63 per cent) and/or conducted in English ($N = 30$, 86 per cent).

Many of the channels had evolved from that of a toy collector into a toy review video channel, especially those focusing on Disney merchandise. Toy collectors are typically aficionados who collect artefacts of certain type as a hobby, and a great deal of merchandise is meant to be collectibles. A number of content creators embarked on producing videos by showing diecasts from Disney Pixar's box office hit *Cars*. Initially, they had an adult interest in collecting merchandise. For example, in 2010 Blu Toys Club Surprise presented a collection of 718 DVDs in an adult voice-over video, including film categories that were not specifically directed at a child audience. Later on, as audience interest grew, more family members were included in the production of the channel and the scope of content evolved from a focus on adult interests to something that is more directed at children.

Toy reviewers who appear as vloggers, too, often have similar beginnings. Ryan's World's first video, on the channel that was then titled Ryan ToysReview, was an unboxing video of a Lego train package. The video was posted on 16 March 2015, and titled *Kid plays with toys Lego Duplo number train*. The video featured three-year-old Ryan picking up a package in a store, opening it at home and building a 'choo choo train'. As is typical in many of the review videos, Ryan's mother asks him questions about the colours and numbers, serving as the dramaturge. Since then, at the same pace as the baby Ryan has grown into a pre-teen and disclosed his real name, the channel has grown in its identity. The videos have gradually developed to include a more carefully designed set-up with an awareness of continuity and more sponsorship, and the early grey-toned thumbnails have become more colourful and carefully designed, reflecting a more general trend in toy videos. In 2019, the channel was renamed and changed its name from Ryan ToysReview to Ryan's World, leaving the pronounced review identity behind. 'We're changing the channel name because we don't just do toy videos. We do science experiments, challenges like *The floor is lava*, educational videos like *Why do floods happen?*, music videos, skits, and lots more', Ryan Kaji stated in an announcement video (Ryan's World, 2019). In a similar fashion, the name changes of popular toy channels illuminate the shift in strategies: for example, DisneyCarToys has become Sandaroo Kids, Awesome Disney Toys has been changed to AWESMR kids, and Brinquedos & Surpresas has switched to Paulinho & Toquinho. There has thus been a gradual transformation from the niched toy presentation videos towards play- and person-driven content, all-inclusive entertainment by child and family influencers (Abidin, 2017). This has partly increased dialogue in production between channel-governing adults and their children, and contributed to increased children's participation in video production. Toy reviews have, however, gained ground as an integral part of channel communication strategies and become established as one way of addressing the world of play.

Toy review videos feature children, parents and other family members as the protagonists, alternating between voice-overs (disembodied) and showing people in front of the camera (bodied). The videos are made by adults; even if children appear as presenters, the production process is controlled by an adult. The trajectories by which these channels have become toy review video producers vary. The three major modes of communication employed by channels include display videos, play videos and vlogs. Display video channels ($N = 12$, 34 per cent) predominantly feature toys by showing them in some way, for example, by unpacking, assembling or just showing the toys one by one to the camera as the person doing so remains in the background and provides voice-over commentary. Play video channels ($N = 4$, 11 per cent) take toy exposure in a more active direction by developing a narrative and/or action with the toys and often show people interacting with the toys. Vlog channels ($N = 19$, 54 per cent) focus more strongly on people and happenings and feature family members talking and doing things or events at home or in other environments, with toys serving a requisite role. Channels may combine different modes from video to video, or they may apply these modes in different categories but, typically, toy review channels seem to rely on these three content modes.

Nevertheless, the majority of toy review videos are very repetitive, displaying the same strategies from one video to another, to the point that most of the soundtracks are composed by a single person who has published his music online under an open licence. The same pattern adds to the recognizability of toy review videos both within and across channels. In addition, channel descriptions typically follow the same pattern: welcoming viewers to 'kid- and family-friendly content', often in two or three different languages, and providing a list of popular global brands to be 'reviewed'.

The general pattern of expression being based on showing toys, the reviewing activity undertaken is often more dependent on the channel's preferences and choices around genre and style than on any community-based consensus of what 'toy reviewing' should imply. All the toy reviews in the sample did, however, feature a space for revealing and addressing toys and play. The videos were very operational, showing action instead of solely focusing on artefacts or people. Content was transferred into action and messages were mediated by *doing* something, for example by trying out a new toy, opening a package, decorating a cake, posing a play challenge, competing between family members, or playing around with a product. In some videos, like those from the channel ToysReviewToys, the showcasing of toys is turned into a play in which toys are anthropomorphized to review other toys. The videos, in other words, form a stage for the play that unfolds in the video, enabling a wide variety of actions. To 'review' something means to showcase it on the playstage. Creating this space is the main aim of the toy review videos.

When examining review videos, it is relevant to note that YouTube is a multi-purpose platform that does not require or suggest that a particular genre, such as review, should be followed. Making judgements about commodities is, however, part of YouTube videos, which often mix and hybridize genres. Nicoll and Nansen (2018) analysed the popular genre of unboxing, a type of review video wherein toys, and related products, are unpacked. Indeed, reviewing is typically coupled with unpacking products and many creators describe their activities as 'unboxing *and* reviewing'. Nicoll and Nansen (2018) found, in their content analysis of toy unboxing videos (based on multiple coding), that 11 per cent of 47 adult-narrated videos (about 5 videos) and 15 per cent of 53 child-narrated videos (about 8 videos) included assessment or reviewing. In toy reviews reviewing is even an embedded activity, often coupled with tutorials, tests, play-throughs, humour shows, relaxation videos and so on.

Actions performed on the playstage are thus patterned in a way that we might refer to as activity categories. Activity categories, of which the most typical ones identified in the toy review video sample are collected in Table 6.4, are motivational affordances implemented in the videos to create suspense, dramaturgy and interest. They reflect YouTube's communication patterns and forms of expression more generally. Reviewing is typically attached to certain activity categories, such as 'play and review' or 'unboxing and reviewing'. Sometimes reviewing is carried out by applying the YouTube-specific activity category and the actual reviewing mode thus stays in the background.

The playstage is a scene for consumptive encounters that typically seem to occur prima vista; the presenters show their first impressions when encountering the product. They often do not know exactly what to expect when opening the package. Presenters are thus usually searching for instructions or assembling the toy at the beginning of a video, thereby involving the viewer in the process of familiarization, which becomes a shared moment of discovery. Indeed, as in amateur vernacular reviews, the video presenters position themselves as fans, aficionados, enthusiasts, hobbyists, collectors and consumers—not as connoisseurs or experts. In this way, they present themselves more as middlemen, a means of exposing toys and brands to their viewers, instead of constructing authority by showing, defining or contextualizing what is being seen on the stage. Comments that presenters make about the toys they are reviewing are

**Table 6.4** The major activity categories of the toy review videos

| *Activity category* | *Description* | *Emic term* |
|---|---|---|
| Opening packages | Unpacking and assembling new toys | Unboxing |
| Preparing surprises | Creating suspense by setting up a scene where something unforeseen unfolds | Giant egg surprises, blind bag surprises, science home experiments |
| Exposing collections | Showing collectibles such as toys, merchandise material or DVDs. | Collector's videos |
| Playing video games | Showing an entire play act on screen | Let's play's, play-throughs |
| Playing in physical environments | Spending time in and/or testing environments designed for play such as private or public playrooms, playgrounds or amusement parks | Pretend plays, toy hunts, toy play reviews, location reviews |
| Showing how to do something | Making something by oneself and showing the making of it | DIY's, how-to's, tutorials |
| Parodizing | Making sketches or humorous stories with or about toys | Toy parodies, parodies with the specific brand name (such as *Cars* or Lightning McQueen parodies) |
| Vlogging | Talking about topics in front of the camera, showing occurrences and events | Vlogs, hauls, my days |
| Challenging and competing | In- or inter-video campaigns to compete in something | Challenges |
| Transformations | Applying makeup or trying out costumes | Makeovers |

often spontaneously expressed personal preferences rather than prepared and informed critiques. For example, the toy reviewer may explain that she likes Mattel's Disney tractor more than Disney Story's tractor without providing any further explanation or revealing possible motivations (Sandaroo Kids, 2012).

Brand names and visual appearances are recognizable and contribute to the appeal of the videos. Showing how toys work, what they really look like (beyond the meta-coverage of advertisements), and how they can be turned into a means of play is, of course, not necessarily contradictory to the traditional roles of institutionalized reviewers, such as the consumer adviser, teacher, judge and primary producer's (artist's/industry's) advocate (Blank, 2007; Orlik, 2016). Seeing a toy in action may, in other words, either contribute to or restrict one's—including a child's—desire to buy the commodity. Besides, everything seen on screen is not necessarily related to (positive) purchasing choices but may stimulate one's fantasy, excite one's curiosity, raise interest in different topics, help in discovering and learning new things, and so on. Still, toy reviews can be characterized by the lack of an attempt to explicitly create critical distance from the industry, or primary producers of the toys. Without this critical distance, communication becomes endorsement, which, in the case of toy reviews, directly targets children.

In other words, what appears to be the most prevalent feature of online toy reviews is a lack of critique, especially when compared to what has traditionally been understood as a 'review' in an institutionalized context. By assuming the mantle of fandom, reviewers can endorse brands without reservations and normalizing their consumer conduct. The primary aim of review videos is not to enhance the consumers' tastes or preferences, or to improve the quality of the toy market in the way professional reviewers aspire to make aesthetic judgements regarding children's literature, thereby improving the quality and output of cultural content for children. Rather, to many toy reviewers, reviewing products is almost synonymous with, simply, making videos about toys. However, to some content creators reviewing toys implies promoting them, making a sort of adreview or branded review, which, given that reviewing should imply the independence of the reviewer, is somewhat of an oxymoron. Only a handful of videos in the sample indicated whether the toys were provided at no cost for review, even if they encouraged contacts from toy marketers on the channel description page. There are, however, exceptions, and one of them is, for example, the channel Working with Lemons, targeting preteens. The creators, a music group of family and friends led by Robbie Bagley in Utah in the United States, indicate possible bias or influence via text that typically appears at the beginning of the video: 'This is an ad for Disney' (Working with Lemons, 2017) or 'Thanks Disney for sending this free Elena toy for review!' (Working with Lemons, 2016). Sometimes, they added a hashtag (#ad) to the video description (Working with Lemons, 2018). Otherwise, very few toy reviewers revealed where the toys came from (whether they were provided at no cost or paid for), what the production context was, or where the toys would end up after the review. Even if some channel owners mentioned something vague about this—for example, Ryan's World claims in his channel description and in public interviews that he donates the toys to friends, local communities or charity—these details were not revealed alongside specific review videos.

Most toy reviews are deeply embedded in a profoundly consumerist culture where acquiring, discovering and using brand new toys becomes the unquestioned priority. When examining what kind of values are mediated and thus incorporated in the contemporary childhood of many, toy review videos may appear problematic. With regard to today's global calls for future sustainable living, articulated in the UN's goals for sustainable development as responsible consumption and production (UN, 2015), socialization into a materialist world appears more or less dubious, to the point of becoming 'miseducation' (López, 2014; Seiter, 2005). The toy review genre combines and blurs the lines between three major genres: review, branded content and entertainment. In general, hybrid genres would not cause major trouble; many products of online culture are hybridized and combine, sample and mix categories to achieve the desired result (Danesi, 2015). Ethical problems arise when different production modes related to a genre are crossed. The same problems arise in society when journalism and branded content are blended, such as in content marketing and, in particular, advertorials and advergames that cannot always be reliably decoded as representing one genre. In these cases, audiences are more often teenagers or adults, not infants and toddlers.

Toy review videos, in other words, present an unconventional, incongruous category compared to similar genres that have child audiences, or to other review videos. Toddlers do not necessarily need or call for critical analysis with their toy endorsements, which means that the argumentation and assessment that play a central role in the review genre do not apply in the same way for toddlers as they do for school-aged children who can evaluate and balance arguments. In literature criticism, review of children's literature, including infants' literature, is typically conducted by an adult reviewer writing for an adult audience with the goal of establishing standards for quality children's books. Toy review videos, however, are not primarily produced in order to advise parents on how to select toys for their children or to assess product quality. Like children's television programmes, toy reviews are produced by adults with the intent of informing, entertaining and educating child audiences by addressing important constituents in the world in which the children are living. Often, children's preferences may differ radically from those of adults (Buckingham, 1995; Schor, 2004).

The production modes of the review, branded content and entertainment are very different from each other and, to a certain extent, even contradictory. If a review implies a third-party assessment of products, conducted with independence and integrity to minimize the influence of the product producer, reviewers should be bound by ethical principles. Branded content, or advertising, constructs its production mode the other way around. Its content is defined by and bound to the commercial interests of the producer and mediator. Even if messages are increasingly embedded and disguised (Hudson & Hudson, 2006), there is an expectation that the context in which the content was created should be revealed. Entertainment implies rather harmless content created for enjoyment, even if it has deeply rooted historic connotations of pacifying audiences and being demoralizing (Harrington, 2017). Toy review videos are mixing up these three categories when a commodity is presented on the playstage (reviewing) as part of a commercial purpose to persuade (branded content) as well as divert the viewer (entertainment).

In addition, in toy review videos the reviewers' production roles oscillate between the institutional, associated with professional production, and the vernacular, associated with lay, amateur or bottom-up production. It would be tempting to generalize that producers of toy reviews are just ordinary people. However, given their massive publicity, which is not just limited to millions of subscribers but also reaches audiences through other platforms such as Instagram and legacy media, and because of their incomes and commercial partnerships, it would be misleading to describe the producers as vernacular amateurs. Even if the quality of the content seems amateur-like, the new online professional amateurs are often trying to mimic amateur authenticity (Nicoll & Nansen, 2018), which Abidin (2017) calls 'calibrated amateurism' and Gaden and Dumitrica (2014) 'strategic authenticity'. By assessing the technical or aesthetic quality, it is thus impossible to assess on which institutional ground the producers are standing. This complexity related to the mash-up character of the genre, together with concealed production contexts, makes toy reviews difficult to position merely by watching the content.

Furthermore, as for their creatorship, it has to be asked whose participatory culture the toy reviews are advancing. The (adult) video producers are promotional intermediaries doing marketing for the brands they are reviewing; at the same time, these intermediaries exploit the (child) audiences' views in order to generate income. In this constellation, the value of the toys is not highlighted by elucidating and explaining it, but the value lies in the co-consuming moment of watching toys in action on the playstage on screen. To convince parents of the good intentions behind the video production, or of the benefits of watching the content, the videos largely deploy some rhetorical strategies primarily targeting adults (parents), attempting to highlight the usefulness of the videos. For example, by highlighting the educative assets of a video that help children to learn colours, numbers or how-to's (how to make something by yourself), educators may be more willing to let children watch these types of videos. Or, besides 'reviewing' the toys, the toy review videos allege to narrate plays with the help of the toys and thus aim at nurturing imagination and fantasy. These parent-convincing strategies are part of strategies counteracting the pure commercialism assumptions and kidbait intentions of the videos, trying to negotiate between more useful purposes and purposes typically seen as less useful, such as the production mode of branded content (exposure to commercial content) and entertainment (diversion and enjoyment).

There is thus no denying that the online toy review business can be financially lucrative. The blurred lines between styles and modes of expression are, however, far less problematic than if production modes—in the case of toy reviews, the disinterested or democratic, and the interest-invested or commercial—are blurred (see Einstein, 2016). In vernacular online cultures, in which communicators are forced to seek solutions for making profit by themselves and not leave it to an employer or commissioner, these lines have become increasingly harder to maintain. Nevertheless, the fact that the word review is borrowed from a disinterested intellectual sphere and used for influencing and marketing purposes strongly undermines the original meaning of reviewing as a critical and independent examination, assessment and evaluation of something. This conceptual transformation contributes to the emergence of the 'promotional review', which seems contradictory in the classical framework of reviewing, while at the same time being part of regular activities of the promotional cultures of social influencers (Davis, 2013; Kozinets et al., 2010).

One of scholars who pointed out these problems already more than a decade ago is Henry Jenkins (2007), who identified challenges in how immediate experiences are transferred into sets of rules and more general guidelines. According to him, there is a 'transparency problem' because children are typically not actively reflecting on their media experiences and cannot articulate what they learn from the participation. There is also an 'ethics challenge', as children cannot on their own develop the ethical norms needed to cope with the complex and diverse social environment online. Educators are thus particularly important in supporting digital cultural citizenship among young children. The hybridity of the content and the mash-up character of the genre, described above, makes it difficult even for adults to establish standards for assessing the quality of toy review video content. Sharpening the definitions of different types of content matters especially in toy reviews, which now seem to blur the lines between disinterested and commercially interested categories.

As branded prosumption, toy review videos are somehow an extreme type of vernacular reviewing. As seen in the examples described above, toy review channels use reviewing as a strategy to expose their audiences to toys and other playful consumer products, often embedded in other modes of play and entertainment, making the toyetic circus into child-targeting reviewtainment (see Sect. 6.4 Reviewtainment: Reviews as Platformized Entertainment). Even if motivated by educational, narrative or dramaturgical factors, such intent is strongly intermingled with marketing and influencing, reinforcing popular brands. The lay, professional or (semi-) professional content producers more or less consciously become promotional intermediaries who are only voluntarily bound by any ethical rules of conduct concerning their sponsorship and production principles. It seems that more transparency is needed from the content creators to make clear in which contexts messages are produced, together with regulation that at the policy level forces vernacular producers in a more ethical and accountable direction. In addition, a more solid incorporation of commercialism and consumerism in discourses of media literacy is needed, not in the way cultural industries have traditionally been dismissed (see, e.g., Buckingham, 1995), which may reinforce misbelief and distrust among parents rather than help them further, but addressing the complexities of producer roles, genres and production contexts so that they can be better dissected and analysed in situated communication. Understandings of how vernacularized commercialism works may thus support families in resisting consumerism and transferring discouraged reactions into something more transformative.

## 6.4 Reviewtainment: Reviews as Platformized Entertainment

Entertaining and 'light' content has always been a rather difficult issue for the intellectual tradition of criticism. Popular forms have only gradually been included in the cultural canon of criticism and journalistic reviewing and legitimacy. Within the journalistic framework of reviewing, review-related forms of entertainment are easily categorized as lifestyle commentary, not as reviewing. Recent academic literature on entertainment has worked towards the denigration of the term and tried to show how entertainment can be valuable to its audiences (Vorderer & Klimmt, 2021; Cunningham & Craig, 2019; Harrington, 2017). Etymologically speaking, entertainment, especially in its German form *Unterhaltung*, entails the meaning of being maintenance—of a way of life, of identities, of a certain culture. The detours from everyday life return to the everyday life by enhancing the everyday experiences of people by allowing them to see things in another way.

Within the tradition of criticism and even journalistic reviewing, it has been an intellectual effort to distinguish good quality from bad. According to a common understanding, the review can ideally be aesthetically pleasing and enjoyable as a textual construct, similar to the artwork that it is covering. However, the boundary beyond the sublime pleasure towards entertainment has been strictly guarded. Entertainment has implied superfluousness, inferiority, ephemerality and other antipodes in terms of how critical intellectualism has typically been defined.

Online cultures typically offer a balance between serious and recreational forms of culture. In the postmodern cultural landscape, 'mashpedia cultures' and 'ever-expanding pastiche cultures' are typical of online communication, where almost anything can be put together through practices of digital production, and the lines between serious and entertainment culture, as well as democratic and commercial, and private and public, become blurred (Danesi, 2015, p. 269; Einstein, 2016). According to Danesi (2015, p. 272), people are 'increasingly more focused on video games, celebrities, sports events, and the like, without distinguishing them from philosophical, artistic, and other forms of culture'. A new mobility across taste hierarchies, the cultural omnivorousness (Peterson & Kern, 1996), does not entirely dissolve aesthetic or social hierarchies or diminish the fact that the added value of reviewing is to be found in the way that the reviewers reduce the cultural distance between the cultural consumer and the cultural object.

A lot of review material, particularly on YouTube, falls into the categories of entertainment, humour, comedy or parody, and reviews are no exception. Reviewers have adopted humour, irony, comedy, parody, satire and sarcasm as rhetorical devices to appeal to their audiences who are often seeking content to enjoy. Reviewers are comedians, and their review shows are imbued with postmodern irony, ambiguity and unseriousness, which detaches reviewing from the basic function of making statements about the worth of a cultural product. Rather than focusing on the product itself, the attention is on the presenter or a story, joke, prank, atmosphere or curiosity. Recreational reviews could perhaps more appropriately be called 'revues'—which, in fact, in some cases might be a productive misinterpretation of the original word 'revue', meaning a theatrical production consisting of brief, loosely connected, often satirical skits, songs and dances. As humouristic or satirical pieces with the purpose of providing an overview or an entertainingly packaged look at a cultural object, review entertainers use reviewing as a way of providing viewers with emotions and experiences rather than trying to persuade them by delivering an informed opinion. 'Revueing', instead of reviewing, means celebrating the joy of consumption.

Entertainment-oriented reviewing is typically a mixture of information transfer, personal reflection, evaluation and a show. The entertaining function can be described as reviewtainment or criticotainment, in the same fashion as the similar hybridized modes of communication and the portmanteau words infotainment (information and entertainment), edutainment (education and entertainment), and politicotainment (political communication and entertainment). These hybrid forms are aimed at providing both substantial information and diversion, regarding them as equally important.

Among user reviewers, in particular in the vernacular domain where the expression is multimodal and not confined to the written language as in user review sites supporting institutional amateurism, three major paths of reviewtainment can be identified: connoisseurial entertainment that is based on the central role of the reviewer as a person; service entertainment that is based on tests and experiments and can thus be called testing reviewtainment; and communication of different types disguised as reviewing, called covert review entertainment. Next, I will briefly describe these three categories.

### *Connoisseurial Reviewtainment*

An extensive volume of review entertainment in the professional vernacular domain is centred around review personalities who need more or less to know their field to be able to turn it into performed acts of diversion, which most typically manifests as a vlog monologue of jokes, gags or satirical comments in front of the camera. The content creators conducting connoisseurial entertainment are entertainers with a personal touch in the field they are covering: comedians, humorists, actors, wits, storytellers. The content they publish is infotainment (from information and entertainment) in the sense of being a mixture of mediating information and facts on cultural products while turning the act of storytelling into a personal performance. Connoisseurial entertainment adopts its basic form in vlogs where a 'talking head' is placed at the centre, delivering his or her reflections, ideas, analyses and experiences to followers. One entertainment-oriented genre, especially prolific on YouTube, is the format of review shows.

Examples of popular connoisseurial entertainment include channels such as The Nostalgia Critic, The Cinema Snob, Ozzy Man Reviews, PewDiePie, Angry Video Game Nerd and Gay Comic Geek. At the centre of these vernacular professionals' production that has found its home in the culture of YouTube typically stands a short-tempered, rageous reviewer figure who preferably delivers commentary on cultural products of low or 'worst' quality. For example, The Nostalgia Critic was one of the channels initiated by Doug Walker (b. 1981) together with his brother Rob Walker on YouTube, a sketch-driven series that started on YouTube with a review of *Transformers* in 2007, before moving to Walker's own site That Guy with the Glasses, and further to the online production company Channel Awesome that also sponsors other review-related channels such as Inked Reality for manga and comic reviews and Barfiesta for bar, club and night-spot reviews. The title character pokes fun at the stereotypical figure of a reviewer, appearing as a bitter and sarcastic reviewer who talks about films and television shows from his childhood in the 1980s and 1990s, usually with comically exaggerated rage. Doug Walker also plays another reviewer character who sprang out of The Nostalgia Critic, Chester A. Bum, on the channel Bum Reviews. The character of a worn out homeless man reviews recent popular releases and typically starts off his reviews, spoken in a squealing tone, by bursting out 'Oh my God! This is the greatest movie I've ever seen in my life!' Throughout the review, he questions many aspects of the film and ends with a verdict introduced with the phrase 'Seriously though'—for example, 'Seriously though, *Hellboy 2* was just plain silly', 'Seriously though, *Narnia* kicked ass!' or 'Seriously though, *The Incredible Hulk* was okay'.

Review spoofs are shows where the opinions of the actual person are hidden or clearly separated from the entertainment content. As a spin-off, though, The Nostalgia Critic generated the vlog series Real thoughts on Nostalgia Critic reviews, where the brothers Doug and Rob, who had also collaborated together on other vlogs, disclosed their actual thoughts on films that the Nostalgia Critic has reviewed. Doug Walker, a versatile reviewer who also contributes with real reviews to the technology and lifestyle site Xomba and has had a solo reviewer channel, Doug Reviews, thus creatively combines the lives of fictional reviewer characters with that of a real-life reviewer person.

In a similar fashion, Ozzy Man Reviews is the entertainment review brand of the Australian social media personality Ethan Marrell (b. 1986) who has published satirical commentary on YouTube and Facebook since 2014. As of the beginning of 2021, Ozzy Man had 4.7 million subscribers on YouTube and 11.3 million followers on Facebook. He also had about 1.7 million followers on Instagram. On his channel description page, he writes that he is reviewing 'wildlife, sport, WTF vids, game of thrones and the odd movie', 'bloody tellin' it straight', 'no bullshit'. Ozzy Man's reviewtainment is based on an intensive and rather aggressive commentary similar to sports commentators, a voice-over on top of a video clip. The commentator's remarks add comedic elements to the original events in the video.

Besides reviewing, for example, *Games of Thrones* episodes, Ozzy Man reviews have covered the royal British wedding in 2018, Oprah Winfrey's interview with the ex-member of the royal British family Meghan Markle, a Korean climbing competition, a Chilean drinking competition, Australian bushfires, a Danish hunting falcon on television, as well as a rat and pigeon's encounter in New York. Delivering his 'bloody thoughts' on trivial events on television underlines the banality of reviewing, while turning the very idea of commenting and reviewing into amusement by exaggeration.

Connoisseurial entertainment plays with fictionalized versions of a reviewer, even if it is occasionally hard to separate the figure from the real-life person with authentic experiences and views. This type of review entertainment draws on the connoisseurial tradition of a knowledgeable, culturally engaged person who can in his presentation—and, indeed, it is often a male person—draw on his vast competence within the field of coverage, yet develop the expression further into a semi-fictional project where the character occasionally transgresses the boundaries of reporting anchored in reality. In a way, reviews in the connoisseurial entertainment style are very postmodernist projects, as they deal with works that do exist, and are, indeed, watched by a real audience, but—in a Baudrillardian sense—develop discourses and tastes that do not unambiguously refer to the shared reality.

Connoisseurial reviewtainment finds its place at the core of vernacularity and vernacular creativity where users contest the institutional forces, namely the overtly serious tradition of legacy media criticism and journalistic reviewing, by creating a parallel universe, a review theatre. The references to institutional forms of reviewing testify to the deeply rooted image of the journalistic reviewer and critic as an admired and glamorous person with influence and intellectual resources but often poor life management and position in the societal hierarchy. Making something new out of this institutional imaginary means resistance and non-institutional power.

The creative re-configuration and stylistic transgression of the review genre relates to the—hardly new—new-literacy practices of poaching (Jenkins, 1992) where users re-make available cultural resources and semantic objects into something new, and re-mixing where 'a range of original materials are copied, cut, spliced, and edited' into something new (Conti, 2013; Lankshear & Knobel, 2011) as part of the vernacular creativity (Burgess, 2006) and mash-up culture (Shiga, 2007). Connoisseurial reviewtainment is partly reinforced and continued by some more general online practices of comedy commentary. For example, the channel The Film Theorists carouses with the idea of creating 'theories' of films through overtly careful analysis, making fun of critical analysis, and the channel CinemaSins focuses on the shortcomings of film releases in their 'Everything wrong with' videos mocking the very idea of critique. These opinionated genres and discourses, followed by audiences of millions, contribute to the reflective consumption of cultural products, although they find some indirect and inversive paths to the core of talking about culture. Especially connoisseurial reviewtainment is strikingly male-dominated. Nevertheless, in this respect it is worth mentioning that Lindsay Ellis (b. 1984) was discovered in a contest organized as a spin-off of The Nostalgia Critic's channel who wanted to find a female host to review female-targeted films and television programmes. Having won the competition under the nickname Dudette, Ellis became in 2008–2014 part of The Nostalgia Chick, sponsored by Channel Awesome, thereafter moving towards long-form video essays. While almost all popular review comedians are men, female reviewtainers are more often found in the field of testing reviewtainment, to be discussed next.

### *Testing Reviewtainment*

A great extent of user reviewing conducted in visual and audiovisual media provides reviewers with possibilities to show how the cultural products look and how they work. Video media typically requires some action, which makes it attractive for reviewers to perform procedures such as unboxing and try-outs of products, as well as tests and experiments. Indeed, many reviews are to a significant extent centred upon the product, showing the reviewer's reactions and first impressions while testing out the mascara, trying to eat something for the first time, or playfully testing products. As an overarching term for these types of reviews, I use 'testing entertainment'. Testing, which involves more or less critical examination, observation and evaluation of a product, occurs in service to the aspiring or real cultural consumer. Service journalism is a category of cultural journalism that addresses audiences as consumers, private persons and clients within a commercial-consumerist framework and is expected to provide these audiences with information, advice and help about the problems of everyday life (Eide, 2017; Eide & Knight, 1999).

Testing entertainment implies reviews based on reactions. As the reviewer deploys some sort of experimental method, testing entertainment comes somewhat close to what Blank (2007) labels procedural reviews. However, while procedural reviews form the counterpart for connoisseurial reviews that are personal reactions of someone with taste, they imply impersonation, or the dissolution of the subjective evaluation by building the evaluation process on a systematic, objectified and measurable method of assessment and rating. Testing entertainment most often does not have a systematic basis for evaluation. Reviews are based on procedures, but these procedures are more or less driven by the entertainment aims.

Being usable or designed for use is the very essence of reviews that are created to answer the question of a product's worth and whether it is something worth purchasing or consuming. Even connoisseurial reviews *experience* a cultural product, and it is thus impossible, or at least not preferable, to create a review without a real and authentic contact with the product, for example writing reviews of art exhibitions solely based on pictures and secondary-source information. A review thus requires exposure to a product through a human or non-human 'test' where its worth can be examined and contested. Review entertainment is utilizing this concept of authentic contact, to pursue the truth through a direct contact and a primary source. The reviewer puts himself or herself in the consumer's place, or adopts the position of the consumer, implying: I will test this product for you and be a substitute for you as a consumer, to find out how it really is. At the same time, the process of familiarizing oneself with the product moves into the foreground and becomes the key narrative or process that unfolds in the review.

While being in the service of the review audience, testing entertainment also has a powerful component of convincing the viewer of being useful to him or her. Review 'utilitainment' fits especially well into reviewing of consumer goods. Utilitainment—from utility and entertainment—is a term used in branded marketing to describe content that provides audiences with entertainment value and a consumer experience that is, above all, useful for them. Successful branded content offers a mix of brand messaging, entertainment and perceived utility—reviews that build the presentation, testing and even critical inquiry of a cultural product or service into a show that could be watched only because of its entertainment value.

In film studies, the concept of 'useful media' has come to refer to a tradition of films that are functional, educational or non-fictional, and somewhat residual in film history—educational and training films, industrials, newsreels, travelogues, home videos and so on. Acland and Wasson (2011, 2) point out that these films are characterized less by their artistic and entertainment aims than by their 'ability to transform unlikely spaces, convey ideas, convince individuals, and produce subjects in the service of public and private aims'. They refer to useful cinema as 'a body of films and technologies that perform tasks and serve as instruments in an ongoing struggle for aesthetic, social, and political capital' (ibid., 3). In this respect, the videos are assigned a political or strategic function. Combined with an entertainment function, as in reviews where the moment of showing counts as much as reasoning, the usefulness and entertainment aspects together make a combination that can be seen as powerfully persuasive.

Testing entertainment in reviewing is typically crystallized in reaction reviews. There is a vast and ever-growing number of different formats—that are, of course, constantly evolving—reflecting review testing entertainment, based on conventions in communicating within a certain genre such as beauty blogging and vlogging or ASMR (a specific genre of relaxation videos). In these formats, as in vlogging where a typical setup includes a person talking in front of the camera, the body of the reviewer is present in the performance, and the embodied performance plays a central role in increasing the pervasiveness of the content. However, even the products under review are physically present, embedded in their contexts of use as much as possible. The context of use can be artificial, such as in staged reaction videos, or authentic, showing how toys or gadgets work in practice.

In *review tests* and *try-outs*, the reviewer puts a product into practice by showing it in front of a camera, describing it and discovering its uses, conforming to the basic constituents of a review such as contextualization, classification, elucidation, interpretation, analysis and evaluation (Orlik, 2016). Reviewers may have access to products prior to their release and create 'sneak peeks' and 'first looks', where the review functions as a preview of a new material artefact available for purchase. Review audiences may not have been in contact with the products under review, or they have only seen them in marketing catalogues, which makes the exposure of the product valuable for them. The reviewer may also have tested a product, like a skincare product, for a longer time in different situations before doing the review.

*First impression reviews* typically occur in the reviewing of beauty products, technological gadgets such as cameras, mobile phones and accessories, video games and cars. In the domain of beauty, reviewers present new products from a certain brand or go through beauty boxes or collections including a number of products. The videos include a surprise moment: Is the product in question good or bad? How does it feel? and How does the reviewer deal with it? *Unboxing* includes a moment of suspension and follows a process of unmasking the product, providing the reviewer with recording time to unpack his or her own experiences and reflections related to consumption, which makes the reviewing process interesting and possibly amusing. Reviews may also have an educational as well as an informative dimension, like in *tutorials* where the reviewer delivers advice, tricks and hacks for interested audiences.

In the *show-and-tell format*, which is applied in different general video genres, the reviewer shows cultural products to the camera while simultaneously talking about them. Audiences are offered information, inspiration and a connection to possibly authentic consumption by the reviewer who often owns the cultural products presented in such review videos. *Play-throughs* are a specific format that originated from gaming communities, where the reviewer records his or her performance onscreen, occasionally commenting on the actions. One of the world's best-known and most subscribed gamer personalities, PewDiePie, Swedish Felix Kjellberg (b. 1989) who had 109 million subscribers on YouTube as of 2021, started in 2010 with the horror and action video games that he regarded as the most horrible. *Pretend plays*, common in toy reviews, are fabricated situations where toys are put into use by creating a play.

Besides different formats such as the abovementioned, service entertainment can be employed as the entire strategy of a video channel. One example of a channel strategy is the YouTube channel Best Ever Food Review Show, created by American, Vietnam-based filmmaker Will Sonbuchner (b. 1984), alias Sonny Side. Offering a food review show for 6.7 million subscribers on YouTube, his production crew of ten members are, in their own words, 'on a mission to hunt down and document the most unique cuisine around the world, encouraging empathy, understanding and appreciation of different cultures through their food'. Using an educational approach, the channel seeks to promote and foster intercultural dialogue through the performative act of testing exotic food. In accordance with reviewtainment, the digital performance around test action becomes a carrier of an expressive function that is enjoyable for its own sake.

### *Covert Review Entertainment*

Another variant of the review is content that is actually not aimed at delivering a judgement of a cultural product but, instead, at marketing and promoting it under the umbrella term 'review', or exposing other ideas than what lies in the focus of a review. Covert review entertainment deals with extended marketing of pseudo- or promotional intermediaries, who do not intend to set themselves as third-party mediators but align themselves with the purposes of primary production. Covert review entertainment may also have to do with recreational or hidden messages disguised in the aesthetics and form of the genre of review. Pseudo reviews may resemble authentic reviews but mock some aspect of a product using humour, becoming play or mock reviews that are part of the creation, dissemination and communal enjoyment of vernacularity (Blank, 2015; de Gregorio et al., 2021). In these types of messages, the review format is a Trojan horse, a camouflage technique, superfluous in terms of the mediated message, or an aesthetic exterior for content that does not socially fulfil the function of reviewing. Covert review entertainment implies imitation, or 'dressing something up with the appearance of authentic replication while it nevertheless functions as an acknowledged aesthetic substitute' (Blank, 2015, p. 287). These types of entertainment-driven reviews are different from sheer fake reviews on user review sites, which are maliciously generated to deliver fabricated opinions and experiences to achieve a biased outcome (see Sect. 7.4 Fake and Pseudo Reviews in Chap. 7).

Pretend reviews are intended to perform another task than reviewing. This applies, for example, for the category of underwear reviews, even if there are certainly reviews that are not intended to mediate covert messages. UNB Blog, a crowdfunded site run by volunteers, publishes video reviews of men's underwear on Vimeo, along with a website dedicated to reviewing and presenting boxer brief-trunks, briefs, jocks, thongs and swimwear. Although the reviewing is carefully conducted to the last detail by discussing the fit, sizing, fabric and style of the clothing, the focus lies in exposing the male body. In a sample of 1273 review videos on Vimeo (see Jaakkola, 2020), there were 56 (4 per cent) male underwear reviews. While sexually explicit material and pornography are prohibited on Vimeo, artistic and non-sexual nudity are allowed by the platform's guidelines (Vimeo, 2018b). According to the guidelines, depictions of sexuality or nudity should 'serve a clear creative, artistic, aesthetic, or narrative purpose' or be of a documentary nature (Vimeo, 2018a). It is thus likely that this erotic type of reviewing was invented to circumvent these rules. Even if the reviews probably do function as a source of information for the niched consumers interested in using these pieces of clothing, it is obvious that the reviews also serve other purposes. 'Reviewing' may thus serve as a narrative excuse to present toned, athletic male bodies, and the videos can be watched with erotic, ironic or humorous intentions, the opinion concerning the use value of the products remaining an irrelevant question. The exploitation of the review genre to use it as camouflaged soft-core pornography demonstrates the flexibility of the functionality of the genre, but also resonates with the long history of non-preferred subcultures being spread to the audience as hidden messages.

Blank (2015), in examining humorous reviews at the user review site Amazon, identifies a number of different products with faux customer reviews from 2014: the Bic 'Cristal for Her' ball pen, a writing utensil marketed exclusively to females, with 1924 fake reviews; the mountain Three Wolf Moon shirt, an epic artistic t-shirt portraying three wolves baying at a full moon, with 2774 reviews; and the Hutzler Banana Slicer, a plastic banana slicer 'written with incredibly specific and outlandish user instructions in a prose style seemingly tailored for imbeciles', which has yielded 4786 reviews. Writing mock or play reviews on silly products becomes a satisfactory tactic of contesting institutional forces. Therefore,

Blank (2015, p. 286) concludes that users 'have managed to carve out a vernacular niche within the institutional confines of Amazon', 'establishing a vibrant digital venue for performative discourse and play'. According to him, the performative frame of faux reviews is enticing individuals to congregate in Amazon's shared virtual space online in order to symbolically interact and ignite a fun and empowering counter-hegemonic discourse.

Finally, it is plausible that covert review entertainment would even include the category of fictitious or *faux* reviews, or review fiction—reviews on imaginary works. As far as the popular online review communities are concerned, this seems not yet to be an established vernacular practice, but the literary history knows examples that may be inspiring for future online content creators. In popular fiction literature, authors have used a metafictional technique called *pseudepigrapha* (from the Greek *pseudes*, false, and *epigraphe*, name or inscription) by writing reviews of books that do not exist. The Argentine author Jorge Luis Borges is known for his short story *An Examination of the Works of Herbert Quain* (1962), discussing and analysing four works of a fictional Irish author. The Polish science fiction author Stanislaw Lem's book *A Perfect Vacuum* (1971) includes reviews of different types for non-existent books; *Les Robinsonades* by Marcel Coscat, *Gigamesh* by Patrick Hannahan, *Odysseus of Ithaca* by Kuno Mlatje and *De Impossibilitate Vitae* by Cezar Kouska share in common that they simply do not exist. Lem also used the same idea in terms of reviews of non-fiction literature in his other books, originally published in magazines, such as *Provocation* (1984) and *One Human Minute* (1986). The genre of review provides an author a discursive cover for discussing a topic with the help of fictitious reviews, but this effort is guided by a creative or an artistic endeavour. As Jorge Luis Borges remarked in the prologue of *Fictions* (1962): 'It is a laborious madness and an impoverishing one, the madness of composing vast books—setting out in 500 pages an idea that can be perfectly related orally in five minutes. The better way to go about it is to pretend that those books already exist, and offer a summary, a commentary on them'. In this respect, the online reviewsphere, with its affordances for such micro-creativity, is a potential review fiction paradise, providing users with rich means of cultivating imaginary culture and intermediary imaginaries.

## References


Abidin, C. (2017). #Familygoals: Family influencers, calibrated amateurism, and justifying young digital labour. *Social Media + Society, 3*(2), 1–15.

Acland, C. R. & Wasson, H. (eds.) (2011). *Useful cinema*. Duke University Press.

Airoldi, M., Beraldo, D., & Gandini, A. (2016). Follow the algorithm: An exploratory investigation of music on YouTube. *Poetics, 57*, 1–13.

Alexanderson, K. (2019). *Barnen och internet 2019*. [Children and the internet 2019.]. The Internet Foundation in Sweden (IIS).

Bainbridge, J. (2017). From toyetic to toyesis: The cultural value of merchandising. In S. Harrington (Ed.), *Entertainment values: How do we assess entertainment and why does it matter?* (pp. 23–39). Palgrave Macmillan.

Baym, N. K. (2015). Connect with your audience! The relational labor of connection. *The Communication Review, 18*(1), 14–22. https://doi.org/10.1080/10714421.2015.996401

Blank, G. (2007). *Critics, ratings, and society: The sociology of reviews*. Rowman & Littlefield Publishers.

Blank, T. J. (2015). Faux your entertainment: Amazon.com product reviews as a locus of digital performance. *The Journal of American Folklore, 128*(509), 286–297. https://www.jstor.org/stable/10.5406/jamerfolk.128.509.0286

Bloom, P. (2013, January 26). Review of the Canon 1DC. *Vimeo*. https://vimeo.com/58263312

Bloom, P. (2014, July 3). The no longer evolving review of the Sony A7S now with extreme low light video. *Philip Bloom*. http://philipbloom.net/blog/a7s/

Blum-Ross, A., & Livingstone, S. (2017). 'Sharenting', parent blogging, and the boundaries of the digital self. *Popular Communication, 2*, 110–125.

Bookishstarlight. (2017, March 4). Top definition: Bookstagram. *Urban Dictionary*. https://www.urbandictionary.com/author.php?author=bookishstarlight

Bruns, A. (2008). *Blogs, Wikipedia, Second Life and beyond*. Peter Lang.

Buckingham, D. (1995). The commercialisation of childhood? The place of the market in children's media culture. *Changing English, 2*, 17–40.

Buckingham, D. (2007). Selling childhood? Children and consumer culture. *Journal of Children and Media, 1*, 15–24.

Burgess, J. (2006). Hearing ordinary voices: Cultural studies, vernacular creativity and digital storytelling. *Continuum: Journal of Media & Cultural Studies, 20*(2), 201–214. https://doi.org/10.1080/10304310600641737

Burroughs, B. (2017). YouTube kids: The app economy and mobile parenting. *Social Media + Society, 2*, 1–8.

Conti, O. (2013). Disciplining the vernacular: Fair use, YouTube, and remixer agency. *M/C Journal, 16*(4) http://www.journal.media-culture.org.au/index.php/mcjournal/article/view/685

Cramer, E. H., & Castle, M. E. (Eds.). (1994). *Fostering the love of reading: The affective domain in reading education*. International Reading Association.

Cunningham, S., & Craig, D. (Eds.). (2019). *Social media entertainment: The new intersection of Hollywood and Silicon Valley*. New York University Press.

Danesi, M. (2015). *Popular culture: Introductory perspectives* (3rd ed.). Rowman & Littlefield.

Davis, A. (2013). *Promotional cultures: The rise and spread of advertising, public relations, marketing and branding*. Polity Press.

de Gregorio, F., Fox, A. K., & Yoon, H. J. (2021). Pseudo-reviews: Conceptualization and consumer effects of a new online phenomenon. *Computers in Human Behavior, 114*.

Dobson, A. S., Robards, R., & Carah, N. (2018). *Digital intimate publics and social media*. Palgrave Macmillan.

Driscoll, B. (2019). Book blogs as tastemakers. *Participations: Journal of Audience and Reception Studies, 16*(1), 280–305.

Duffy, B. E. (2016). The romance of work: Gender and aspirational labour in the digital culture industries. *International Journal of Cultural Studies, 19*(4), 441–457. https://doi.org/10.1177/1367877915572186

Duffy, B. E. (2017). *(Not) getting paid to do what you love: Gender, social media, and aspirational work*. Yale University Press.

Edensor, T., Leslie, D., Millington, S., & Rantisi, N. (Eds.). (2009). *Spaces of vernacular creativity: Rethinking the cultural economy*. Routledge.

Eide, M. (2017). The culture of service journalism. In N. N. Kristensen & K. Riegert (Eds.), *Cultural journalism in the Nordic countries* (pp. 195–204). Gothenburg.

Eide, M., & Knight, G. (1999). Public/private service: Service journalism and the problems of everyday life. *European Journal of Communication, 14*(4), 525–547. https://doi.org/10.1177/0267323199014004004

Einstein, M. (2016). *Black ops advertising: Native ads, content marketing, and the covert world of the digital sell*. OR Books.

Ferris, I. (2009). Book-love and the remaking of literary culture in the Romantic periodical. In I. Ferris & P. Keen (Eds.), *Bookish histories: Palgrave studies in the enlightenment Romanticism and cultures of print* (pp. 111–125). Palgrave Macmillan.

Gaden, G., & Dumitrica, D. (2014). The 'real deal': Strategic authenticity, politics and social media. *First Monday, 20*(1) https://doi.org/10.5210/fm.v20i1.4985

Geff, G. (2012). *Venture labor: Work and the burden of risk in innovative industries*. The MIT Press.

Gibbs, M., Meese, J., Arnold, M., Nansen, B., & Carter, M. (2015). #Funeral and Instagram: Death, social media, and platform vernacular. *Information, Communication & Society, 18*(3), 255–268.

Goffman, E. (1959). *The presentation of self in everyday life*. Doubleday.

Harrington, S. (Ed.). (2017). *Entertainment values: How do we assess entertainment and why does it matter?* Palgrave Macmillan.

Hjarvard, S. (2004). From bricks to bytes: The mediatization of a global toy industry. In I. Bjondeberg & P. Colding (Eds.), *European culture and the media* (pp. 43–63). Intellect.

Holland, D., Lachicotte, W. S., Jr., Skinner, D., & Cain, C. (2001). *Identity and agency in cultural worlds*. Harvard University Press.

Holzenberg, E. J. (2019). Book collecting. In S. Eliot & J. Rose (Eds.), *A companion to the history of the book* (2nd ed., pp. 815–826). Wiley & Sons.

Hudson, S., & Hudson, D. (2006). Branded entertainment: A new advertising technique or product placement in disguise? *Journal of Marketing Management, 22*(5–6), 489–504.

Hunter, A. (2016). Monetizing the mommy: Mommy blogs and the audience community. *Information, Communication & Society, 9*, 1306–1320.

Ito, M. (2010). The rewards of non-commercial production: Distinctions and status in the anime music video scene. *First Monday, 15*(5).

Jaakkola, M. (2015). *The contested autonomy of arts and journalism: Change and continuity of the dual professionalism of cultural journalism. Doctoral dissertation*. Tampere University Press.

Jaakkola, M. (2018). Journalistic style and writing. In J. Nussbaum (Ed.), *Oxford Encyclopedia of Journalism Studies*. Oxford University Press.

Jaakkola, M. (2020). Oman lukukokemuksensa visualisoijat: käyttäjälähtöiset kirjallisuusarvostelut Instagramissa. [Visualizers of their own reading experience: The user-generated literature reviews on Instagram.]. *Kulttuurintutkimus, 36*(3–4), 31–44.

Jenkins, H. (1992). *Textual poachers*. Routledge.

Jenkins, H. (2007). Confronting the challenges of participatory culture: Media education for the 21st century (part one). *Nordic Journal of Digital Literacy, 2*, 23–33.

Johansen, S. L. (2018). Everyday media play: Children's playful media practices. *Conjunctions, 4*(1), 1–10.

Karlsten, E. (2017, March 7). Här är svenskarna som bygger egna barn-tv-imperium – på Youtube. [Here are the Swedes who are building up their own kid tv imperium – on YouTube.] *Breakit*. https://www.breakit.se/artikel/6781/de-drar-in-miljoner-pa-hemmagjorda-barnfilmer-pa-youtube

Kim, J. (2012). The institutionalization of YouTube: From user-generated content to professionally generated content. *Media, Culture & Society, 34*(1), 53–67.

Kolehmainen, M., & Mäkinen, K. (2021). Affective labour of creating atmospheres. *European Journal of Cultural Studies, 24*(2), 448–463.

Kozinets, R. V., de Valck, K., Wojnicki, A. C., & Wilner, S. J. S. (2010). Networked narratives: Understanding word-of-mouth marketing in online communities. *Journal of Marketing, 74*(2), 71–89.

Lange, P. G. (2014). *Kids on YouTube: Technical identities and digital literacies.* Left Coast Press.

Lankshear, C., & Knobel, M. (2011). *New literacies: Everyday practices and social learning* (3rd. ed.). Open University Press.

Lauzen, M. M. (2018a). *The celluloid ceiling: Behind-the-scenes employment of women on the top 100, 250, and 500 films of 2017.* Center for the Study of Women in Television and Film. https://womenintvfilm.sdsu.edu/wp-content/uploads/2018/01/2017_Celluloid_Ceiling_Report.pdf

Lauzen, M. M. (2018b). *Thumbs down 2018: Film critics and gender, and how it matters.* Center for the Study of Women in Television and Film. https://womenintvfilm.sdsu.edu/wp-content/uploads/2018/07/2018_Thumbs_Down_Report.pdf

Layne, S. L. (Ed.). (2009). *Igniting a passion for reading: Successful strategies for building lifetime readers.* Stenhouse Publishers.

Leadbeater, C., & Miller, P. (2004). *The pro-am revolution: How enthusiasts are changing our society and economy.* Demos.

Leaver, T., Highfield, T., & Abidin, C. (2020). *Instagram: Visual social media cultures.* Wiley.

Livingstone, S. (2013). Online risk, harm and vulnerability: Reflections on the evidence base for child internet safety policy. *ZER: Journal of Communication Studies, 18*, 13–28.

Livingstone, S., Mascheroni, G., & Staksrud, E. (2018). European research on children's internet use: Assessing the past and anticipating the future. *New Media & Society, 20*, 1103–1122.

López, A. (2014). *Greening media education: Bridging media literacy with green cultural citizenship.* Peter Lang.

Luckman, S. (2015). Women's micro-entrepreneurial homeworking: A 'magical solution' to the work–life relationship? *Australian Feminist Studies, 30*(84), 146–160.

Nakamura, L. (2015). The unwanted labour of social media: Women of colour call out culture as venture community management. *New Formations, 86*, 106–112.

Naseem, F. (2018, May 17). Bookstagram for beginners! *The guy with the book.* http://theguywiththebook.com/2018/05/17/bookstagram-for-beginners

Nicoll, B., & Nansen, B. (2018). Mimetic production in YouTube toy unboxing videos. *Social Media + Society, 3*, 1–12.

Olave, M. A. T. (2020). Book love: A cultural sociological interpretation of the attachment to books. *Poetics, 38*(1). First published online 27 February 2020.

Orlik, P. B. (2016). *Media criticism in a digital age: Professional and consumer considerations.* Taylor & Francis.

Oswell, D. (2013). *The agency of children: From family to global rights.* Cambridge University Press.

Peterson, R. A., & Kern, R. (1996). Changing highbrow taste: From snob to omnivore. *American Sociological Review, 61*(5), 900–907. https://doi.org/10.2307/2096460

Pocket.watch. (2018, February 13). Major apparel and toy companies jump on board Pocket.watch media brand. Press Release. https://pocket.watch/press/press-release-february-13-2018

Quora. (2018). How is Vimeo similar to and different from YouTube? https://www.quora.com/How-is-Vimeo-similar-to-and-different-from-YouTube

Robehmet, N., & Berg, M. (2018, December 3). Highest-paid YouTube stars 2018: Markiplier, Jake Paul, PewDiePie and more. *Forbes*. https://www.forbes.com/sites/natalierobehmed/2018/12/03/highest-paid-youtube-stars-2018-markiplier-jake-paul-pewdiepie-and-more/#6e3606ba909a

Rodger, N. (2019). From bookshelf porn and shelfies to #bookfacefriday: How readers use Pinterest to promote their bookishness. *Participations, 16*(1), 473–495.

Ryan's World. (2019, October 24). No more Ryan ToysReview... *YouTube*. https://www.youtube.com/watch?v=VObZz6LquuY&feature=emb_imp_woyt

Sandaroo Kids. (2012, December 25). Disney Frank combine die cast REVIEW new in BOX McQueen & Mater tractor tippin' diecast kids toys. https://www.youtube.com/watch?v=CdWfq2YOJdo

Schneider, N. (2003). *Still life: Still life painting in the early modern period*. Taschen.

Schor, J. B. (2004). *Born to buy: The commercialized child and the new consumer culture*. Scribner.

Seiter, E. (2005). *The internet playground: Children's access, entertainment, and miseducation*. Peter Lang.

Shiga, J. (2007). Copy-and-persist: The logic of mash-up culture. *Critical Studies in Media Communication, 24*(2), 93–114. https://doi.org/10.1080/07393180701262685

Smith, A. & Anderson, M. (2018). Social media use in 2018. Pew Research Center, March 1, 2018. Available at http://www.pewinternet.org/2018/03/01/social-media-use-in-2018/

Statista. (2019). Most popular children-themed YouTube channels as of January 2019, ranked by number of subscribers (in millions). https://www.statista.com/statistics/785626/most-popular-youtube-children-channels-ranked-by-subscribers/

Statista. (2021). *Estimated annual earnings of selected YouTube channel creators as of June 2020 (in million U.S. dollars)*. https://www.statista.com/statistics/373772/youtubers-monetization-earnings-celebrity/

Steiner, A. (2008). Private criticism in the public sphere Personal writing on literature in readers' reviews on Amazon. *Participations: Journal of Audience and Reception Studies, 5*(2).

Steiner, A. (2010). Personal readings and public texts: Book blogs and online writing about literature. *Culture Unbound: Journal of Current Cultural Research, 2*(2), 471–494.

Strangelove, M. (2010). *Watching YouTube: Extraordinary videos by ordinary people*. University of Toronto Press.

Thrift, N. (2000). Still life in nearly present time: The object of nature. *Body & Society, 6*(3–4), 34–57. https://doi.org/10.1177/1357034X00006003003

UN, the Committee on the Rights of the Child. (2021). *General comment on children's rights in relation to the digital environment*. https://www.ohchr.org/EN/HRBodies/CRC/Pages/GCChildrensRightsRelationDigitalEnvironment.aspx

UN, United Nations. (2015). *Transforming our world: The 2030 Agenda for Sustainable Development*. https://sdgs.un.org/2030agenda

VanDeGraph. (2016, September 15). Why toy videos get hundreds of millions of views on YouTube explained. *Medium*.

Ville, V.-I., de la Garnier, P., & Brougère, G. (Eds.). (2021). *Cultural and creative industries of childhood and youth: An interdisciplinary exploration of new frontiers*. Peter Lang.

Vimeo. (2018a). How does Vimeo determine the difference between pornography and artistic or non-sexual nudity? Legal FAQs. https://help.vimeo.com/hc/en-us/articles/224978088-How-does-Vimeo-determine-the-difference-between-pornography-and-artistic-or-non-sexual-nudity-

Vimeo. (2018b). *Vimeo guidelines*. https://vimeo.com/help/guidelines

von Bonsdorff, P. (2018). Children's aesthetic agency: The pleasures and power of imagination. In J. Delafield-Butt, A.-W. Dunlop, & C. Trevarthen (Eds.), *The child's curriculum: Working with the natural values of young children* (pp. 126–138). Oxford University Press.

Vorderer, P., & Klimmt, C. (Eds.). (2021). *The Oxford handbook of entertainment theory*. Oxford University Press.

Watson, R. (2019). Some non-textual uses of books. In S. Eliot & J. Rose (Eds.), *A companion to the history of the book* (2nd ed., pp. 645–660). Wiley & Sons.

Wiedmann, K. P., Hennings, N., & Langner, S. (2010). Spreading the word of fashion: Identifying social influencers in fashion marketing. *Journal of Global Fashion Marketing, 1*(3), 142–153.

Wisner, W. (2016). YouTube surprise toy videos are basically toddler crack. *Scary Mommy*. https://www.scarymommy.com/youtube-surprise-toy-reviews-toddler-crack/. Jaakkola, M. (2020). Useful creativity: Vernacular reviewing on the video-sharing platform Vimeo. *Culture Unbound, 12*(2): 1–20.

Working with Lemons. (2016, August 12). Elena of Avalor – toy review. https://www.youtube.com/watch?v=Xzb_VP4xndk

Working with Lemons. (2017, December 19). Your favorite Star Wars Sith Lord and Jedi Master Centerpiece unboxing and review. https://www.youtube.com/watch?v=AQqjoTDmS5Y

Working with Lemons. (2018, October 20). Squirrel girl from Marvel Rising: Secret warriors | toy review. https://www.youtube.com/watch?v=WSIuLfA6CP8

WordStream (2017). 33 mind-boggling Instagram stats & facts for 2018. Available at https://www.wordstream.com/blog/ws/2017/04/20/instagram-statistics

CHAPTER 7

# Characteristics of Vernacular Reviewing

Discussing post-professional reviewing as intermediation in the context of post-institutional cultural production, my focus in this book has been on vernacular reviewing, which I localize as forms of reviewing outside the institutional practices related to maintaining professionalism (the critics and journalistic reviewers, Sect. 4.1 From Criticism to Reviewing) and amateurism (amateur and customer reviewers on specific user review sites, Sect. 4.2 User Reviewing). These reviewers are mostly organized on the social web that is lacking the hierarchical organizational characteristic of institutional professionalism. Reviewing, organized within vernacular online lifestyle communities, adopts different forms and shows great diversity, but there are some dimensions in common that can be identified in these non-professional forms of reviewing.

As reflected in the concepts of cultural intermediation and intramediation (Chap. 3 Reviewing as Post-Institutional Cultural Production), reviewing is a value-creation process. However, 'value' or 'quality' are neither one-directional concepts nor do they imply linear progress; rather, negotiation of what counts as a value is at the heart of social communities of all reviewers (see also Bolin, 2019). There are different values that are being created, and they mean different things to individuals and groups of people. Value creation also produces values of different types that are at different stages of development. Wenger-Trayner and Wenger-Trayner (2020) distinguish between immediate, potential, applied, realized, enabling, strategic, orienting and transformative value in social processes.


M. Jaakkola, *Reviewing Culture Online*,
https://doi.org/10.1007/978-3-030-84848-4_7

The value(s) created through the content production of reviewing can be identified, above all, as aesthetic-artistic, economic, individual and social. These are important dimensions especially for constructing the social phenomenon of non-professional reviewing. While the focus of institutional professional reviewing has typically strictly been on aesthetic value creation—even if the other values have equally been present—non-professional forms of reviewing make the importance of the other value-creation processes more prevalent. When looking at the dimensions of aesthetic-artistic, economic, individual and social value creation separately we can make the following remarks about the fundamental conditions of vernacular and amateur reviewing:

*Aesthetic-artistic value creation*: Institutional forms of reviewing are directed towards defining art—distinguishing it from non-art—and recognizing the quality of the new pieces of art or culture that are recognized as art. Kjørup (in Bille & Olsen, 2018, p. 231) distinguishes between four conceptions of artistic quality: objective, instrumental, psychological and sociological understanding. Artistic quality can thus be regarded as inherent qualities possessed by art (objective understanding), the aesthetic experience that the work elicits (instrumental understanding), effects of art on people who are experiencing it (psychological understanding), and actions by groups of people who are experiencing art and who feel that the particular form of art they are experiencing is 'for them' (sociological understanding). Reviews, created by people who are particularly sensitive towards the question of artistic-aesthetic quality, attempt to identify these qualities by analysing works in public. The new knowledge that is produced is, above all, descriptive, historically situated and normative, helping audiences and institutions locate the new works in existing contexts of arts.

*Economic value creation*: The production of reviews and reviewer identities is largely dependent on the platform logics and their way of supporting the gaining of profit. While amateur reviewers on user review sites are typically directed by symbolic profits, the social web encourages and urges individuals to develop revenue, to be able to develop their activities and make them more sustainable. Post-Professional reviewers are thus far more embedded in the commercial structures of the review market than their institutional professional counterparts who are essentially lifted from the direct economic circulation, being able to develop a disinterested intermediary identity.

*Individual value creation*: Reviewing fulfils some fundamental functions for individuals. Being engaged in processes of reviewing provides individuals with the satisfaction of acquiring symbolic capital and raising one's status in the eyes of others by acquiring attributes that are highly valued. As aspirational work, it also involves the promise of providing individuals with new career possibilities, which does not mean that reviewing may be their first career choice but rather a stepping stone into the cultural industries. For professional or professionalizing actors, reviewing provides a direct economic asset by abolishing the need to pay for a performance or a product. For amateurs, reviewing offers the possibility to become more structured in their leisure time, to make use of their competences in a way that benefits others and to gain recognition that they would otherwise not receive in their private cultural engagement. As identity work, reflexive consumption and maintenance of a lifestyle, reviewing is an individualist project that supports the self-development of an individual. Lifestyle communities are resources for individuals to construct their everyday.

*Social value creation*: Non-professional forms of reviewing provide an alternative for professional reviewing in their measurability and volume; big data based on reviewers' assessments may deliver insights into consumer behaviour and cultural trends, and the amateur's insights on cultural products, which traditionally have not received a lot of space in the professional institutional framework of reviewing, become visible and tangible. Sharing one's own ideas and thoughts based on the reception of cultural products creates meaning, shared understanding and social coherence between individuals who, then, get emotionally connected and engaged.

Along with the established institutional professional reviewing, vernacular and amateur reviewing are increasingly influential practices that need to be considered as forms of cultural intermediation, yet as distinctive practices in their own right in their respective fields of institutional amateurism and vernacular professionalism and amateurism. A major distinction between institutional professional reviewing and non-professional forms of reviewing (see Chap. 5 Post-Professional Reviewers) is the mechanics of value creation. The main aim of professional institutional reviewing is to generate something of value towards making a difference in the historico-aesthetic value of a new piece of art. This is seen in the reviewer's intention to act as cultural intermediary in the cultural value chain by negotiating between poles of primary production and reception, to arrive at an evaluation outcome. Non-professional, user-generated forms of reviewing, in contrast, aim at taking something of value and doing something with it. This can be seen in processes of cultural intramediation where user reviewers generate value as part of their local community and by relating new pieces of art to their situated experiences and practices of reception rather than placing themselves in historico-aesthetic traditions. However, many reviewers, especially in the vernacular and, in particular, in the vernacular professional domain, fluctuate between positionings, and distinctions are not clear-cut in practice. Distinguishing between grades of professionalism helps to place different reviewers on the map, and recognizing the fact that there are a number of different positionings in the intermediary chain of cultural mediation delivers us a more specific idea of what kind of reviewing is addressed.

The local, situated reception knowledge, which results in everyday expertise possessed by 'experts by experience' or 'everyday amateur experts', is generated in processes of value creation in lifestyle communities, as part of their ongoing reflective work. To capture the character of the reviewing that is enacted in these communities it is appropriate to ask what their dominant features are. As I have so far been largely underlining the differences between the various categories of reviewers, it is worth asking what kind of similar features are shared by vernacular and amateur forms of reviewing. As an answer to this, it can be noted that reviewing is a performative act that can be observed as shared value creation that I call *co-consumption*, affective individualized lifestyle work that can be subsumed as *me-viewing*, and transformative creativity that I have termed *re-creational work*. A prevalent feature of user reviewing is its ethical instability, which makes *fake and pseudo reviews* a common but unpleasant offshoot of user reviewing. I will go through these three features of non-professional review production next, to bring together some important dimensions that in general characterize vernacular and amateur reviewing.

## 7.1 Co-consumption

The prosumptive work of value creation conducted by vernacular and amateur reviewers on online platforms is communal, connective and collectivist in its character. User reviewers are acting as part of an imagined community, sharing central ideas and following each other's practices. Whether a form of institutional amateur, professional vernacular or amateur vernacular reviewing (Chap. 5 Post-Professional Reviewers), content is produced in proximity with the audience that consumes the reviews and, potentially, the cultural products under review. Creative vernacular processes have frequently been portrayed in terms of their communal character, as reflected in the wider frameworks of participatory culture, vernacular creativity and cultural engagement discussed earlier. Across different disciplines, users' engagement in media processes has further been described as both a process and a method to support collaborative processes, in the form of co-creation (Potts et al., 2008; Cova & Dalli, 2018; Ramaswamy & Ozcan, 2014), collective creativity (Weijo et al., 2018) and co-production (Kolehmainen & Mäkinen, 2021; Brandsen et al., 2018). These processes are depicted to include intrinsic processes of co-construction, which refers to the contextualization of the services in the user's own life, where value may be influenced by current and past experiences of the service or associated services, and co-experience, the user experience created together by individuals in virtual interaction (Strokosch & Osborne, 2020). Social phenomena of sharing products and experiences online have also been addressed as collaborative consumption, the peer-to-peer-based activity of obtaining, giving or sharing access to goods and services, coordinated through community-based online services as part of the principles of a sharing economy (Botsman & Rogers, 2010; Hamari et al., 2015). The idea of developing reflexivity and shared practices based upon a shared mission—or a certain lifestyle related to following a certain form and type of culture—lies at the core of the participatory nature of reviewing cultures, which has previously been conceptualized as communities of practice (Wenger, 1998) and, as a more recent extension of these, to make them more connected to social value creation, social learning spaces (Wenger-Trayner & Wenger-Trayner, 2020). Here, the fundamental idea is that the common consumption of cultural goods can become a shared experience when carried out on an online platform. *Co-consumption* is the shared undertaking in which amateurs and professionals beyond institutional professional reviewing are involved.

As co-consumption is not based on a shared professional framework supported by a hierarchically managed organizational structure and pertinent professional infrastructures, vernacular and amateur co-consumption presupposes local cultures of knowledge. The production of cultural consumer expertise unfolds in the community and platform-specific practices of multimodal metadiscourse (discourse on the discursively constructed objects, i.e. existing discourses). When comparing professional institutional and non-professional forms of reviewing, there is a difference that Bernstein (1999) calls a difference between vertical and horizontal discourses of knowledge and respective knowledge structures. According to him, horizontal discourses are local, segmentally organized, context-specific and dependent on maximizing encounters with persons and habitats. Vertical discourses take the form of a coherent, explicit, systematically principled, hierarchically oriented structure, with specialized criteria for the production and circulation of texts and specialized language conventions, as in sciences and even journalism. He sees them as oppositional, the former creating symbolic and the latter practical mastery. In this respect, the formalization of amateur media, or the professionalization of amateur reviewing, implies verticalization of knowledge, which is typically accompanied by a strengthened intermediary position, as the reviewer is seeking a more independent positioning in discourse.

User-generated processes are typically idealized and romanticized as processes of sharing and mutual support, which may be a true experience by the reviewers involved. Nevertheless, although they address the same material and epistemic objects that cultural products constitute, such as books or music albums, or any consumer goods, reviewing communities do not necessarily develop intellectual socialization or pursue any shared knowledge-creating inquiry. They do not necessarily have a shared epistemic paradigm, and do not attempt to gain a consensus on new insights concerning the products, or develop ideas based on each other's texts. It seems that the shared and common feature is the experiential dimension, the feeling of being part of a reviewing community, and getting inspiration and support for personal development. Amateur reviewing communities thus remain segmental in their organization of knowledge. However, their value lies in the social and individual management and, eventually, empowerment, of cultural consumers. The status of the reviews as separate texts is not as distinct and articulated as in professional institutional reviewing. Although vernacular reviews are stand-alone textual products, they can be more aptly seen as part of longer processes, as unfinished products (Bruns, 2013) and pieces of continuing learning and reflexive maintenance processes internal to fan communities (Ito, 2010)—processes of co-consumption.

What follows from the above is that co-consumption does not necessarily need to be connected to the question of quality of the products that are being reviewed. As highlighted earlier, answering the question of a product's worth—determining whether the product is good or bad—seems not to be the ultimate objective of the vernacular or amateur review. The notion of articulating a quality assessment of a product is based on the idea of reviewing as a meaning making and transfer process. More than a societal mission, co-consumption, reviewing, especially in its vernacular forms, is more a set of individually oriented practices of cultural citizenship for the cultivation of critical cultural literacy or competence, enhanced familiarity with the cultural form in question. Value resides in the actions and interactions that make possible or support lifestyle work as me-viewing and re-creational work, the two concepts to be discussed next.

## 7.2 Me-viewing

User reviewers' work is strongly linked to the individualized, self-centred, autobiographical work carried out in the context of their own reception process and history by bloggers and other social media users (Chia, 2012), and thus connects to the technologies of the networked self (Papacharissi, 2013; Bakardjieva & Gaden, 2012), such as the projects of self-branding (Scolere et al., 2018) and micro-celebrity or online fame (Djafarova & Trofimenko, 2018). Reviewing also strongly underordinates itself to digital intimate publics (Dobson et al., 2018), with characteristics of production cultures such as affective labour (Gregg, 2009) and affinity spaces (Gee, 2004; Hayes & Gee, 2010). Felski (2020) argues that the 'captivated audiences' make use of cultural products of both high arts and popular culture, above all, through identification, attunement and interpretation, which are all emotional and self-centred processes deviant from the critical aloofness that is associated with criticism (Felski, 2015).

I thus want to address reviewing performed by non-professional reviewers as a specific form of reviewing that dismisses some central dimensions of cultural intermediation and does more justice to intramediational processes, me-reviewing. Instead of looking back at production related to a cultural product—re-viewing its production trajectory and history—user reviews are more involved in looking at themselves, their own experiences and lifeworlds. Me-viewing is performative and affective lifestyle work, typically shared with like-minded users within the cycles of cultural intramediation. It is more prominent in amateurs' activities, as professionalization essentially means phasing out individual and seemingly contingent treats, systematizing the methods of communication. However, even vernacular professionals work on emotions by drawing on themselves as persons and personalities, which is an integral part of self-celebrification practices. Instead of viewing the work and its diverse contexts, the focus is more often on the project of the self, essential for sustaining the reviewership. Me-viewing manifests in three major dimensions in reviewers' labour that I have labelled the love of culture, self-journaling and life staging. Being engaged as a reviewer, or a me-viewer, has a self-observing, self-developmental and self-therapeutic function.

*The love of culture* lies at the heart of being an *amateur*, a lover of a certain form of culture. As shown in the case studies presented in previous chapters, the reviewer attributes are to a large extent related to intense and deep feelings of affection, passion, satisfaction, joy, happiness and pleasure. The presentation and performance of a loving and caring self offers individuals an output channel for individual experiences and feelings. At the same time these are raw material for a reviewer who intends to record, structure and analyse his or her reading, watching or listening experience, or more generally a sensory experience that is in the foreground of the review discourse. Manifesting one's private and intimate relationship with culture of a certain form also functions as self-authoring of the reviewership, supporting the making of a narrative of the reviewing self to oneself and others.

*Self-journalling* is a common practice known from early blogs, social bookshelves or book, music or film cataloguing services where the material-symbolic repository of cultural goods collected and owned by an individual becomes visible to others. Tracking what one has been reading, listening to or following lets the personal history become accumulated, delivering a more coherent narrative of one's cultural learning path and profile than what would perhaps be observable otherwise. Tracking also serves as an affirmation for having done the right thing; one common idea widely shared by user reviewers is that they are convinced that they are living a healthy cultural life.

Reviewing on social platforms often has its origins in coping with anxiety, loneliness, frustration, stress or personal problems, helping an individual to develop inner balance and better mental health. To follow one Instagram book reviewer respondent's (see Sect. 6.1 Prettifying Books: Book Reviewers on Instagram) answer: 'I began reviewing because I'm a homeschool housewife who was bored. I'm also an author, so reading the works of others assisted in the growth of my own voice'. This normative discourse manifested even as advocacy for reading, as many reviewers conceived of themselves as change agents, encouragers of 'new generations' to read, 'making more people read and learn', as survey respondents noted. This discourse connects the reviewing and reading of books to part of their wellbeing and discourses of self-help, self-care and self-improvement, which are also intrinsically individually centred. Being conscious of one's reading self underlies the possibility of self-tracking, -quantifying and -optimizing one's engagement with the help of an increasing number of social cataloguing tools, self-tracking tools for reading and social recommendation systems (Lupton, 2016; Yoo et al., 2017; Chen, 2008). Cultural engagement—taking one's own time and dedicating it to a good individual cause—is a way of taking care of oneself, and when talking about their reviewing activities, the respondents promote themselves as advocates of a good cause. This discourse, popular more generally in advocating the benefits of consuming arts (see, e.g., Stickley & Clift, 2017), can be connected to creating personal autonomy as part of cultural citizenship (cf. Rimke, 2000). By self-identifying with an active, engaged and enlightened reader, individuals can feel more confident and empowered as cultural consumers (Grodin, 1991).

*Life staging* has to do with domesticating a lifestyle and making it one's own by creating a virtual space for oneself. This often manifests concretely by making a profile, a reviewer's page or a reviewer account somewhere, but more generally it appears to reviewers as bulldozing a personal space in the reviewsphere; it may be the cosy corner of a bibliophile or the professional portfolio of a filmmaker. It can be described as making a home in the reviewsphere. This home, as it is public and consciously performed to others, becomes a window into or showcase of one's situated lifestyle. The virtual space created through the strategic rituals of intimacy resembles a condition that Gee (2004) calls the 'affinity space'. Gee examines the affinity space with regard to informal learning and sees it as being in contrast to formal classroom settings, but the affinity space is, to a large extent, the constructed community that occurs in creative online communities. In affinity spaces, the interaction between the participants occurs 'only secondarily through shared culture, gender, ethnicity, or face-to-face relationships' and with the common goal of 'sharing practices, patterns of consumption, and ongoing relationships to businesses and organizations' (ibid., p. 98). In this shared-interest group, with the common endeavour primarily being one's status, competence or looks do not matter.

The idea of a space, or a place, is important for user reviewers who are envisioning their activities as part of communities such as Bookstagram (Sect. 6.1 Prettifying Books: Book Reviewers on Instagram) or creating a personal virtual space such as the playstage (Sect. 6.3 At the Playstage: Toy Reviewers on YouTube). Oldenburg and Brissett (1982) argued that 'third places' are crucial for civil society, democracy and civic engagement by establishing feelings of a sense of place and belonging to a community (see also Potter & McDougall, 2017). According to Oldenburg and Brissett, the home, the place where people live, is the first place, and the workplace, the place where people tend to spend most of their time, is the second place. Third places, as public places, exist beyond (private) homes and places of economic production, and as settings for socializing with each other on a voluntary basis, they constitute the anchors of community life, such as cafes, churches, public libraries, parks, community houses or virtual communities. Characteristics of third places are that they offer free access and thrive on emotional expressiveness and social roles, and qualifications play a smaller role. Sharing moments of consumption that used to be private or shared in one's immediate physical settings only provides users with new possibilities for creating a common third place that, for its part, can offer a route into arts and culture beyond the formal institutions of media and education.

## 7.3 Re-creational Work

As discussed and demonstrated in previous chapters, among the institutional and non-institutional contexts, there are user reviewers with a wide range of different profiles. There are connoisseurial-critical reviewers, who are located closer to the cultural intermediary role of institutional professionals, yet discovering new platform-specific dimensions in reviewing, often in a dialogue with younger audiences and subcultures. They are contrasted with promotional 'influencer' reviewers where it is not always clear whether the reviewing process is independent and the reviewer's integrity ensured or if the reviewer puts himself or herself on the primary producers', the sellers', side, using reviewing as an aesthetic or functional excuse to come across with interested cultural audiences. Moreover, there are entertaining or (micro-)celebrity reviewers, building a personality that attracts audiences. They are contrasted with service-minded or educational reviewers, who are more disinterested, democratic and 'serious' when it comes to talking about art and aesthetics and who intend to help cultural consumers in their choices. In other words, there is a broad scale of orientations within the post-professional map of reviewers. What is common to them all is that they are taking cultural products and services as their starting point to 'do their stuff' and want to make a difference.

Characteristic of all non-professional reviewers is that they are conducting their work in their leisure time, which makes the leisure culture an appropriate context for user reviewing (Albrechtslund & Albrechtslund,

2014). Leadbeater (2007) remarks that most pro-am activities take place outside normal working hours in the evenings, on holidays and at weekends, in leisure time. Leisure, seen as an antithesis of work, is defined as a form of relaxation that allows people to recuperate from work. Yet user reviewers' activity is characterized by—to use Leadbeater's words—a sense of compulsion and effort, being more serious than being located in a zone of pure freedom and spontaneity. According to Leadbeater, pro-ams feel 'they have to do it', 'get up early', 'make sacrifices', 'put in the hours'. Stebbins (1992) calls this voluntary work with obligations 'serious leisure'. These features bring us back to aspirational and relational work, addressed earlier. However, there is something more: not all reviewing activity needs to result in professionalized activity, which is especially the case for the vast numbers of amateurs who have no plans for a future professional career. The work of amateurs is more self-maintaining and -supporting with regard to the activity they are doing, and with aims that are not directly related to the idea of professionalism and professional growth.

With regard to the self-supporting but socially transformative learning processes that are at stake in vernacular and amateur reviewing, I call non-professional reviewing *re-creational work*. This type of online labour has three key dimensions. First, 'recreation' refers to activities undertaken when one is not working. Reviewing is essentially a voluntary leisure time activity, and the typical user reviewers do not make any claims in terms of becoming professionals. Whatever the original reason for starting the reviewing activities, the activity of reviewing remains meaningful only as long as it is regarded as a hobby. Treating reviewing as a hobby keeps the standards and requirements set for a professional away and enables users to review products that they simply happen to like and when they have time.

Second, tightly related to the hobbyist dimension, 'recreation' is a diversion from the pressures of the job—pastime that feels fun. The 'meviewers' strongly indicate that they perform reviews because it makes them feel happy and satisfied, and it is an activity that allows them to cherish their love of culture. The affective features in amateur and vernacular reviewing are highly prominent, as both vernacular professional reviewers and vernacular and institutional amateur reviewers are characterized by a noticeable emotional investment. They tend to describe themselves with terms filled with love, passion and affection, and review texts are often emotional, atmospheric and intimate, humorous and witty.

Third, if seen as 're-creation'—the creation of something new—reviewing means the constant reconstruction of the reading activity. By 'domesticating' a new book, or making it fit into one's own life and lifestyle, the user reviewers try to create situated meaning for a certain book. The domestication framework, traditionally applied in media studies and in particular in the studies of information and communication tools, examines how technologies enter and find their place in people's everyday lives (Haddon, 2016). Recreation thus means a value-creation process that is based on an attempt to singularize a product into one's life. Each act of recreation thus resonates with the book love that is supported by the reviewing readers' community.

User reviewers are undertaking aesthetic, economic, individual and social re-creation. User reviewers' discovery of and creative adjustment to platform affordances create forms of expression and engagement that may even be completely foreign to the institutional professionalism of reviewing. Questions of making a living or how to establish an ethically sustainable independence as a reviewer may renew the economic conditions and result in innovation. Recreational work bears significance for identity formation and politics in the individualized life projects of reviewers. The community building involved in reviewing produces metacoverage that may imply work and potential re-work on values and norms.

As for the transformative power of the lifestyle work conducted by user reviewers, many scholars have remained sceptical regarding the re-creational potential of digital labour, regarding the capitalization on voluntary and lay work as exploitation (Petersen, 2008) and as reinforcement of prevailing power structures rather than the culmination of creativity and freedom (Petersen, 2008; Ouellette & Wilson, 2011; Duffy, 2015). Re-creational work shall thus not be celebrated as automatically transformative, empowering and cultivating, but remains to be critically inspected. However, the pedagogical potential of review as a genre and practice paves the way for development, experimenting and re-education in terms of values and power structures (see Chap. 8 Conclusions: Towards a Pedagogical Agenda).

## 7.4 Fake and Pseudo Reviews

The reviewspheres online are experiencing increased levels of false or biased information circulating in reviews through social media and user review websites. They represent disruptive communication that is intentionally or unintentionally misleading, distorting the standard function of reviewing. The misuses of the umbrella concept of review connect to aesthetic, economic, individual and social purposes. Three basic forms of non-review can be distinguished: fake reviews, pseudo reviews and fabled reviews. *Fake reviews* are usually understood as review content that is intentionally biased, counterfeit or false. For example, user review sites may accommodate reviews that have been written for the sake of skewing the effect of ratings and the review outcome of a specific product or service, usually to do harm through negative reviews or to boost a product through positive reviews. *Pseudo reviews* refer to content that mimics the review format, pretending to deliver a third-party assessment of a product or service, but being dedicated to promoting this product or service and thus being marketing instead of reviewing. This is often the case for branded content that has not been reported as such, as when social influencers do 'reviews' of consumer products that they have received. *Fabled reviews* are fictive, imaginary reviews, false or faux reviews, that fabricate both their content and storytelling approach (genre, format or mode). These reviews are easier to detect and less or not at all harmful in their effects, as they are typically created for artistic instead of malicious purposes, like the covert review entertainment addressed earlier (Sect. 6.4 Reviewtainment: Reviews as Platformized Entertainment). These form of reviews deals with benevolent, creative and productive misuse of the content and approach.

Reports studying fake reviews have discovered that, for example, Amazon is amassed with reviews that are not genuine (He et al., 2021; ReviewMeta, 2019). Among almost 6 million customer reviews from 2019, more than a half were unverified reviews that, moreover, seemed to have a more positive rating than verified reviews (ReviewMeta, 2019). In 2015, approximately 20 per cent of online reviews on Yelp.com were suspected of being fake (Luca & Zervas, 2016). Advertising standards agencies have reacted to high volumes of reviews on popular user review sites such as TripAdvisor and Skytrax that seem to be fake (Schmidl, 2012). The trend seems to be increasing, although Amazon has taken legal action against reviewers and sellers (Trecul, 2019).

Fake reviews can be automatically generated (Juuti et al., 2018), resulting in large-scale AI-aided production of malicious review content, 'automated crowdturfing' (Yao et al., 2017). User studies indicate that users have difficulties in detecting machine-generated fake reviews and distinguishing them from real reviews (Juuti et al., 2018). Fake reviews also essentially intervene in the automatically generated indices, contributing to rating and ranking results and affecting the image that is mediated to a user of a certain cultural product.

Fake reviews have higher importance for customer product reviews that are more clearly connected to usability that is transferable from person to person than art-related reviews where individual opinion- and taste-formation plays a role. Already more than a decade ago, researchers estimated that a one-star rating increase affects business revenue by 5–9 per cent on Yelp.com (Luca, 2010). Because of the monetary impact of beneficial review content, businesses can rely on so-called crowdturfing agents (Wang et al., 2012; Yao et al., 2017) who are dedicated to delivering positive ratings written by workers to a customer in exchange for monetary compensation. Platforms do prohibit crowdturfing in their community guidelines, for example explicitly not allowing user reviewers to buy content related to promotions. However, the act of writing fabricated content is not considered illegal, nor is matching reviewers to producers and mediators of products.

Because of extensive fraudulent and malicious uses of reviews, but also to detect quality in reviews, an urgent question becomes who reviews the reviews. The question of developing practices and platforms for meta-reviewing in turn conjures the question of what kind of structures for organizing, curating and monitoring could be developed across platforms to help cultural consumers orientate in a contradictory landscape. In legacy media, the editorial control and, more broadly, the self-regulation of mass media is supposed to make metareviewing unnecessary—as a sheer fake detection; media criticism as part of democratic discussion is, of course, always a welcomed feature—and perhaps just a matter of professional self-reflection of the community of practitioners. In user reviewing, there is no centralized ethical code but micro-systems of ethics at work. Besides the standard regulation of content on platforms that applies for all content, not only reviews, the review content available is continuously ranked and organized in different ways. As mentioned earlier (Sect. 4.2 User Reviewing), platform providers, especially within the institutional amateur framework, tend to maintain in-built site-intern report and flag functions to detect fake reviews. User review sites also act proactively by setting rules for valid reviews and moderating the publishing of reviews. This is, however, obviously not enough, and many scholars have high hopes for platform-independent automatic detection (see, e.g., Yao et al., 2017). The online services Fakespot, founded by Saoud Khalifah in 2016, and ReviewMeta, founded by Tommy Noonan in the same year, detect fake reviews and potential biases by automatically analysing Amazon's online product reviews. Fakespot's browser plug-in identifies suspicious reviews on Amazon and eBay. ReviewMeta's online tool, which according to the company a couple of years ago collected a dataset of over 18 million reviews (ReviewMeta, 2016), gives reports on any product on Amazon, recalculating the product rating after filtering out the suspicious reviews. It can be anticipated that the solutions developed for validating news and detecting disinformation in fact-oriented or informative-genre coverage, such as debunking communities and authorized fake news detectors' networks, can help here.

Thus far, review assessment communities that would produce metadiscourse and contribute to metareviewing in the vernacular and amateur domains remain relatively low in number. The endeavour to counteract the problem of fake or low-quality review content typically co-exists with the aim to help review audiences to navigate in the abundance of user reviews. Customer services sites such as Consumer Reports and Trustpilot include reviews on review services and sites in their content. Metacritic is an example of services pursuing overviews of reviews on different platforms. Meta-reviewing can also be regarded as an essential mission of media education. For example, the American non-profit organization Common Sense Media produces ratings and reviews of YouTube channels, including review channels, for parents and guardians, with the slogan 'Reviews for what your kids want to watch (before they watch it)'. Based on user-generated content, adults and children can assess a channel's content across different categories by rating it, for example, in terms of a channel's 'consumerism', and by leaving written commentary.

Reviewers' activities as promotional intermediaries or pseudo-intermediaries pose another challenge. The point of departure is that reviewers are de facto not marketers, yet as part of platformized production they are allowed to manage commercial partnerships that institutional reviewing is not directly committed to. The tolerance for branded content varies from culture to culture, some societies being less restrictive than others (see, e.g., Steenkamp, 2001). The international self-regulatory standards and codes for marketers, to be complemented with national frameworks, highlight advertisers' social responsibility, truthfulness and substantiation, identification of marketed content and transparency (ICC, 2018). Reviewers should in their conduct show autonomy and self-determination in the management of their review activities and make visible all sponsorships and partnerships entered. While covert advertising can be reported by users for consumer ombudsmen and advertisement regulators, it is not always straightforward to define marketing and distinguish it from different forms of reviewing, which applies to pseudo-intermediaries oscillating between promotion and judgemental commentary. In every case, the review audiences should be aware of the motives behind the reviewer's intent to review products, how the reviewer has acquired the products, and how independent the reviewer's position is; in case there are any connections that may cause a bias affecting the reviewer's integrity, these contextual bounds should be clearly reported. Incentivized reviews, where the reviewer receives a free or discounted product to make a review, became prohibited on Amazon in 2016 unless they are facilitated through Amazon's own Vine Program (Amazon, 2016), but they regularly occur in the vernacular reviewsphere. ReviewMeta's (2016) data indicated that about 20 per cent of Amazon product reviews were incentivized and provided with the disclaimer 'I received this item in exchange for an honest review', but consumers who receive a free or discounted product in exchange for a review were more likely to leave a positive review. While the average rating for a product on Amazon was 4.4 stars, for non-incentivized reviews it was 4.3 stars and incentivized 4.7 stars. The positive tone in the review not only stems from the fact that the reviewer would be paid or corrupt, but boils down to the good purchase or deal bias discussed in Sect. 6.2 Judging Gadgets: Filmmaker Reviewers on Vimeo.

Recently, in Sweden, an investigative journalistic project drew attention to the boundaries between democratic and promotional intermediaries by filing a complaint with the national advertising ombudsman against 14 well-known social influencers, resulting in six of the influencers being condemned for violating the ethical code of conduct and performing clandestine advertising (Winberg & Lundin, 2019). The reaction by one of the central influencers was indignant and aggressive, describing investigative journalism of old media as an insult towards the influencers and their fan community (Törnblom, 2019). The relatively young branch of social influencers is thus still seeking their place in the ethical framework. Some media authorities, like the Norwegian Media Authority (2019), have published guidelines for bloggers and vloggers concerning how to mark advertising content in blog and video entries. User-generated content, however, often falls into a grey zone of persuasiveness where the scale from evaluation to promotion, from reviewership to social influencership, is a gliding one. The dimension that makes the situation even more complex is that the boundary between evaluation and advocacy has been quite fluid even in journalistic reviews. Even journalistic reviewers may feel that they are promoters and advocates of the cultural form, lifestyle or product family they present (Harries & Wahl-Jorgensen, 2007). Some vernacular reviewers produce contextual material that addresses their review approach, such as the acquisition of a good and the rating and evaluation system applied, thus increasing their transparency, but it is by far not the standard practice for all aspiring reviewers in the vernacular and amateur domain. The genre of review thus forms an easy pathway into false marketing, as reviewers may not always be fully conscious of the consequences of their 'recommendations' and 'endorsements', or of the lack of transparency, contextualization and critique. Professionalization of social influencers has brought about influencers' associations such as Influencers of Sweden, but as employee interest organizations, their preliminary objective is to support members in acquiring profit and managing their partnerships rather than developing an ethical code, let alone for the—from their perspective—marginal group of reviewers. It is evident that in the long run, to ensure the independence and truthfulness of reviewing, social mechanisms to detect bias and ethical self-consciousness and transparency from the producers' side need to be fortified.

## References


Albrechtslund, A.-M. B., & Albrechtslund, A. (2014). Social media as leisure culture. *First Monday, 19*(4). https://doi.org/10.5210/fm.v19i4.4877

Amazon. (2016, October 3). Update on customer reviews. *Amazon*. https://www.aboutamazon.com/news/innovation-at-amazon/update-on-customer-reviews

Bakardjieva, M., & Gaden, G. (2012). Web 2.0 technologies of the self. *Philosophy and Technology, 25*(3), 399–413.

Bernstein, B. (1999). Vertical and horizontal discourse: An essay. *British Journal of Sociology of Education, 20*(2), 157–173.

Bille, T., & Olsen, F. (2018). Measuring the quality and impact of arts and culture. In K. O. Eliassen, J. F. Hovden, & Ø. Prytz (Eds.), *Contested qualities: Negotiating value in arts and culture* (pp. 229–256). Fagbokforlaget.

Bolin, G. (2019). Value production in media industries and everyday life. In M. Deuze & M. Prenger (Eds.), *Making media: Production, practices, and professions* (pp. 111–119). Amsterdam University Press.

Botsman, R., & Rogers, R. (2010). *What's mine is yours: The rise of collaborative consumption*. Harper Collins.

Brandsen, T., Verschuere, B., & Steen, T. (Eds.). (2018). *Co-production and co-creation: Engaging citizens in public services* (pp. 18–26). Routledge.

Bruns, A. (2013). Exploring the pro-am interface between production and produsage. In F. L. F. Lee, L. Leung, J. L. Qiu, & D. S. C. Chu (Eds.), *Frontiers in new media research* (pp. 241–258). Routledge.

Chen, Y.-F. (2008). Herd behavior in purchasing books online. *Computers in Human Behavior, 24*(5), 1977–1992.

Chia, A. (2012). Welcome to me-mart: The politics of user-generated content in personal blogs. *American Behavioral Scientist, 56*(4), 421–438.

Cova, B., & Dalli, D. (2018). Prosumption tribes: How consumers collectively rework brands, products, services and markets. In O. Kravets, P. Maclaran, S. Miles, & A. Venkatesh (Eds.), *The SAGE handbook of consumer culture* (pp. 235–255). Sage.

Djafarova, E., & Trofimenko, O. (2018). 'Instafamous' – Credibility and self-presentation of micro-celebrities on social media. *Information, Communication & Society, 22*(10), 1432–1446.

Dobson, A. S., Robards, R., & Carah, N. (2018). *Digital intimate publics and social media*. Palgrave Macmillan.

Duffy, B. (2015). Amateur, autonomous, and collaborative: Myths of aspiring female cultural producers in web 2.0. *Critical Studies in Media Communication, 32*(1), 48–64.

Felski, R. (2015). *The limits of critique*. The University of Chicago Press.

Felski, R. (2020). *Hooked: Art and attachment*. The University of Chicago Press.

Gee, J. P. (2004). *Situated language and learning: A critique of traditional schooling*. Routledge.

Gregg, M. (2009). Learning to (love) labour: Production cultures and the affective turn. *Communication and Critical/Cultural Studies, 6*(2), 209–214. https://doi.org/10.1080/14791420902868045

Grodin, D. (1991). The interpreting audience: The therapeutics of self-help book reading. *Critical Studies in Mass Communication, 8*(4), 404–420.

Haddon, L. (2016). The domestication of complex media repertoires. In K. Sandvik, A. M. Thorhauge, & B. Valtysson (Eds.), *The media and the mundane: Communication across media in everyday life* (pp. 17–30). Nordicom.

Hamari, J., Sjöklint, M., & Ukkonen, A. (2015). The sharing economy: Why people participate in collaborative consumption. *Journal of the Association for Information Science and Technology, 67*(9), 2047–2059. https://doi.org/10.1002/asi.23552

Harries, G., & Wahl-Jorgensen, K. (2007). The culture of arts journalists: Elitists, saviors or manic depressives? *Journalism, 8*(6), 619–639.

Hayes, E. R., & Gee, J. R. (2010). Public pedagogy through video games: Design, resources, and affinity spaces. In J. A. Sandlin, B. D. Schultz, & J. Burdick (Eds.), *Handbook of public pedagogy: Education and learning beyond schooling* (pp. 116–124). Routledge.

He, S., Hollenbeck, B., & Proserpio, D. (2021, January 22). *The market for fake reviews*. https://ssrn.com/abstract=3664992 or https://doi.org/10.2139/ssrn.3664992

ICC, International Chamber of Commerce. (2018). *ICC advertising and marketing communications code: Building consumer trust through responsible marketing*. https://iccwbo.org/content/uploads/sites/3/2018/09/icc-advertising-and-marketing-communications-code-int.pdf

Ito, M. (2010). The rewards of non-commercial production: Distinctions and status in the anime music video scene. *First Monday, 15*(5).

Juuti, M., Sun, B., Mori, T., & Asokan, N. (2018). Stay on-topic: Generating context-specific fake restaurant reviews. *European Symposium on Research in Computer Security*, 132–151.

Kolehmainen, M., & Mäkinen, K. (2021). Affective labour of creating atmospheres. *European Journal of Cultural Studies, 24*(2), 448 –463.

Leadbeater, C. (2007). *We think: Why mass creativity is the next big thing*. http://charlesleadbeater.net/wp-content/uploads/2010/01/We-Think-charles-full-draft.pdf

Luca, M. (2010). *Reviews, reputation, and revenue: The case of Yelp.com*. Working paper 12-016. Harvard Business School.

Luca, M., & Zervas, G. (2016). Fake it till you make it: Reputation, competition, and Yelp review fraud. *Management Science, 62*(1), 3412–3427.

Lupton, D. (2016). *The quantified self: A sociology of self-tracking*. Polity Press.

Norwegian Media Authority. (2019, March 18). Veileder til youtubere og videobloggere om merking av reklame [Guidelines for youtubers and vloggers on marking of advertisement]. https://www.medietilsynet.no/globalassets/dokumenter/veiledere/190318-yt-veileder-kommersielt-innhold.pdf

Oldenburg, R., & Brissett, D. (1982). The third place. *Qualitative Sociology, 5*(4), 265–284.

Ouellette, L., & Wilson, J. (2011). Women's work: Affective labour and convergence culture. *Cultural Studies, 25*(4–5), 548–565. https://doi.org/10.1080/09502386.2011.600546

Papacharissi, Z. (2013). A networked self: Identity performance and sociability on social network sites. In F. L. F. Lee, L. Leung, J. L. Qiu, & D. S. C. Chu (Eds.), *Frontiers in new media research* (pp. 207–221). Routledge.

Petersen, S. M. (2008). Loser generated content: From participation to exploitation. *First Monday, 13*(3) https://doi.org/10.5210/fm.v13i3.2141

Potter, J., & McDougall, J. (2017). *Digital media culture and education: Theorizing third-space literacies*. Palgrave Macmillan.

Potts, J., Hartley, J., Banks, J., et al. (2008). Consumer co-creation and situated creativity. *Industry and Innovation, 15*(5), 459–474.

Ramaswamy, V., & Ozcan, K. (2014). *The co-creation paradigm*. Stanford University Press.

ReviewMeta. (2016, September 19). *Data proves Amazon reviews with 'free or discounted disclaimer' are extremely biased.* https://www.youtube.com/watch?v=kdLI62JKpCk

ReviewMeta .(2019, March 28). Growing unverified review problem: Amazon flooded with millions of fake reviews in 2019. *ReviewMeta.com.* https://reviewmeta.com/blog/amazon-flooded-with-millions-of-fake-reviews-in-2019/

Rimke, H. M. (2000). Governing citizens through self-help literature. *Cultural Studies, 14*(1), 61–78.

Schmidl, E. (2012, November 13). Advertising standards authority calls out TripAdvisor and Skytrax for fake user reviews. https://www.smartcompany.com.au/finance/economy/advertising-standards-authority-calls-out-tripadvisor-and-skytrax-for-fake-user-reviews/

Scolere, L., Pruchniewska, U., & Duffy, B. E. (2018). Constructing the platform-specific self-brand: The labor of social media promotion. *Social Media + Society, 4*(3), 1–11.

Stebbins, R. A. (1992). *Amateurs, professionals and serious leisure.* McGill-Queen's University Press.

Steenkamp, J. E. M. (2001). The role of national culture in international marketing research. *International Marketing Review, 18*(1), 30–44. https://doi.org/10.1108/02651330110381970

Stickley, T., & Clift, S. (Eds.). (2017). *Arts, health and wellbeing: A theoretical inquiry for practice.* Cambridge Scholars Publishing.

Strokosch, K., & Osborne, S. P. (2020). Co-experience, co-production and co-governance: An ecosystem approach to the analysis of value creation. *Policy & Politics, 48*(3), 425–442. https://doi.org/10.1332/030557320X15857337955214

Törnblom, C. (2019, May 23). Influencers måste finna sig i att bli ifrågasatta [Influencers need to accept to be questioned]. *Resumé.* https://www.resume.se/nyheter/artiklar/2019/05/23/casper-tornblom-influencers-maste-finna-sig-i-att-bli-ifragasatta-insikt/

Trecul, E. (2019, July 9). Amazon fake reviews: A problem and a 5-star industry. *Red Points.* https://www.redpoints.com/blog/amazon-fake-reviews/

Wang, G., Wilson, C., Zhao, X., Zhu, Y., Mohanlal, M., Zheng, H., & Zhao, B. Y. (2012). Serf and turf: Crowdturfing for fun and profit. In *Proceedings of the 21st International Conference on World Wide Web (WWW).* Association for Computing Machinery (ACM).

Weijo, H. A., Martin, D. M., & Arnould, E. J. (2018). Consumer movements and collective creativity: The case of Restaurant Day. *Journal of Consumer Research, 45*(2), 251–274. https://doi.org/10.1093/jcr/ucy003

Wenger, E. (1998). *Communities of practice: Learning, meaning, and identity.* Cambridge University Press.

Wenger-Trayner, E., & Wenger-Trayner, B. (2020). *Learning to make a difference: Value creation in social learning spaces.* Cambridge University Press.

Winberg, Y., & Lundin, J. (2019, May 22). Samir Badran-stormen visar varför influencers vägrar att bli granskade [The storm around Samir Badran shows why influencers refuse to be investigated]. *Resumé.* https://www.resume.se/nyheter/artiklar/2019/05/22/samir-badran-stormen-visar-varfor-influencers-vagrar-att-bli-granskade/

Yao, Y., Viswanath, B., Cryan, J., Zheng, H., & Zhao, B. Y. (2017). Automated crowdturfing attacks and defenses in online review systems. In *Proceedings of the 2017 ACM SIGSAC Conference on Computer and Communications Security.* ACM.

Yoo, S., Lemos, J., & Finn, E. (2017). Nellodee 2.0: A quantified self reading app for tracking reading goals. In P. Zaphiris & A. Ioannou (Eds.), *Learning and collaboration technologies: Technology in education.* LCT 2017. Lecture Notes in Computer Science, vol 10296. Springer.

CHAPTER 8

# Conclusions: Towards a Pedagogical Agenda

User-generated review content is sometimes hard to relate to professional criticism and reviewing. Reviews created by non-professionals or aspiring professionals may be met with dismissive attitudes downplaying their importance and quality when juxtaposed and compared with the ideals of professional or established criticism and reviewing.

In 2012, Booker Prize head judge Peter Stothard made it to the headlines by warning that book bloggers are harming literature (Flood, 2012). At another extreme, professional institutional reviews are regarded as elitist and inaccessible and, as such, losing their importance. Recently, the television channel HBO Nordic published a Facebook post that stated, 'Honest reviews from real people. Are you fed up with exaggerated, hard-to-read and unnecessarily long reviews? Here you can find a selection of genuine recommendations of series—from fans like you' (Pallas, 2018; translation by the author.) After critical commentary by journalists who regarded the characterization of journalistic reviews as dismissal of professional reviewers (Pallas, 2018), they re-wrote the post: 'Spontaneous reviews from our fans. Here you can find a selection of recommendations of series—from fans like you' (HBO Nordic, 2018).

This book has aimed to work vernacular reviewing into the broader theoretical framework of reviewing, locating non-professional forms of reviewing closer to consumption and learning paradigms while at the same time highlighting its relationship to the existing understandings of review professionalism. Drawing a synthesis and underlining the continuities


M. Jaakkola, *Reviewing Culture Online*,
https://doi.org/10.1007/978-3-030-84848-4_8

between the critical discourses and practices available has entailed the intention to put user reviewing into a context that is more historically embedded and institutionally legitimate than the way it is typically conceptualized in everyday discourses. Envisioning user reviewing as part of the historical continuity and layered contemporaneity of post-professional reviewing enables us to see reviews created by ordinary people beyond the binary of the professional and amateur, or citizenship and customership.

Positioned at the consumption end of the cultural mediation chain, vernacular book reviews are not simply challenging or replacing the longer book-review format, especially not the institutionalized professional book review. Rather, vernacular reviews may essentially mark diversification and democratization in the reviewsphere—diversification by introducing new, more processual and participatory practices for reviewing and democratization by enabling users of different degrees of expertise and agency to be involved in public communication. Development in the vernacular domain may also imply re-organization and professionalization of reviewing if different reviewspheres interact and develop intensified exchange and interdependence. While the institutionalized domain of reviewing places great emphasis on the reviewer's role and legitimacy when delivering judgements, in the vernacular domain of reviewing, the focus is more on collective learning processes to create critical communicative agency as part of reflexive consumption.

It lies in the core of reviewing that review—as a mode of communication and a genre—is a *counter-promotional practice*. The counter-promotionalism marks the distinction of the reviewer from a content creator and social influencer. Reviewing entails the ambition of not taking imposed meanings for granted but creating an independent picture of the product or service under review, based on the empirical work of the reviewer as an experiencing subject. While doing this, user reviews are balancing between sustaining integrity and being put under pressure from the primary producers. There are, however, many levels of address, including different understandings of quality—ranging from simple recommendations similar to putting the thumbs up to refined tasting where the experience of receiving is deconstructed and clarified to the audience. Different communities also develop different standards of ambitions and quality. As value-creation can be based on another types of value than the aesthetic-artistic, reviewers may depart from the original understandings of institutional professional reviewing where aesthetic quality is central to the reviewing act, while still remaining valuable to the social group of people. Despite the multifaceted value-creation processes, there are, at large, shortcomings in user reviewing, such as the ethical instability and misuses of the genre, as well as blurring of communication modes and gender biases, which all make the system of reviewing less rigorous, accountable and functional. The question is, then, what to do to these shortcomings, and how to develop the genre.

Developing the ethical basis and standards for reviewing remains a rudimentary task. Becoming engaged as a reviewer implies ethical involvement, but the ethical framework for reviewing, such as a dispersed and incongruent universe of practices, is lacking shape. At the point of analysis, the vernacular practices of reviewing such as 'instareviewing' and 'toy reviewing' were evidently still in their infancy. Even if reviewing has deeper traditions than the history of social networking sites and platforms, the creative work of discovering and making use of affordances to invent new methods of communication and social organization is very young. It seems, above all, that more transparency is needed from the content creators to make clear in which contexts messages are produced, together with regulation that at the policy level forces vernacular producers in a more ethical and accountable direction. In addition, a more solid incorporation of commercialism and consumerism in discourses of media literacy is needed, not in the way cultural industries have traditionally been dismissed (see, e.g., Buckingham, 1995), which may reinforce misbelief and distrust among parents rather than help them further, but addressing the complexities of producer roles, genres and production contexts so that they can be better dissected and analysed in situated communication. Understandings of how vernacularized commercialism works may thus support communities in resisting consumerism and transferring discouraged reactions into something more balanced and transformative.

Furthermore, even misuses of and biased content in reviews prompt educational interventions. Not only critical prosumption of arts and culture but also critical reception and uses of reviews of different types need pedagogical guidelines and frameworks to develop policies, pedagogies and practices. Critical review literacy is a citizen competence related to media literacy, with a focus on valid source criticism. Guardians and other adult gatekeepers of child viewers, however, need support and tools for developing literacy for online genres. For example, toy reviewing also involves a great deal of potential for addressing toys, play and children's worlds in a way that supports children's voices and agency. Enhancing support for child agency across all three categories of media literacy (content reception, produsage/prosumption and production) is a twenty-first-century objective for media and information literacy actors.

However, the idea of user reviews entails a great pedagogical potential in terms of creative uses of the genre (see, e.g., Suárez & González Argüello, 2020; Dezuanni, 2021; Jerasa & Boffone, 2021). The pedagogical uses of the review could be more systematically developed into a genre pedagogy that is not focused on the aesthetic-stylistic features of the textual category or uses of a certain medium or a platform, but places the cultural engagement within the genre to the foreground. Ideally, reviewing new cultural products and services advances reflection and verbalization of experiences. The vernacular forms of reviewing indicate that review can be used creatively and fruitfully to support individuals' ability to communicate across various social contexts, and, with regard to the rich body of reviewtainment, also in terms of counterstorytelling and bending (re-writing and transforming critical ideas). Reviewing is to a large extent work with various contexts, and as such, reviewing enables opening up new contexts for one's consumption that are beyond the immediate reaction, and even sharing one's reactions may empower cultural consumers to become more conscious of the ground on which they are standing as consumers, citizens and individuals. In this way, reviewing could be more efficiently harnessed to a pedagogical resource for developing individual relationships with art and culture. Indeed, in the domain of arts and different cultural forms, the personal and individual relationship is crucial. We do not typically ask whether a person likes 'culture' in a general sense, but we do ask what kind of music or literature or which artist or author one is interested in or follows. By supporting reflexive evaluation of one's interests, reviewing could thus be regarded as a pedagogical toolkit to support the development of a critical and reflexive relationship with cultural forms and their consumption more generally.

Review pedagogy is an ideal post-media literacy practice. In his book *The Gutenberg Galaxy* (1962), Marshall McLuhan introduced the idea of a post-literate society in which multimedia technology has advanced to the point where the ability to read or write typographic texts is no longer the dominant form of literacy. The traditions of reviewing seem to be at this turning point between the typographic and electronic era. A great extent of more recent user reviewing is based on oral presentation, coupled with online interaction, rooted in the everyday agency of cultural citizens and consumers. The multimodal media spaces require a renewal of our sensory existence to live up to spatial multimodal presentations where texts are non-linear and consist of processes rather than products, and writing is no longer the dominant skill required from the reviewers.

Once the medium no longer constitutes the core of literacy practice—or in this case, reviewing—post-media reviewing underlies a way of thinking and pedagogical practice that resists recourse to the idea of 'the media', or the 'text', as external to the media-literate agents in social practice (Kendall & McDougall, 2012; Bennett et al., 2011). Instead of making and understanding textual presentations within a certain genre, we need to think of enacting this genre in different production spaces, and to recognize the conditions of meaning making we need to be able to identify the basic elements of which these conditions consist: the professional positionings of the communicators who identify themselves as reviewers, the emic understandings of the review genre, the perceived and used affordances within the community to make reviewing happen, and the tactics of resisting imperatives imposed from the internal logics of cultural intermediation and platformized production. This theoretical shift could be translated into a new pedagogical model that would move forward from unmasking properties of a contained text towards 'curating a moment in time of textual meaning-making' (Andrews & McDougall, 2012; Bennett & McDougall, 2016). These creative processes are an outcome of the interplay of emotions, values and behaviours.

In the development of the review genre in the institutional professional domain, the vernacular professionals and amateurs may count as forerunners of post-literate and post-media practice. Ideas from the play with platform affordances can be transformed to institutional communication, as well, and while the early digitalization meant for professional reviews to be shuffled into web editions of newspapers as such, reviews are contemporarily being developed to make use of digital affordances in a more effective way. However, even if most of the newest development of reviewing occurs online, the future of reviewing does not necessarily need to be virtual only. With the participatory turn of cultural organizations, especially in the aftermath of the global Covid-19 pandemic around 2020 that made the world take a digital leap in organizing its activities, hybrid environments can be increasingly anticipated even for the cultural sector engaging potential reviewers. Combining virtual and physical methods of engagement for their audiences, cultural organizations can harness audience reviewers in more versatile ways. Even today, reviews are occasionally organized as physical scene events such as review slams and battles, or as live events in physical form where the genre finds new forms, practised as part of different forms of journalism, curation and other public pedagogy, perhaps even by new practitioners and audiences.

The abovementioned shifts have as a consequence meant that reviewing of cultural products has become an integral part of our mediatized everyday life to many, and an increasing number of individuals can be part of evaluation processes affecting our understandings, uses and valuation of contemporary culture. Online reviews attract audiences in the millions and become embedded in communication patterns that shape tastes and lifestyles, not remaining a distant institutional practice reserved for the few. However, this book documents evolvements that are of a relatively young age. The features and terms and conditions of use of a social networking platform may also change abruptly, as shown by the 'APIcalypse' in 2018, a data scandal caused by the British company Cambridge Analytica that acquired personal data about Facebook users for political purposes by alleging that were using it for academic research, which made Facebook accelerate the curtailment of its Application Programming Interface (API) for non-commercial partners (Bruns, 2019). Historiographies of the online genre trajectories are important in order to outline a historical perspective of the turbulent evolvement in cultural communication and online engagement and to achieve more general perspectives on cultural and digital citizenship and the industry—platform relationships (see, e.g., Helmond & van der Vlist, 2019).

Seeing reviewing as a field that encompasses diverse practices followed by various groups of people who have diverging motives, incentives and cultures enables us to see the whole breadth of reviewing practices in society, which are, indeed, far away from activities reserved for a few. Globally, reviewing is embedded in using a wide variety of consumer and citizen services, from shopping items to tourist destinations, from borrowing books from the library to sharing leisure services, from assessing people's behaviour to doing activities at home. We are all reviewers now, and we should take it seriously, while remaining sensitive to the fact that while value-creation is a multifaceted process and can elicit values of various types, not everyone's opinion has equal worth. By refining our view on the various forms of reviewing across various contexts and being able to tell what form of reviewing we are dealing with we can better develop an understanding of the social action and agency in question, and ensure that reviewing will gain a sustainable ground for its future existence.

## References


Andrews, B., & McDougall, J. (2012). Curation pedagogy – Further towards the inexpert. *Medijske Studije (Media Studies), 3*(6), 152–156.

Bennett, P., & McDougall, J. (Eds.). (2016). *Doing text: Media after the subject*. Auteur.

Bennett, P., Kendall, A., & McDougall, J. (2011). *After the media: Culture and identity in the 21st century*. Routledge.

Bruns, A. (2019). After the 'APIcalypse': Social media platforms and their fight against critical scholarly research. *Information, Communication & Society, 22*(11), 1544–1566. https://doi.org/10.1080/1369118X.2019.1637447

Buckingham, D. (1995). The commercialisation of childhood? The place of the market in children's media culture. *Changing English, 2*, 17–40.

Dezuanni, M. L. (2021). TikTok's peer pedagogies: Learning about Books through #Booktok videos. AoIR Selected Papers of Internet Research, 2021. https://doi.org/10.5210/spir.v2021i0.11901

Flood, A. (2012). Books bloggers are harming literature, warns Booker prize head judge. *The Guardian*, 25 September 2012. Available at https://www.theguardian.com/books/2012/sep/25/books-bloggers-literature-booker-prize-stothard

HBO Nordic. (2018, August 19). A Facebook post. https://www.facebook.com/HBOSweden/posts/1089369744558796

Helmond, A., & van der Vlist, F. N. (2019). Social media and platform historiography: Challenges and opportunities. *TMG – Journal for Media History, 22*(1), 6–34.

Jerasa, S., & Boffone, T. (2021). BookTok 101: TikTok, digital literacies, and out-of-school reading practices. *Journal of Adolescent and Adult Literacy*, published online before print 8 October, 2021. https://doi.org/10.1002/jaal.1199

Kendall, A., & McDougall, J. (2012). Critical media literacy after the media. *Comunicar, 19*(38), 21–29.

McLuhan, M. (1962). *The Gutenberg galaxy: The making of typographic man*. University of Toronto Press.

Pallas, H. (2018). HBO:s kritikerförakt ligger i tiden [HBO's dismissal of critics is reflects the current climate]. *Göteborgs-Posten*, August 21.

Suárez, M. d. M., & González Argüello, M. V. (2020). Becoming a good BookTuber. *RELC Journal, 51*(1), 158–167. https://doi.org/10.1177/0033688220906905

# Index




M. Jaakkola, *Reviewing Culture Online*,
https://doi.org/10.1007/978-3-030-84848-4

The manufacturer's authorised representative in the EU is Springer Nature Customer Service Centre GmbH, Europaplatz 3, 69115 Heidelberg, Germany. If you have any concerns regarding our products, please contact ProductSafety@springernature.com

Printed and bound by CPI Group (UK) Ltd, Croydon, CR0 4YY

30/09/2026

02225499-0008